California
Wine
FOR
DUMMIES

California Wine For Dummies®

Cheat Sheet

California's Main Varietal Wines

Wine Name	Color	Taste
Chardonnay	White	Usually dry or fairly dry; full-bodied, smooth-textured; flavors can include ripe apple, tropical fruits, butter, or toasty oak
Sauvignon Blanc	White	Fairly dry; medium-bodied; pronounced aromas and flavors that can include white fruits (pear, apple), citrus, herbal notes, or fresh grass; usually no oaky character
White Zinfandel	Pink	Medium-sweet; smooth-textured; fruity flavors such as berries, melon
Cabernet Sauvignon	Red	Dry; medium- or full-bodied, with some firmness of texture; medium-intense flavors that can include dark fruits, herbal notes, and smoky oak
Merlot	Red	Dry; medium- or full-bodied with fairly soft texture; medium-intense flavors that can include plum, tea leaves, chocolate
Pinot Noir	Red	Dry; fairly full-bodied, with silky texture; pronounced aromas and flavors generally of red berries, dark berries, cherry
Syrah/ Shiraz	Red	Dry; fairly full-bodied with smooth texture; flavors include juicy red or dark fruits, sometimes with earthy, spicy, or herbal notes
Zinfandel	Red	Dry or fairly dry; medium- or full-bodied, sometimes with firmness of texture; flavors of berries and herbs

Main Wine Regions and Their Specialties

Region	Wine Specialty
Anderson Valley	Pinot Noir, Chardonnay, Riesling, Gewurztraminer, sparkling wine
Carneros	Pinot Noir, Chardonnay, Merlot, sparkling wine
Monterey	Chardonnay, Pinot Noir, Cabernet Sauvignon
Napa Valley	Cabernet Sauvignon, Chardonnay, Sauvignon Blanc
Paso Robles	Cabernet Sauvignon, Merlot, Zinfandel, Petite Sirah, Syrah
Santa Barbara	Pinot Noir, Chardonnay, Syrah
Sonoma County	Zinfandel, Pinot Noir, Chardonnay

For Dummies: Bestselling Book Series for Beginners

California Wine For Dummies®

Wine Pronunciation Guide

- Barbera (bar-*bear*-a)
- Cabernet Sauvignon (cab-er-nay so-vee-nyohn)
- Gewurztraminer (gheh-*vertz*-trah-mee-ner)
- Grenache (greh-nahsh)
- Merlot (mer-lo)
- Mourvedre (more-ved'r)
- Pinot Grigio (pee-no *gree*-jo)

- Pinot Gris (pee-no gree)
- Pinot Noir (pee-no nwahr)
- Riesling (*rees*-ling)
- Roussanne (roo-sahn)
- Sangiovese (san-joe-*vay*-see)
- Sauvignon Blanc (so-vee-nyohn blahnk)
- Tempranillo (tem-pra-*nee*-yoh)
- Viognier (vee-oh-nyay)

Wines for a Change of Pace

Try these white wines:

- **Dry Chenin Blanc:** Medium-bodied with rich texture and a crisp backbone
- **Gewurztraminer:** Full-bodied, soft, with medium-intense to intense floral and lychee flavors
- **Pinot Blanc:** Dry, medium-bodied with crisp acidity and subtle flavors of apple and minerals

- **Pinot Gris/Grigio:** Dry to fairly dry, fairly full, with pronounced peach, citrus, and floral flavors
- **Roussanne:** Dry, full-bodied, with rich texture and white-fruit flavors
- **Viognier:** Full-bodied, dry, flavorful (peaches, floral notes)

Try these red wines:

- **Barbera:** Medium-bodied, fairly soft, with tart-cherry flavors
- **Cabernet Franc:** Medium-bodied and dry with expressive red-fruit flavors and medium tannin
- **Malbec:** Medium- or full-bodied with velvety texture and rich plum flavor
- **Petite Sirah:** Full-bodied, dry and firm, with ripe dark-fruit flavors and spicy notes

- **Petit Verdot:** Full-bodied, dry and firm with tannin; flavors of blueberry with violet notes
- **Sangiovese:** Fairly full-bodied, with firm tannin and red-fruit and herbal flavors
- **Tempranillo:** Full-bodied, with dryish texture and flavors of dark fruits and herbs

Copyright © 2009 Wiley Publishing, Inc. All rights reserved.

Item 7607-2.

For more information about Wiley Publishing, call 1-800-762-2974.

For Dummies: Bestselling Book Series for Beginners

California
Wine
FOR
DUMMIES®

by Ed McCarthy & Mary Ewing-Mulligan

WILEY

Wiley Publishing, Inc.

California Wine For Dummies®

Published by
Wiley Publishing, Inc.
111 River St.
Hoboken, NJ 07030-5774
www.wiley.com

Copyright © 2009 by Wiley Publishing, Inc., Indianapolis, Indiana

Published simultaneously in Canada

For general information on our other products and services, please contact our Customer Care Department within the U.S. at 877-762-2974, outside the U.S. at 317-572-3993, or fax 317-572-4002.

For technical support, please visit www.wiley.com/techsupport.

Wiley also publishes its books in a variety of electronic formats. Some content that appears in print may not be available in electronic books.

Library of Congress Control Number: 2009924128

ISBN: 978-0-470-37607-2

Manufactured in the United States of America

10 9 8 7 6 5 4 3 2 1

WILEY

About the Authors

Ed McCarthy and **Mary Ewing-Mulligan** are two wine lovers who met at an Italian wine tasting in New York City's Chinatown and subsequently merged their wine cellars and wine libraries when they married. *California Wine For Dummies* is the seventh wine book that they co-authored in the *For Dummies* series — including the best-selling *Wine For Dummies* and two of their favorites, *French Wine For Dummies* and *Italian Wine For Dummies.* They also wrote *Wine Style: Using Your Senses to Explore and Enjoy Wine* (Wiley) in 2005. Together, they have taught hundreds of wine classes, visited nearly every wine region in the world, run five marathons, and raised 12 cats. Along the way, they amassed more than a half a century of wine experience between them.

Mary is president of International Wine Center, a New York City school for wine professionals and serious wine lovers. As U.S. director of the Wine & Spirit Education Trust (WSET), the world's leading wine-education organization, she works to make the courses she offers in New York available in more and more parts of the United States. She is also a freelance wine writer. Mary's most impressive credential is that she was the first female Master of Wine (MW) in the United States and currently is one of only 26 MWs in the U.S. (with 277 MWs worldwide).

Ed, a New Yorker, graduated from the City University of New York with a master's degree in psychology. He taught high school English in another life, while working part time in wine shops to satisfy his passion for wine and to subsidize his growing wine cellar. In 1999, Ed went solo as author of *Champagne For Dummies*, a topic on which he's especially expert. He is contributing editor of *Beverage Media,* a trade publication. Both Ed and Mary are also columnists for the online wine magazine WineReviewOnline.com and are Certified Wine Educators.

When they aren't writing, teaching, or visiting wine regions, Mary and Ed maintain a busy schedule of speaking, judging at wine competitions, and tasting as many new wines as possible. They admit to leading thoroughly unbalanced lives in which their only non-wine pursuits are hiking in the Berkshires and the Italian Alps. At home, they wind down to the tunes of k.d. Lang, Sarah Brightman, Bob Dylan, and Neil Young in the company of their feline roommates, Dolcetto, Max, Ponzi, and Pinot.

Authors' Acknowledgments

This book would not be possible without the amazing team at Wiley. We thank Publisher Diane Steele, who along with Acquisitions Editor Stacy Kennedy engaged us and encouraged us to write *California Wine For Dummies*. And special thanks to our Project Editor, Chrissy Guthrie, for her patience with us and for her invaluable suggestions to improve the text — and make it all fit!

We thank our Technical Editor, fellow wine writer and esteemed California wine expert Alan Goldfarb, for his expertise. It's a better, more accurate book because of you.

Special thanks to Steve Ettlinger, our agent and friend, who brought us to the *For Dummies* series in the first place and who is always there for us.

We thank all our friends in the wine business for your input and suggestions for this book; the book reviewers whose criticism of our previous books has been so generous; and our readers, who have encouraged us with your enthusiasm for our earlier books. We are inspired when we recall how many of you have told us that *Wine For Dummies* was the first wine book you ever read.

Mary gives special thanks to Linda Lawry and everyone else at International Wine Center who enabled her to have the time and peace of mind to work on this book. Thanks, also, to Elise McCarthy; E. J. McCarthy and his fiancée, Kim Espinosa; and Cindy McCarthy Tomarchio and her husband, David, for their encouragement and support. And thanks to Jason and Michael Tomarchio for the joy they bring us.

Publisher's Acknowledgments

We're proud of this book; please send us your comments through our Dummies online registration form located at `http://dummies.custhelp.com`. For other comments, please contact our Customer Care Department within the U.S. at 877-762-2974, outside the U.S. at 317-572-3993, or fax 317-572-4002.

Some of the people who helped bring this book to market include the following:

Acquisitions, Editorial, and Media Development

Senior Project Editor: Christina Guthrie

Acquisitions Editor: Stacy Kennedy

Senior Copy Editor: Danielle Voirol

Assistant Editor: Erin Calligan Mooney

Editorial Program Coordinator: Joe Niesen

Technical Editor: Alan Goldfarb

Editorial Manager: Christine Meloy Beck

Editorial Assistants: David Lutton, Jennette ElNaggar

Art Coordinator: Alicia B. South

Cover Photos: © Gerald French/CORBIS

Cartoons: Rich Tennant (`www.the5thwave.com`)

Composition Services

Project Coordinator: Kristie Rees

Layout and Graphics: Samantha K. Allen, Reuben W. Davis, Christine Williams

Special Art: Interior maps by Lisa Reed

Proofreader: Nancy L. Reinhardt

Indexer: Potomac Indexing, LLC

Publishing and Editorial for Consumer Dummies

Diane Graves Steele, Vice President and Publisher, Consumer Dummies

Kristin Ferguson-Wagstaffe, Product Development Director, Consumer Dummies

Ensley Eikenburg, Associate Publisher, Travel

Kelly Regan, Editorial Director, Travel

Publishing for Technology Dummies

Andy Cummings, Vice President and Publisher, Dummies Technology/General User

Composition Services

Gerry Fahey, Vice President of Production Services

Debbie Stailey, Director of Composition Services

Contents at a Glance

Table of Contents

Introduction

Do California wines need demystifying? At one time, we believed they didn't. In a universe of wines with complicated foreign-language place names, California's wines, named for their grape varieties, were a beacon of simplicity, welcoming uninitiated wine drinkers to the pleasures of wine.

These days, California wines are still welcoming (they don't get to dominate wine consumption in the U.S. by being difficult to enjoy!), but the number of wineries in California has exploded to more than 2,000, and the map of wine regions has expanded to include pockets of vineyard land that were literally off the map only 15 years ago. What's more, California now grows dozens of grape varieties beyond its traditional Big Six mainstays for fine wine.

California wine is still easy to understand, but scratch the surface, and you can discover a wealth of fascinating nuances. Nuances of climate, of grape varieties and *clones* (subvarieties), of vineyard soils and altitudes and proximity to the sea, of winemaking beliefs and goals — each of these enriches the landscape of California wine and the drinking pleasures that it holds.

California today is truly a land of opportunity for wine lovers. Come discover it with us.

About This Book

Over the past few years, we came to realize that a serious gap existed in our *Wine For Dummies* series — California! This gap is especially gaping when you consider that almost 70 percent of all the wine consumed in the U.S. is California wine. This book is our attempt to fill that gap and to help you complete your wine knowledge and increase your wine-drinking pleasure.

You probably drink California wine already, because wines from California are the top-selling wines in the U.S. Could you find other wines from California — other grape varieties, other tastes — that you might enjoy even more than what you already know? We bet you can. Will discovering the various wine regions that specialize in making your favorite type of wine increase your appreciation of the wine? We hope so. We hope that our passion and the passion of our favorite winemakers will become contagious so that you can find your own passion for California wines.

In every other *For Dummies* wine book that we've written, we took a geographic approach to the wines, moving from one wine region to the next and discussing the kinds of wines that you find in each. In *California Wine For Dummies*, however, we take a different approach. We move from grape variety to grape variety, because that's the structure we're accustomed to in approaching California wines. Within each grape-variety chapter, we discuss the regions of California that grow that variety and the signature each region gives to the taste of the wine.

Of course, we also name our favorite producers for each type of wine. Because California makes wines at every price level, from affordable to downright luxury pricing, we give our wine recommendations in specific price ranges — including top wines to try in the under-$15 category.

Conventions Used in This Book

Here are a few conventions you should be familiar with as you read this book:

- New terms appear in *italics* and are followed by brief, easy-to-understand definitions.

- Web addresses appear in a particular typeface called monofont.

- Keywords in bulleted lists appear in **boldface.**

- In pronunciations, the stressed syllable is *italicized.* (***Note:*** French words technically don't have stressed syllables.)

In making our specific wine recommendations throughout this book, we usually divide the wines into three price categories. We use the wines' average retail prices as the basis for placing them in each category, to the extent that we're able to determine that from Internet listings; in some stores, the wines cost more, and in restaurants, they tend to cost at least two to three times the retail price. The prices we use are based on the currently available vintages at the time of our writing this book; subsequent vintages and older wines can cost more.

The actual price ranges we use vary slightly from wine to wine, but here are the general categories:

- ✔ **Moderately priced:** Wines that retail for less than $20
- ✔ **Moderate-plus:** Wines that retail between $20 and $50
- ✔ **High-end:** Wines that retail mainly between $50 and $100

We list the actual average retail prices for individual wines that cost over $100. In rare situations, when we recommend several wines over $100, we categorize them as *Luxury* wines. You'll also see some sidebars naming some top-value wines that cost under $15.

Other "rules" that we apply in our listings of recommended wines include the following:

- ✔ Within each price category, we alphabetize our recommended wines according to the names of the producers. Sometimes we list more than one recommended wine per producer.
- ✔ After every wine, we indicate, in parentheses, the American Viticultural Area (AVA) or other location where the grapes grow; this might or might not be the same as the location of the winery.
- ✔ When the name of a particular wine isn't the name of a vineyard, we place the name of the wine in quotation marks.
- ✔ We do not include small-production wines that are available only in California. (We do, however, recommend some small-production wines that have limited national distribution. We suggest that you check www.wine-searcher.com to help you find the retail stores where the wine is available and to comparison-shop for the lowest prices.)

Finally, any given lodging or meal prices might have changed since publication. Visit Web sites or contact the hotel or restaurant in question for the most up-to-date information.

What You're Not to Read

Because we wrote this book, we obviously believe that every single bit of information will be useful to you. But you might not care to know the same level of detail as we care to give. The Technical Stuff icon marks details or background explanation that you can ignore, if you like, or come back to later when you have more time.

Likewise, our sidebars amount to color commentary on the text; you can skip over these gray boxes if you want to know just the facts. Some sidebars offer basic background information about wine specifically for readers who feel their wine basics could use some brushing up.

Foolish Assumptions

In writing this book, we had to make some assumptions about you, the reader. We assume that

- You drink wine already or are interested in becoming a wine drinker.

- You already know something about wine. But just in case you don't, we use simple language and explain things clearly, and we include fundamental information such as what wine is and how to taste it. (For more thorough coverage of the basics, check out our other book, *Wine For Dummies,* 4th Edition [Wiley].)

- You're looking for more than a travel guide. You might also want information on California wine history, characteristics of wines from certain regions, or recommendations for specific wines. Of course, if you are looking for travel info, we do include some text from *Frommer's Portable California Wine Country,* 5th Edition, by Erika Lenkert (Wiley), as well as some of our own suggestions for hotels, restaurants, and wine country attractions.

How This Book Is Organized

We divide this book into five parts, which we describe here. This part structure allows you easy access to the information you need, whether you want to know about California wine in general, the state's most popular wines, or some of its more minor (but still excellent) players.

Part 1: The Big Picture of California Wine

In this meaty section, we give you the lay of the land for California wines, both historically and geographically. We explain how California names its wines, how the state's vast vineyard areas break down into specific regions known as AVAs, and how to recognize a wine's AVA and other important phrases on a label.

Chapter 1 provides an overview of California wine today — the range of wines that California makes and how California's geography makes the wines unique — and then it looks back in time to the origins of today's wine scene in the Golden State. Chapter 2 reveals what a varietal is and what varietal wines represent (or don't) in terms of quality; it also explains the exceptions, wines that are blends of various grape varieties. Finally, it provides snapshot descriptions of California's main white and red grape varieties.

Chapter 3 in effect is a line-by-line explanation of the language of a California wine label. Chapter 4 gets down and dirty: It covers all the major wine regions of California, telling you what's special about each, from the soil to the climate to the types of wine the region makes.

Part 11: The Headliners

The four chapters in this part cover the six varietal wines that you most need to know about to be fluent in California wine: Chardonnay, Sauvignon Blanc, Cabernet Sauvignon, Merlot, Pinot Noir, and Zinfandel. For each type of wine, we explain the various regions where the grapes for that wine grow, we describe the taste of the wine, we profile a few storied producers, and we name our recommended brands in several different price categories — including special-value wines under $15.

Part III: More Reds, Whites, Pinks, and Bubblies

Yes, there's more — much more! California makes a tempting range of white and red wines from grape varieties that are more obscure than the main six covered in Part II, as well as fascinating blended white and red wines inspired by the wines of classic European wine regions. We cover those wines in this part of the book, along with California's rosé (pink) wines, sparkling wines, and sweet dessert wines. In Chapter 9, you read about Pinot Grigio/Pinot Gris, white Rhône-style wines, Riesling, and other white wines. Chapter 10 introduces you to Syrah/Shiraz, Petite Sirah, red Rhone-style blends, and Italian-inspired blends. And Chapter 11 covers California's sparkling wines, rosé wines, and sweet wines.

Part IV: Enjoying California Wines

This part of the book brings all that information about California wines home — home to your table, your neighborhood wine shop, your guests at dinner, and your vacation plans. Chapter 12 reveals our secrets for pairing wine and food and tells you which California wines go best with which types of dishes. We also describe the ins and outs of California's recent vintages and counsel you on when to drink which types of wine. Chapter 13 offers practical advice on visiting wineries and getting your souvenir bottles back home safely.

Part V: The Part of Tens

We put our heads together and prioritized all the questions that people ask about California wines so we could answer the ten top frequently asked questions for you in Chapter 14. Then we fantasized about our most romantic, inspiring, fun, not-to-be-missed travel experiences in California wine country and laid out our top ten picks for your consideration in Chapter 15.

Icons Used in This Book

We use icons throughout the book to emphasize certain points about wine. Also, we alert you to information that might be particularly interesting to you (or not).

This bull's-eye marks advice and information that will make you a wiser wine drinker.

You don't need to memorize everything you read in this book, but some issues in wine are so fundamental that you should keep them in mind every time you pull out a wine glass or pick up a bottle. We mark the essential information with this symbol.

This odd little guy is a bit like the 2-year-old who constantly insists on asking, "Why?" If you don't have the same level of curiosity that he has, feel free to skip over the information that follows. Wine will still taste just as delicious.

Wine snobs practice all sorts of affectations designed to make other wine drinkers feel inferior. But you won't be intimidated by their snobbery if you pay attention to the Snob Alert icons and see it for what it is. (And you can find out how to impersonate a wine snob!)

To our tastes, the wines we mark with this icon are bargains because we like them, we believe them to be of good quality, and their price is low compared to other wines of similar type, style, or quality.

Unfortunately, some of the finest, most intriguing, most delicious wines are made in very small quantities. These wines have limited distribution, and you can't always get your hands on a bottle, even if you're willing to pay the price. We mark such wines with this icon and hope that your search proves fruitful. (*Tip:* You might be able to find some leads at www.wine-searcher.com, a search engine that scours the price lists of thousands of retailers.)

In certain sections of the book, we add valuable travel info, including tips on restaurants, hotels, happening events, and so forth, from *Frommer's Portable California Wine Country,* 5th Edition, by Erika Lenkert (Wiley).

Where to Go from Here

You can start reading anywhere in this book. Jump right into Chardonnay (Chapter 5) or Pinot Noir (Chapter 7) or whatever sounds inviting. But when you have a moment, read the opening chapters that explain the words you find on wine labels and name all California wine regions. If you're fairly new to wine, these chapters will be all the more helpful. And don't overlook our final chapters dealing with practical matters, such as pairing wine and food and traveling to wine country.

Part I
The Big Picture of California Wine

In this part...

California is a big place, and the big picture of its wines is no small snapshot! The kinds of wine that California makes, the importance of these wines on the world stage, California's major grape varieties and wines — right there, you have plenty of wine background to chew on (or more precisely, to slurp and swallow). But we don't stop there. This is the part where you discover the meaning behind the names of California's wines and the other words that appear on the wines' labels, as well as follow the fascinating history of California wine from its origins to the present day. Most important of all, you can travel vicariously from one wine region to the next and discover what makes each one special.

Chapter 1

Introducing California Wines

- -

In This Chapter

▶ The gamut of California's wine production

▶ California wine's international status

▶ Why the region is ideal for producing wines

▶ California's colorful wine history

- -

All 50 U.S. states make wine — mainly from grapes but in some cases from berries, pineapple, or other fruits. Equality and democracy end there. California stands apart from the whole rest of the pack for the quantity of wine it produces, the international reputation of those wines, and the degree to which wine has permeated the local culture. To say that in the U.S., wine *is* California wine is not a huge exaggeration.

If you want to begin finding out about wine, the wines of California are a good place to start. If you're already a wine lover, chances are that California's wines still hold a few surprises worth discovering. To get you started, we paint the big picture of California wine in this chapter.

Covering All the Bases in Wine Production

Wine, of course, is not just wine. The shades of quality, price, color, sweetness, dryness, and flavor among wines are so many that you can consider *wine* a whole world of beverages rather than a single product. Can a single U.S. state possibly embody this whole world of wine? California can and does.

Whatever your notion of wine is — even if that changes with the seasons, the foods you're preparing, or how much you like the people you'll be dining with — California has that base covered. We would be the last people to suggest that you forever-after drink the wines of only one state or wine region, because we believe in constant experimentation; however, if that curse were to befall you, you could rest assured that within the boundaries of California, you could find just about any type of wine you might desire.

The color and type spectrums

California makes a huge amount of white wine and red wine — the split is about even these days — and yet one of California's best-selling types of wines is actually pink, or *rosé*. (That would be the wine called White Zinfandel, and yes, that name is illogical.) California also produces plenty of rosé wines besides White Zinfandel.

Sparkling wine — wine with bubbles in it — and really sweet like-dessert-in-a-glass wines are two classic types of wine beyond regular *still* (nonsparkling), *dry* (not sweet) wines. California's sparkling wines range in price from super-affordable to elite, and in quality, they range from decent to world-class. They also encompass a range of styles, from sweet and easy-to-enjoy to classically dry and complex. Sweet dessert wines are one of California's smallest wine categories, but nevertheless, you can score. Your options range from delicious red Port-style wines (*fortified* wines, made by adding extra alcohol) to rich, seductive golden-colored wines made from grapes that shriveled into an extra sweet state.

Have we missed anything? We hope not, because California doesn't! We cover white and red wines in Chapters 5 through 10, and we cover rosé, sparkling, and dessert wines in Chapter 11.

The wallet spectrum

For some wine drinkers, love of wine is color blind as long as the price is right — and the wine producers of California are completely obliging. At their most affordable, California's wines cost as little as $2 for the equivalent of a standard bottle. (The volume of a standard wine bottle is 750 milliliters, which is a little more than 25 ounces.) And a few elite wines boast prices of up to $750 a bottle. Yes, that's $1 per milliliter, or $30 an ounce.

In terms of the dollar value of sales, the booming segment of the market is in the $15-and-up wines. But a greater quantity of wine sells in the under-$8 price tier. Bottom line: plenty of wine at whatever price you choose.

Defining wine

If you're new to the whole wine experience, we proudly recommend that you take a look at our book, *Wine For Dummies*, 4th Edition (Wiley), because it provides a wealth of information about wine in general that can help you appreciate our favorite beverage. But the last thing we want to do is halt your momentum in discovering California's wines, so for now, here's a quick summary of what wine is and how a wine gets to be the way it is.

Wine is grape juice that underwent fermentation, a biological process in which microscopic fungi called yeasts transform the sugar in the juice into alcohol and carbon dioxide (which usually dissipates). A *dry* wine is a wine whose grape sugar converted totally or almost totally into alcohol so that little or no sugar remains in the wine. Wines that retain some natural grape sugar are categorized as off-dry, medium-dry, medium-sweet, or sweet, depending on how much sugar they contain.

A dry wine is mainly water, with about 12 to 16 percent alcohol (ethanol), 0.5 to 1 percent glycerol (a sweet alcohol), 0.5 to 0.7 percent tartaric acid (from the grapes), and hundreds of minor components. These minor components include other acids, *tannin* (a natural substance in the grape skins and seeds), the grapes' coloring matter, unfermented grape sugar (called *residual* sugar), minerals, aromatic compounds that create the wine's aromas and flavors, and so forth.

Most of the components of wine come from the grapes. Others come from the fermentation process, the materials that the wine or juice comes in contact with (such as oak barrels), and the wine's aging process before and/or after the wine is bottled and sold. The winemaker also often adds certain substances, such as sulfur dioxide (which helps prevent the wine from turning to vinegar) or extra acid, in tiny amounts.

Even though wine is mainly water, it's an amazingly complex liquid. Different wines can be similar in taste, but no two wines are exactly the same. The taste of any one wine is a function of

✔ The grapes

✔ The winemaking technique, such as the temperature or duration of fermentation and the type of container used for fermentation or aging

✔ How young or old the wine is when you drink it

✔ How you store it and how it was stored before you bought it (heat can age a wine prematurely, for example, or ruin it)

Even the type of closure on the bottle — natural cork, plastic "cork," composite cork, or a screw-off cap — can affect the wine's taste. Even the type of glass that you drink it from can affect its taste!

What's a quality wine, anyway?

You can't read this book — or any other book on wine, for that matter — without stumbling across frequent references to wine quality. If you conclude that some wines are higher in quality than others, you're right. But how much should quality matter to you in choosing your wine?

First of all, you can take comfort in knowing that very few poor-quality wines exist today. The quality scale of California's wines, for example, runs from acceptable to superb, and most wines fall into the *good* range. Secondly, you should remember that the quality of a wine is ultimately less important than the enjoyment the wine brings you. When a wine is satisfying, what more can you ask of it?

Wine experts assess the quality of a wine by evaluating all its characteristics, deciding how well the various aspects of the wine work together, and measuring all this against their mental yardsticks of what they consider to be wine perfection. Some of the issues might not be important to you. For example, a wine that seems to be capable of developing great complexity of flavor as it ages can earn bonus points from an expert, but you might plan to drink the wine in the next 24 hours. Or a wine can lose points because its taste doesn't follow through to the rear of your mouth (it doesn't have *length*); but if you tend to simply drink a wine rather than analyze it as it flows across your tongue, the initial impression of flavor is more important to you.

Many of the wines that experts consider to be lower down the quality scale are wines that are made purposely to appeal to certain groups of wine drinkers. They have characteristics such as intense flavor that hits you immediately, soft *texture* (the tactile feeling of the wine against your tongue and gums), and a slight note of sweetness — all of which make the wine taste delicious — but they lack the nuances of flavor or texture that a finer wine would have.

The packaging spectrum

For several generations, until the mid-1970s, California specialized in making red, white, and pink wines that sold in large jug-like bottles at very affordable prices. These were easy wines for everyday life, with screw-off caps so that you could pour two glasses and then close up the bottle for the next day. You can still find these California *jug wines* in most places where wine is sold, although their sales have declined.

Today's large-volume, easy-open option is the 3-liter box with a collapsible bag of wine inside and a spigot attached to the bag for easy serving. Some California wines even come in *Tetra-Brik* packages, which are compact, plasticized paper containers like you see for cooked tomatoes, generally about 1 liter in size — 33 percent bigger than a standard wine bottle. They don't require a plastic bag inside them to hold the wine, and they're super portable, not to mention eco-friendly and a great value. California is certainly not the only place that's packaging wine in innovative ways like this, but California's wine repertoire definitely includes plenty of wines in this category.

User-friendly wine options from California now also include premium wines — the good stuff — in regular-size wine bottles that are sealed with screw-off caps. Some winemakers, concerned that the screwcaps might confuse wine drinkers because of California's long tradition of making inexpensive jug wines with that type of closure, aren't embracing screwcaps for fine wine the way that Australian and New Zealand winemakers are. But some are, so California has that, too.

Leading the Market in Popularity

The Golden State makes more wine than all other U.S. states combined. Not only that: Its wine production is huge even on a world scale. The U.S. as a whole ranks fourth for the quantity of wine it produces. But California owns that number-four spot even all by itself, producing 7 percent of the world's wine — more than Argentina, Chile, Australia, Germany, and every other country except for Italy, France, and Spain.

In 2007, California made almost 566 million gallons of wine. That's equivalent to more than 2.8 billion standard-size bottles.

All that production reflects a big demand for California wine. Two out of every three times that someone in the U.S. grabs a bottle of wine to take home, points to a wine name on a restaurant wine list, or clicks on the computer screen to buy wine, that wine comes from California.

A driving force behind the popularity of California wine is the way the wines taste. We're about to make a generalization here, but we feel that it's a safe one: California wines are very fruity (that is, they have aromas and flavors that suggest fruits) and very flavorful (those fruity flavors are intense and easy to notice when you taste the wine), and these characteristics appeal to the typical American palate. When Americans taste California wines, they like them, and they come back to them again and again. Well, two out of three times, anyway.

Another factor feeding the popularity of California wines is the smart marketing that the wineries practice. Winemakers in California understand what people want and make wines that fill those needs. That's why California wines run the whole gamut of styles and types: Wine drinkers themselves run the whole gamut in taste and price preferences. Whether you're a glass-of-Chardonnay-at-the-bar drinker, a fine wine collector, or a passionate Pinot Noir hobbyist, California makes wines that can appeal to you.

Of course, quality plays a role also. Starting in the 1970s, California pioneered many winemaking innovations that improved wine quality. Flaws that used to exist in wines all over the world are now rare because the highly trained winemakers of California discovered how to prevent them, and other winemakers followed suit. In terms of fundamental quality, California wines are among the most reliable in the world.

Golden Resources in the Golden State

Could the success story of California wines have happened just anywhere, or is there something about California itself that's an integral part of the picture?

Actually, the place itself is always part of the picture when you talk about wine. Wine is an agricultural product: The grapes that are the raw material for wine come from vineyards that have certain growing conditions — certain soil fertility, certain moisture, certain sunshine and heat, and so forth. These growing conditions affect the quality and, to some extent, the style of the final wine. If California makes quality, flavorful wines, that's due in no small part to the place called California. We discuss the various regions of California in Chapter 4, but for now, read on to find out what makes the state as a whole so ideal for producing wine.

California climate

Of the various factors that influence vineyard regions and determine their suitability for growing wine grapes, one of the most important is climate. *Climate* is the general meteorological pattern of a large area. *Microclimate*, a term you hear frequently in wine circles, is the particular meteorological pattern of a smaller area, such as a certain hillside.

In wine terms, what matters is having a good, long stretch of months with temperatures above 50°F, not-excessive amounts of rain, and few, if any, frosts or hailstorms. Beyond those basic requirements, winemakers look for special characteristics, such as fog or winds that moderate high temperatures, long sunshine hours, or abundant winter rains that supply groundwater. Every nuance in a microclimate affects the grapes that grow there. Even if California wines are generally very fruity and flavorful, nuances of taste occur as the result of differences in climate — and these differences are part of the reason California makes wines in every conceivable style.

The French use the word *terroir* to describe the combination of climate and soil factors that affect the grapes and thereby influence the style of an area's wines. California's winemakers sometimes use this term themselves.

Rainfall and the need for irrigation

California has a Mediterranean-type climate, which means that rains fall in the winter but not during the summer growing season. We can still remember our disappointment the first time we went to Northern California during the summer, expecting to see green landscapes and finding brown grass and parched fields instead. (At least the vines themselves were green and gorgeous.)

To supply the water grapevines need, most wineries in California rely on irrigation. Generally they use *drip irrigation*, a system that feeds drops of water to each vine through a small hose that stretches along the base of the vines. These days, irrigating the vines is a complex balancing act between conserving water and giving the vines enough.

Some vineyards, particularly those on steep slopes where irrigation installations are difficult, survive on only the water that the ground holds. California has these *dry-farmed* vineyards, but they're the exception rather than the rule.

Hot but cool, cool but hot

Apart from their common lack of growing-season rain, California's winemakers face many differences in weather patterns, depending on where in the state their vineyards are situated. For example, in the huge Central Valley, which lies mainly south of the state capital of Sacramento, the temperatures can be very high all summer. In contrast, the vineyards in Napa and Sonoma Counties that lie across the San Pablo Bay north of San Francisco experience many mornings that are so cool and foggy you might forget that it's summer.

More than 60 years ago, two eminent scientists in California devised a method for categorizing the climate of various wine regions according to the average monthly temperatures from April through October. They defined five temperature bands, calling the coolest one Region I and the warmest, Region V. Different *heat*

summation regions, as they're called, are appropriate for growing grapes to make different types of wines. California's finest wines come from the cooler regions, Regions I and II.

Ocean breezes, elevation, and other influences on climate

Picture what California looks like on a map. (If you're having trouble, turn to Chapter 4 for a map of California's wine regions.) With its long coastline, mountains, and deserts, the state has an amazing range of altitudes and other features that influence temperature, humidity, and rainfall patterns. The Pacific Ocean to the west represents a moist, cooling influence, whereas the deserts that occupy the state's eastern border, adjacent to Nevada and Arizona, represent a hot, dry weather influence.

In California, one of the key determinants of local climate is not how northerly or southerly a vineyard is but how close it is to the Pacific Ocean. Ocean breezes and fog moderate the temperature downward. Interior vineyard areas experience no moderating influence from the ocean, except in special cases when a mountain range funnels ocean air far inward or through some such anomaly.

California also boasts a wide range of altitudes, from Death Valley, which lies at 282 feet below sea level, to Mount Whitney, which rises 14,505 feet above sea level. You won't find any wineries or vineyards at either extreme, of course, but the state's diversity of altitudes has an impact on its wines nonetheless.

Altitudes vary even within a single wine region of California. Napa Valley, for example — California's most famous wine region — has vineyards on flat, low-lying land close to the Napa River; on hillsides that rise gently to the west and east of the river; and on mountains that rise above the hills. And that's just one of California's wine regions, of which there are dozens.

Soil matters

In grape-growing circles, not all dirt is equal. The particular soil that a vineyard has is an important element in the overall ecosystem of that vineyard, affecting the availability of water and nutrients to the vines, the depth to which the roots grow, the rate of vine growth, and so forth.

Different soils can require different irrigation treatments, different pruning techniques, or different *rootstocks* (the rooting part of the vine, which, through grafting, is usually a different species from the part of the vine that produces the fruit). Subtly or not-so-subtly, the soil affects the way the grapes grow and therefore the wine that the grapes make.

The vineyard temperature dynamic

How much can vineyard temperature affect the taste of the final wine? Actually, quite a lot. Generally speaking, the warmer the temperature of the vineyard, the riper the grapes get. The riper the grapes get, the more sugar and the less acidity they have; they taste sweeter and less tart, just as for any other fruit.

In the winemaking process, the sugar that accumulates in the grapes changes into alcohol — therefore, the riper the grapes, the higher the alcohol content of the wine. Besides being high in alcohol, wines from very ripe grapes have flavors of very ripe fruit or sometimes even baked fruit. And because the acidity of the grapes is lower, the acidity of the wine is lower (unless the winemaker adds acid to the juice); the lower acidity makes for a softer texture in the wine.

Grapes that are somewhat less ripe, as they can be in cooler vineyards, tend to make wines with medium alcohol levels, fresh fruity flavors, and enough acidity to bring vibrancy to the wine. Either style of wine can be delicious, but each is distinct from the other because of the vineyard temperature.

In California, many of the least expensive wines come from grapes grown in fertile soils, and plenty of the fine wines come from grapes grown in soils of medium or poor fertility. Mountain vineyards in particular tend to have poor soils, resulting in grapes that are concentrated in color and flavor.

California's winemakers tend to place less emphasis on soil than many European winemakers do, but that doesn't mean that soil variations don't exist throughout the state. In Napa Valley alone, scientists have documented more than 30 different types of soil.

The human factor

Another element in California's unique combination of wine resources is its people. Even if Californians joke that very few of them were born actually in California, the fact is that California's climate and lifestyle have attracted an impressive pool of winemaking talent. Or to be perfectly correct, California has attracted the people, and its universities have nurtured the winemaking talent.

California boasts two major universities that specialize in teaching winemaking and *viticulture* (that's *grape growing* to the rest of us). The two schools are the California State University at Fresno (www.csufresno.edu) and the University of California at Davis (www.ucdavis.edu), each known in wine circles by just its location name. A high percentage of California's own winemakers have launched their careers by studying at these universities.

Davis, in particular, is world famous. Seldom do we visit wine regions in Europe — even the most established, elite winemaking regions — without meeting a winemaker who studied at Davis. The stellar reputation of the university's technical wine programs has made Davis a destination of choice for those who could go anywhere in the world.

Besides studying in California, winemakers from abroad often spend time working in California's wineries, particularly when they're young and just getting started in their families' wine businesses. This is a boon for everyone involved, because the sharing of traditions and winemaking philosophy that results enriches the experience of California's winemakers as much as it does the visitors'.

California's Wine Timeline

We've visited the vineyards of Greece and Israel, which both have histories of grape growing and wine production that date back 4,000 to 5,000 years. By those standards, California is a baby. Wine grapes have grown in California for no more than 250 years. (That's one reason you might hear California referred to as a *New World* wine region, as opposed to Europe's vineyards, which are part of the *Old World* of wine.)

California's youth doesn't imply a lack of history, however. Those 250 years have seen several distinct phases of wine production and an impressive growth trend.

Planting the seeds in the 18th century

Wine grapes first came to California via Mexico. After Mexico became part of the Spanish Empire in the early 1500s, Spanish missionaries, both Jesuits and Franciscans, planted vineyards in Mexico. Gradually, as Spain expanded its reach, the missionaries moved up to "New Mexico," an area that spread from what's now Texas to California.

Franciscan Father Junípero Serra, the greatest Spanish wine missionary of all, planted the first California vineyard at Mission San Diego in 1769. Father Serra established eight more missions and vineyard sites as he traveled north in California. He died in 1784 and is justifiably known as the Father of California Wine.

The variety Father Serra planted, descended from Spanish vines growing in Mexico, became known as the Mission grape, and it dominated California wine production until about 1880, when the grape variety called Zinfandel became established (refer to Chapter 8 for more on Zinfandel's heritage).

The founder and other pioneers

In 1833, a Frenchman named Jean-Louis Vignes planted other European vines in Los Angeles. But the person who did the most to establish California wine — the founder of the California wine industry — was a Hungarian immigrant named Agoston Haraszthy.

In the 1850s and 1860s, Haraszthy, a merchant and ultimately a promoter of California wine, made several trips to Europe, returning with vine cuttings from 165 of Europe's best vineyards. Although he did obtain grants from California to cover some of the expenses, he covered much of the cost personally. Haraszthy introduced about 300 grape varieties to California, an amazing feat.

Haraszthy also fostered vine planting all over Northern California, promoted hillside planting, dug caves for cellaring wine, and championed dry-farmed (nonirrigated) vineyards. And he founded Buena Vista Winery in Sonoma's Carneros region in 1857. Buena Vista is the oldest continually operating winery in California.

Other early wineries include the following:

- **Charles Krug:** Napa Valley's first commercial winery, Charles Krug, opened in 1861. Robert Mondavi's parents later acquired it (see the upcoming section "Reinventing itself in the 1960s"). Today, the Peter Mondavi family owns and operates the winery.

- **Schramsberg:** In 1862, Jacob Schram, a German immigrant, founded the Schramsberg winery on Napa Valley's Diamond Mountain. About a century later, the late Jack and Jamie Davies stumbled upon the long-abandoned winery and began California's first modern sparkling wine business at Schramsberg — today better than ever under the tutelage of the Davies' son, Hugh. (*Note:* In the 1890s, French immigrant Paul Masson probably pioneered California sparkling wine in the Santa Cruz Mountains.)

- **Simi:** In 1876, two Tuscan immigrant brothers, Giuseppe and Pietro Simi, began making wine in San Francisco from Sonoma County grapes. In 1881, the Simi brothers planted vineyards in Sonoma's Alexander Valley and founded the historic Simi Winery.

✔ **Wente:** In 1883, Wente Vineyards opened in Livermore Valley, east of San Francisco. It's the oldest continuously operating family-owned winery in California.

By 1889, more than 140 wineries existed in California, including Beringer (1876) and Inglenook (1879). By the 1900s, nearly 800 wineries existed in the United States; a good number of these wineries were in California, but they were also in New York, New Jersey, Ohio, and Missouri. California wines found export markets as far away as Australia.

Surviving Prohibition

California winemaking was forced to take a big time-out on January 16, 1920, when the 18th Amendment to the U.S. Constitution — the Prohibition amendment — went into effect. Through a technicality, home wine production of up to 200 gallons a year remained legal. Although many growers of wine grapes in California went out of business, others were able to survive by making grape juice or by growing grapes for this new home winemaking market. Trainloads of wine grapes went outward from California to major Midwest and Eastern cities, where private citizens, many of them immigrants from countries that had strong wine cultures (such as Italy), bought the grapes for wines they produced in their basements.

When the 21st Amendment repealed the 18th Amendment effective December 5, 1933, and alcohol production again became legal, the California families who managed to keep their vineyards going were poised to produce wine for the thirsty nation. The number of wineries had dwindled to only 140, however.

Inexpensive *generic* wines — wines named for wines from other countries — became big business in the post-Prohibition era through the 1950s. Dessert wines (sweet wines) and fortified wines (wines strengthened with extra alcohol) became the dominant style from California. Not until 1963 did U.S. consumption of dry table wines (from California and elsewhere, including Europe) exceed consumption of rich, sweet wines. But then things began to change.

Reinventing itself in the 1960s

What happened to the California wine industry and the image of California wines starting in the 1960s was nothing short of revolutionary. It didn't begin suddenly — a few wineries in Napa Valley,

Sonoma County, and surrounding areas had already made inroads in a new direction as early as the 1930s. But by the 1960s, the movement had achieved critical mass.

What exactly was this movement? It was a focus on quality and on varietal wines. A *varietal* wine is a wine named for the single or dominant grape variety that makes the wine. By naming wines *Chardonnay* or *Cabernet Sauvignon* instead of using meaningless generic names borrowed from famous wine regions outside the U.S., California's wine producers suddenly brought new legitimacy to their wines. Varietal naming was not the norm then — the majority of European wines were, and still are, named for the place where the grapes grew rather than the grape variety — and California caught the world's eye in adopting this practice.

A pivotal moment in California's wine revolution was the decision of the late Robert Mondavi to leave his family's winery, Charles Krug, and start his own winery. Robert Mondavi Winery opened in 1966, and from day one, its focus was on quality. Mondavi himself became an unofficial ambassador for California wines, particularly those of Napa Valley, and he convinced elite wine producers from all over the world that California was indeed one of the world's finest wine regions. The reputation of Napa Valley and the appeal of the wine business became such that a winery boom occurred in California, and it continues to this day. In 1960, California had 256 wineries, and by 1980, it had almost double that number, 508. Today, California boasts more than 2,600 wineries — and most likely twice as many brands of wine.

Another pivotal moment came in 1976 at a Parisian blind wine-tasting. At what came to be known as the *Judgment of Paris,* a group of expert French wine tasters ranked a Napa Valley Chardonnay higher than the prestigious French white wines featured in the event, and they ranked a Napa Valley Cabernet Sauvignon higher than the elite French red wines they tasted. The wine world was shocked by the success of upstart California. A whole new era began for California wine.

Expanding in the late 20th and early 21st centuries

The growth of California wine from the 1980s to the present has occurred on two fronts: qualitative and quantitative. Statistics testify to the growth in numbers:

- ✔ By the end of 2007, California wineries numbered 2,687.

- ✔ Vineyard land in California covered more than 475,000 acres in 2007, a growth of 43 percent since the late 1980s.

- ✔ California wineries shipped more than 541 million gallons of wine in 2007.

Part of the backstory behind these numbers is the fact that since the 1980s, owning a winery in California has become an aspiration of successful individuals from other walks of life. Doctors, airline pilots, film magnates, corporate executives, and technology millionaires have all poured their fortunes and their hearts into California wine country.

As for quality, much of California's growth in recent years has been an increased awareness of the importance of vineyard sites and a better understanding of how to maximize the potential of specific plots of land.

It was a crisis that instigated this growth in knowledge. In the 1980s, many vines in California began to die because of a tiny louse called *phylloxera* that was gradually destroying the vines' roots. Phylloxera had visited California before, in the late 19th century. The solution then was to graft the *Vitis vinifera* vines — the dominant wine grape species — onto rootstocks of other vine species that were phylloxera-resistant. In the 1980s, California's most prevalent rootstock unexpectedly fell victim to the bug. Except for a lucky few, vineyard and winery owners were forced to make the difficult decision to uproot their vines and replant their land.

In hindsight, this crisis was a great opportunity. It enabled vineyard owners to undo any mistakes of the past and to take advantage of all the knowledge about grape growing that had developed in the years since they had first planted their fields. Awareness of the vineyard's role in producing fine wine increased among winemakers. Today, when winemakers discuss their wines, they're likely to spend as much time talking about the vineyard as about how they make their wine.

Today, California wine country and California wines are so famous and so popular that 14.5 million tourists visit California wine country each year. To put that in perspective, that's fewer tourists than Disneyland gets but more than Hollywood does.

Chapter 2

What's in the Bottle

*O*ver the years, the expression that we've probably heard more than any other from people in the wine business — those who sell wine and those who make it, too — is "it's what's in the bottle that counts." This expression can serve many purposes. For example, if a label is ugly but the wine itself is good, it can suggest that the unattractive label is really of no consequence. (We happen to disagree with that: Why should a wine drinker even try a wine and discover that it's good if the packaging isn't inviting?) But mainly, people use this statement to underscore the fact that wine is a beverage for people to drink and enjoy, and in the end, "what's in the bottle" must taste good to the people who purchase and drink that wine.

What's in California's wine bottles? Lots of good-tasting, people-pleasing wines, to be sure. But what are these wines exactly? What are they made from, and how do winemakers construct them to bring you positive taste experiences? We're not about to launch into a technical treatise on winemaking techniques in this chapter — just offer some insight into what you're actually drinking when you sip a glass of California wine.

The Grape Names the Wine

When you drink most wine, you're essentially drinking grapes. As raw material goes, however, grapes are an extremely mixed lot. Thousands of grape varieties exist just within *Vitis vinifera,* the wine grape species. And winemakers can use grapes from other species, as happens in parts of the U.S. where the climate is unsuitable for growing *Vitis vinifera.* Any one grape variety can become a wine in itself, or it can be combined with another variety or multiple varieties. The number of possible permutations of the raw material, "grapes," surely runs into the millions.

For California wines, the situation is less chaotic. That's because in the 1960s and 1970s, the winemakers of California began to focus on specific grape varieties to make their wines. Today, almost every California wine comes from the juice of a single, dominant grape variety — with the juice of other grape varieties sometimes added, in smaller quantities, to make the wine tastier, higher in quality, or more affordable. And that dominant grape variety is named on the wine label. In fact, in most cases, the name of the grape variety is the name of the wine. (We identify California's major grape varieties and describe their wines later in this chapter.)

Varietal wine: A wine that is what it (mostly) is

A wine that's named after its sole or dominant grape variety is a *varietal* wine, and that's the main type of wine California produces. When you pick up a bottle of California wine, the name of the wine (most of the time) tells you which grape variety is the dominant one in that wine. You more or less know what you're drinking.

To maintain truth in labeling, regulations have emerged to control the use of grape names. The regulations mainly govern the amount of the dominant grape variety that a wine must contain in order for that wine to carry the grape variety name. Early on, a wine could derive as little as 50 percent from a particular variety — and therefore 50 percent from *other* varieties — and still carry that grape variety name. Fortunately, that regulation changed. (We say *fortunately* because — let's face it — half of something just isn't enough to define a whole.) Now, U.S. federal regulations dictate that a wine must derive at least 75 percent from the variety that's named on the label.

Generally speaking, the less expensive a wine is, the more likely it is to contain grapes other than just the named variety. This happens for a couple of reasons:

✓ **Cost of grapes:** The most popular, best-selling grape varieties, such as Chardonnay, are also the most expensive varieties for wineries to purchase from grape growers. By limiting the quantity of that expensive variety to only 75 percent of the wine and blending in 25 percent of wine from less expensive varieties, a winery can bring down its production costs and sell the final wine at a lower price. This cost savings is particularly important for less expensive wines, especially wines that cost $10 a bottle or less, because these wines are often produced in very large volumes so that they can reach wine drinkers across the U.S.

✔ **Flavor appeal for the mass market:** Winemakers carefully engineer the taste of every inexpensive, mass-market wine so that the wine will appeal to as many wine drinkers as possible. Combining other grape varieties with the popular named variety is a valuable tool for winemakers to tweak the taste of their wine and make it distinctive from that of other brands of wine.

Regardless of the wine's price, certain varietal wines almost always contain grapes other than the main variety that's named on the label. That's because winemakers traditionally blend certain grape varieties with certain other varieties to enhance the taste of the wine. For example, Cabernet Sauvignon and Merlot are classic partners: Most Merlot wines contain some Cabernet Sauvignon, and most Cabernet Sauvignon wines contain some Merlot. A bit of Merlot nicely softens a Cabernet wine, and a bit of Cabernet helps make a Merlot wine more substantial.

At face value, whether a wine contains grape varieties other than the main variety that's the name of the wine is neither positive nor negative. The real test of the winemaker's decision to blend multiple grapes is the taste of the wine. If you like the wine, does it really matter how many grape varieties work together to create that taste? (No, it doesn't.)

Variety or varietal?

Want to catch your favorite wine know-it-all in an error? Just listen to how he or she uses the terms *variety* and *varietal,* and you'll probably get the opportunity you're looking for. Lots of people mistakenly use these words as synonyms. They might explain, for example, that "three varietals are in this wine." Technically, the noun *varietal* refers to a wine named for a grape variety; the grape is a *variety,* not a *varietal.* Using *varietal* as an adjective is also correct, as you would if you were to refer to a grape's varietal characteristics, for example.

Quality claims: What varietal does not imply

Generic is the term that U.S. regulations use for wines with borrowed place names, such as the name of a French wine region (Bordeaux, Chablis, and so forth) on a California wine. Back in the 1960s and 1970s, when varietal wines from California were emerging on the U.S. market and wines with generic names were the norm, you could safely say that varietal wines were of a higher quality than other California wines. One reason was that the wineries pioneering varietal naming were all serious, quality-oriented wineries.

The great nature versus nurture debate

Because grapes are the raw material of a wine and because every grape variety has its own set of taste characteristics, it would be logical to think that every wine from a particular grape variety would taste very similar to other wines made from that grape variety. But the situation is actually more complex than that.

For one thing, not all grapes of the same variety taste exactly the same: The farming practices used in the vineyard can influence their taste. When a grape grower prunes the vines in such a way that they produce a very large crop of grapes, for example, those grapes can have less flavor than grapes that come from vines with a smaller crop load. Likewise, flavor may be less intense if one grower irrigates the vines a lot more than another grower. Differences in weather from one year to the next can also affect the taste of the grapes so that in one year, for example, the Cabernet grapes have very ripe fruity flavors and in another year, they have herbal notes in their flavor profile.

Winemaking techniques also can cause wines made from the same grape to taste different from each other. If oak barrels or other forms of oak (boards, chips, or powder that sit in the wine briefly) are part of the winemaking regimen, the wine can have different flavors than a wine from the same grape variety that's made entirely in stainless steel tanks. And that's just one example. The temperature of the fermentation, the type of yeast that's used, the amount of sweetness (if any) that the winemaker retains in the wine, filtration techniques, and many more winemaking practices influence the taste of a wine.

That said, the grape variety dictates the wine's DNA, and therefore wines from the same variety will have quite a lot in common. Each variety has a predictable range of aromas and flavors, for example, as well as a tendency to make wines of a certain depth of color and *weight* in the mouth (how light or full they seem when you drink them).

Today, varietal names are so commonplace among California wines that the presence of a varietal name means absolutely nothing in terms of a wine's quality. You can find varietal wines that sell for $3 a bottle and others that sell for hundreds of dollars a bottle. Obviously, the quality of what's inside the bottle varies tremendously in each case, despite the fact that both wines carry a grape variety name.

To some extent, a varietal name can help you predict what the wine will taste like — but less than you might think. Wines named *Chardonnay* are a perfect example. Some Chardonnay wines are on the sweet side; these tend to be the least expensive wines designed to appeal to large numbers of wine drinkers. Other Chardonnays are completely dry, for those who have classic tastes in wine. Some are soft and made for immediate enjoyment. Others are very serious wines that will improve as they rest in the bottle for a few years. Some — most, in fact — have toasty, smoky aromas and flavors that come from aging in oak barrels (if the wine costs more than $15, approximately) or from absorbing the flavor of chips of oak or oak powder that infuses in the wine for a brief period (the inexpensive wines). But some Chardonnays have no toasty, smoky flavors from oak because they're made without any oak treatment. Grab a bottle of "Chardonnay," and you can't be entirely sure what the wine will taste like. But at least you'll know that at least 75 percent of it derived from Chardonnay juice.

Wines without Varietal Names

The varietal wine concept has penetrated the California wine industry — and the American wine-buying culture — to such an extent that probably over 95 percent of the California wines that you see on store shelves carry varietal names and are made mainly from the grape variety that's the name of the wine. But not every bottle of wine wears a varietal label. The following sections discuss the main situations in which wines have other types of names.

Blends: Naming when the point is multiple grape varieties

Sometimes a winemaker doesn't want to use a full 75 percent of any one grape variety in a wine but prefers instead to blend several types of grapes to achieve exactly the style of wine that he or she seeks. In these cases, the wine carries a clever name that has nothing to do with the grape varieties used to make the wine. For example, Turnbull Wine Cellars in Napa Valley makes a wine called

Old Bull Red that contains, in the 2006 vintage, 44 percent Merlot, 18 percent Tempranillo, 16 percent Sangiovese, 9 percent Cabernet Sauvignon, 6 percent Barbera, 5 percent Cabernet Franc, and 2 percent Syrah. Wines like this can be lots of fun for the winemaker to blend, and they offer wine drinkers something different from the standard varietal wines.

Sparkling wines are another example of blending for success. California's finest sparkling wines are mainly blends of Chardonnay and Pinot Noir grapes, often in approximately equal proportions. (**Note:** The tradition of blending the juice of white and red grapes to make sparkling wines goes back to the Champagne region of France, where it's the norm.) Their labels carry the winery name and the word *brut,* which indicates a dry style, or sometimes a proprietary name, such as Étoile, the top-of-the-line bubbly from the Domaine Chandon winery. You can occasionally come across a sparkling wine that's entirely Chardonnay and carries the grape variety name on its label, but that's an exception to the rule. Many California sparkling wine producers make a *blanc de noirs,* which is a white wine that's usually all Pinot Noir, but the grape variety seldom appears on the front label. (Chapter 11 gives you much more information about California's fine sparkling wines.)

Emulating European classics

Certain classic European wines are blended wines. When wine-makers take those wines as their inspiration, they naturally blend together wines from several different grape varieties. Two types of blends that are common in California are those inspired by the wines of France's southern Rhône Valley and those inspired by red or white wines from France's Bordeaux region.

The fine art of blending

How exactly do winemakers blend different grape varieties together? Most of the time, they *vinify* (make into wine) the juice of each grape variety separately so that they have a certain number of tanks of Chardonnay, for example, and other tanks of French Colombard or Chenin Blanc or whatever other grape they might possibly blend with the Chardonnay. Then, when the time is right, the winemaking team gathers to taste prototype blends — different variations of possible blends that they mix in beakers, just like in chemistry lab. They continue experimenting with different formulations until they find one that has the right taste and is also financially feasible.

Southern Rhône Valley reds are generally blends of lesser-known grape varieties such as Grenache, Mourvedre, Cinsault, and Carignan, as well as the better-known Syrah grape. In the Rhône Valley, the blends vary tremendously, some being Grenache-dominant, some being Syrah-dominant, and everything in between. Today, a nonprofit organization, called the *Rhone Rangers,* exists to promote these wines (www.rhonerangers.org). More than 200 wineries are members, although some of those wineries aren't in California. You generally don't see the name Rhone Ranger on a bottle of blended red wine, but you might see a reference to France's Rhône Valley on the back label. What you'll find inside the bottle is usually a full-bodied, fairly soft red wine with very ripe fruit flavors and a certain earthy note.

Advocates of the style of wine produced in France's Bordeaux region banded together more than 20 years ago to form the Meritage Association (www.meritagewine.org). The red wines are blends of two or more varieties from a group of eight; the principal ones are Cabernet Sauvignon, Merlot, Cabernet Franc, Malbec, and Petit Verdot. The whites are blends of two or more of the following varieties: Sauvignon Blanc, Sémillon, and Sauvignon Vert. In both cases, no single variety can make up more than 90 percent of the blend. More than 100 wineries in California belong to the Meritage Association. Some of these wineries name their top wines with the trademarked name Meritage, and many of them use proprietary names, with or without the name Meritage. One example is the wine called Trilogy, from Flora Springs Winery in Napa Valley, which is a blend of Cabernet Sauvignon, Merlot, and Cabernet Franc. Often, Meritage blends are the most expensive wines that a particular winery makes.

Period pieces, generically speaking

One situation in which California wines are not named varietally occurs when the producer decides to use a generic name. *Generic names* include, in the language of U.S. government regulations, "names of geographic significance which are also the designation of a class or type of wine." These names include Burgundy, Chablis, Champagne, Chianti, Port, and Sherry, among others. Although these names are all names of real wines from real places outside the U.S., producers can legally use them for their California wines provided that the actual origin of the wine appears "in direct conjunction" with the (phony) place name, such as California Burgundy, California Chianti, or California Champagne. (Actually, to be perfectly correct, the regulations refer to these names as *semigenerics,* but we don't really know what that means, and so for simplicity we call them *generic* names.)

What all this bureaucratese means is that you can still find California wines that have those borrowed place names from famous European wine regions. Fifty years ago, these wines represented the majority of California's production, but now they occupy a distinct minority. Generally, you find these wines packaged in large gallon-size jugs or in bag-in-a-box containers. They're a throwback to once-upon-a-time, and they serve a diminishing clientele. The wines are usually sweet, and they're the most inexpensive segment of California's wine production.

The In-Crowd: California's Major Varietal Wines

If you scour the shelves of a good wine shop, you can probably find more than a dozen distinct types of varietal wine from California. But the list of varietal wines is top heavy: A handful of wines are by far the most popular, most widely available, and best-known varietal wines from the Golden State. These are Chardonnay and Sauvignon Blanc (both white wines), Cabernet Sauvignon and Merlot (red wines), and Zinfandel (a red wine and also a pink wine). Pinot Noir and Syrah/Shiraz are also fairly popular varietal wines.

Chardonnay

The Chardonnay grape is a white grape that makes white table wines and sparkling wines. Because the Chardonnay grape is easy to grow in a wide range of climates and types of soils, it grows throughout California's wine regions. The fact that Chardonnay wine is the number one best-selling varietal wine from California is no small incentive to grape growers to continue growing this grape wherever they can.

Chardonnay wines usually have some toasty, smoky aromas and flavors that come from oak. Depending on the individual brand, the oaky character can be intense, moderate, or subtle. (Some California Chardonnays are made without using oak at all, but they're in the minority.) Chardonnay wines have fruit aromas and flavors that include apple, citrus fruit (especially lemon), and tropical fruits such as mango or pineapple. You can also sometimes find aromas and flavors that suggest butter, butterscotch, vanilla, or caramel; these particular aromas and flavors come from oak or winemaking processes, not from the grapes.

White versus red: Tannin makes the difference

For many wine drinkers, the choice of which wine to drink boils down to a very fundamental decision: white or red? The main difference between white wine and red wine is that white wines generally come from white grape varieties and red wines come from red (or "black") varieties. But there's a greater difference than meets the eye: Red wine contains more tannin than white wine does.

Tannin is a substance that can produce a drying sensation, sometimes described as *grip,* in the wine's texture. It exists naturally in the skins, seeds, and stems of grapes, and it can also come from oak barrels that the wines age in. (It also exists in other foods, such as tea.) The presence of tannin in red wines is the main reason they don't taste as good when they're served cold: Chilling the wines can make the tannins taste bitter.

Not only do red grapes contain more tannin than white grapes do, but the process of making red wines — specifically the fact that the grape skins must soak in the juice in order to give their color to the wine — means that more of the grape tannins find their way into red wine.

Some red wines have more tannin than others (Pinot Noir wines tend to have less tannin than Cabernet Sauvignons, for example), and some wines have softer, less-drying tannins than others, but most red wines do contain tannin.

The wines tend to be full-bodied. Although the world's classic Chardonnay wines — the white wines from the Burgundy region of France — are very dry, California's Chardonnays range from dry to rather sweet. The least expensive brands, those that sell for about $10 a bottle or less, are most likely to be somewhat sweet, probably because the wineries are targeting a broad audience that appreciates a wine that's not truly dry. For more information on California Chardonnay, including lists of our recommended wines, turn to Chapter 5.

Sauvignon Blanc

The Sauvignon Blanc grape variety accounts for only about 8 percent of California's white wine production (compared to a whopping 43 percent for Chardonnay), but after Chardonnay, it's the number two most popular domestic white varietal wine. Some wines based on the Sauvignon Blanc grape call themselves Fumé Blanc, which U.S. authorities recognize as a synonym for Sauvignon Blanc. (Chapter 5 tells the whole story of how this wine came to have two different names.)

We find it hard to generalize about the taste of Sauvignon Blanc wines because they vary so much according to where the grapes grow, how ripe the grapes get before they're harvested, how the winemaker chooses to vinify the juice, and how he or she ages the Sauvignon Blanc wine. Not only that — many winemakers like to blend some Sémillon wine into their Sauvignon Blanc, which can alter the taste of the wine a lot by making it softer, fuller, richer in texture, and less intense in flavor.

Generally, Sauvignon Blanc wines are crisper than Chardonnay and medium-bodied rather than full-bodied, with more vivid, pronounced fruit flavors, which include citrus, pear, or passion fruit. The wines can also have herbal or vegetal aromas and flavors, such as mowed grass or green peppers. Also, many Sauvignon Blanc wines are made without any use of oak, and therefore they lack the smoky, toasty, vanilla-like aromas and flavors of Chardonnay.

You can find some Sauvignon Blanc wines from California that are truly dry, but in our experience, more and more of them taste rather sweet; we place them at the sweet end of the spectrum that's commercially considered dry wine.

Cabernet Sauvignon

The Cabernet Sauvignon grape variety is California's most-planted red wine grape, representing about 23 percent of California's red wine production. It grows well in most parts of the state, with the exception of the very coolest regions, such as many coastal areas.

Most of California's elite red wines are either varietal Cabernet Sauvignons or blends such as Meritage wines that are predominately Cabernet Sauvignon (see the earlier section "Emulating European classics"). But you can find plenty of varietal Cabernet Sauvignon wines at every price, including in the $10-and-under price tier.

At the least expensive end, Cabernet Sauvignon wines are very fruity, medium-bodied, fairly flavorful wines that have a bit of sweetness. At medium to high price levels, Cabernet Sauvignon wines are fairly full-bodied with firm tannin and are often capable of aging for a few years after you purchase them. That's because with age, the wines' tannins become softer and the flavors become more complex and a bit subdued. (See the sidebar "White versus red: Tannin makes the difference" for more on tannin.)

In general, Cabernet Sauvignon wines have aromas and flavors of black currants or other small black berries, sometimes a minty or other herbal note, and often toasty, smoky, or vanilla-like suggestions from the oak that's used in making the wine. Most Cabernet Sauvignon varietal wines contain some Merlot or sometimes other red wines such as Cabernet Franc, Petit Verdot, or even Syrah.

In general, we consider Cabernet Sauvignon wines to be California's most reliable red wines. Whenever we're in a situation in which we don't know the particular brands that are available — on an airplane, for example, or at a catered event — we opt for the Cabernet Sauvignon as the safest bet.

Zinfandel

Zinfandel wines are a special case because the majority of them are not red wines but sweetish pink wines, labeled as White Zinfandel. The grape itself is red, and the Zinfandel wines that aren't labeled as "white" are in fact usually very hefty red wines.

White Zinfandel is one of the most popular types of wine in California. It emerged in the early 1970s and became a big hit, especially with wine drinkers who find most red and white wines to be too dry for their tastes. Winemakers produce White Zinfandel by draining the grape juice from the dark skins before the juice has had the chance to absorb more than a pale pink color.

Zinfandels (the red versions are labeled simply Zinfandel, never Red Zinfandel) have rich flavors of berry fruit, particularly *brambleberries* (those berries whose plants contain thorns, such as blackberries and loganberries). The wines are medium-bodied or full-bodied and very fruity, with spicy or sometimes jammy flavor. They tend to be even higher in alcohol than other red wines. The less expensive Zinfandels are generally moderate in tannin and meant for drinking young, whereas the pricier Zinfandels have a firm tannin backbone that enables them to age.

Zinfandel today occupies both the moderately priced tier and the high-end price tier of red wines. The elite wines often come from special vineyards where the vines are 80 or even 100 years old. Old vines produce a smaller crop of grapes that are concentrated in flavor and prized for top-quality wines.

Merlot

California Merlot took a bad rap in the movie *Sideways* and is now somewhat less popular than it was in the early years of this century. But the Merlot grape is still California's third red grape variety, after Cabernet Sauvignon and Zinfandel. The Merlot grape doesn't grow well just anywhere, however, and the quality and taste of Merlot wines can vary quite a lot depending on whether the grapes grew in an area that's more or less suitable for this variety.

Merlot wines are generally full-bodied and have aromas and flavors of plums, other dark fruits, and sometimes tea or chocolate. Because the Merlot grape has less tannin than the Cabernet Sauvignon grape, Merlot wines tend to be a bit softer in texture than Cabernet Sauvignon, which is one reason that they appeal to many wine drinkers.

Some inexpensive Merlots can be fairly light in body (the weight of the wine in your mouth) with flavors that suggest tea and herbal notes more than fruity character. The best Merlot wines give an impression of plumpness in your mouth, with rich flavors of dark, plump fruits.

Pinot Noir

California's Pinot Noir wines are extremely popular, but these red wines are also small-time compared to Cabernet Sauvignon, with only about 20 percent as much production as Cabernet.

The Pinot Noir grape grows at its best only in certain vineyard areas, and it doesn't do well in the warm conditions that characterize many of California's regions for inexpensive wines, such as the Central Valley (refer Chapter 4 for information on this region). Therefore, decent inexpensive Pinot Noir wines from California are rare. But at the medium and high end of the price scale, plenty good-quality Pinot Noirs exist, mainly from cool coastal vineyards.

Two key characteristics of Pinot Noir wines are their abundance of fruity aromas and flavors and their relatively low amount of tannin, which makes them fairly soft and silky-textured for red wine. Typical fruit flavors include red berries, black berries, and cherries, and these are often accompanied by spiciness from oak and sometimes by earthy aromas and flavors. The wines are usually fairly full-bodied and high in alcohol, which gives them smooth texture as well as a slight suggestion of sweetness.

Traditionally, Pinot Noir wines contain only Pinot Noir grapes. But lately, many California Pinot Noirs contain some Syrah or Merlot. Winemakers are using these other grapes in some cases to beef up the color of their Pinot Noir wine, which generally isn't very dark on its own, and in the case of inexpensive wines, winemakers use the other grapes to reduce their production costs. Unfortunately, these other grapes don't have nearly as much seductive aroma as Pinot Noir, and their presence diminishes the wine's aromas and flavors. If your Pinot Noir is very deep in color, it may contain one of these other grapes.

Syrah/Shiraz

The Syrah grape has grown in California for several decades, but varietal Syrah wine has really taken off only recently — particularly if it calls itself *Shiraz* instead of Syrah. The name Shiraz is a synonym that originated in Australia, and the popularity of Australian Shirazes in the U.S. motivated many California winemakers to rename their own Syrah wines as Shiraz.

Syrah or Shiraz varietal wines are generally moderate in tannin and full of berry flavors — sometimes with nuances of spiciness (such as black pepper), earthy notes, or smoked meat flavors, but more often than not, just juicy fruitiness. Syrah is also frequently part of blended wines such as Rhône-style reds (see the section "Emulating European classics," earlier in this chapter).

Other California Varietal Wines

About 110 different wine grape varieties grow in California, and you could theoretically see any one of them as the name of a varietal wine. But in practice, you'll find fewer than two dozen varieties among the varietal wines from California (unless, of course, your hobby is discovering unusual or obscure types of wine).

In the preceding section, we describe the seven most commonly seen varietal wines from California. In the following sections, we name 10 varietal wines that occupy something like a second tier in terms of how common they are and another 18 wines that are even less common.

Whites

In addition to the white wines that we name in the earlier sections, other varietal whites wines that you're likely to see include the following, which we list alphabetically:

- **Chenin Blanc:** This is one of the world's classic white wine grapes, but it has little recognition among wine drinkers because its most famous wines (from the Loire Valley region of France) don't carry the grape name. In California, Chenin Blanc wines generally range from medium-dry (even though some are labeled *dry*) to medium-sweet and are fairly full-bodied, with rich texture. Most of the Chenin Blanc juice in California ends up in inexpensive blended wines, but some good varietal wines do exist.

- **Gewürztraminer:** Only a small amount of this flavorful grape grows in California, mainly in cooler areas such as Mendocino County and parts of Sonoma County. The wines are generally full-bodied, unoaked, richly textured, and rich in perfumed aromas and flavors that can include lychee fruit, rose, peach, apple, and citrus fruit. Usually, they're not fully dry, but they often taste dryer than they technically are.

- **Pinot Blanc:** California boasts a few very fine wines from the white Pinot Blanc grape. These wines are dry, fairly full-bodied, and unoaked or gently oak-influenced, with subdued aromas and flavors.

    For many years, many of what was thought to be Pinot Blanc plantings in California were actually another grape entirely, Melon de Bourgogne (the grape that makes Muscadet in France).

- **Pinot Grigio/Gris:** This one's a biggie. Sometimes these white wines are called Pinot Gris, and sometimes they're called Pinot Grigio, the Italian name for the wine (to take advantage of the huge success of Italian Pinot Grigio wines in the U.S.). California Pinot Grigios tend to be sweeter than the Italian versions, less crisp, and fruitier in flavor. Sometimes when a winery names the wine Pinot Gris, it signifies a fuller-bodied, more flavorful style of wine — but you really need to taste the wine or read reviews of it to be sure.

- **Riesling:** California makes a few very good wines from the white Riesling grape variety and some fairly sweet wine that's made to appeal to wine drinkers who don't like truly dry wines. The best wines come from cooler regions such as Mendocino County, Monterey County, and cool sections of

Napa Valley. They're dry to medium-dry and unoaked, with rich fruity aromas and flavors (peach, apricot, citrus, melon, apple, and so forth).

✔ **Viognier:** This white variety makes full-bodied, dry white wines that are rich in aroma and flavor, particularly peachy and floral notes, sometimes with evident minerally character. These wines can be unoaked or made using oak barrels, but they usually don't taste oaky.

Reds

Red varietal wines that you might encounter in the California section of your wine shop — besides the five big names that we discuss earlier in this chapter — include the following:

✔ **Cabernet Franc:** This red grape is, as the name suggests, related to Cabernet Sauvignon, and it's used in many varietal Cabernet Sauvignons, some varietal Merlots, and many red Meritage blends. As a varietal wine in its own right, it tends to have notes of red fruits rather than the black-fruit character common in Cabernet Sauvignon and Merlot. It's somewhat less tannic and firm and is somewhat fruitier than comparably priced Cabernet Sauvignons. You'll find varietal Cabernet Francs only from serious producers, and you won't find this varietal wine at inexpensive, mass-market prices.

✔ **Grenache:** This red grape variety is common in blended Rhône-style red wines. On its own, it makes full-bodied red wines that are high in alcohol and not very tannic, unless they have tannin from aging in oak barrels. Actually, much of the varietal Grenache wine that you might find from California is White Grenache, a somewhat sweet pink wine in the style of White Zinfandel.

✔ **Petite Sirah:** This grape variety — not to be confused with Syrah, which is a different variety — is an old-timer and something of an original in California. The French know it as the Durif variety, and it's fairly obscure. But it has a loyal following in California among some winemakers and some wine drinkers. The wines are deeply colored, full-bodied, tannic, and powerful, with aromas and flavors of dark fruits and often black pepper.

✔ **Sangiovese:** Some winemakers once had big plans for varietal Sangiovese wines in California — and some still pride themselves in this wine, although it has proven to be challenging to make. Sangiovese is Italy's major red grape, particularly famous in wines from the region of Tuscany, such as Chianti. In California, the wines are fairly full-bodied and firm in tannin.

Even less-known varietals

Still other grape varieties are even less common as the basis of varietal wines in California — but we mention them here just in case you encounter one of these wines and wonder what it is. Unusual white varieties that a few producers do make as varietal wines include Arneis and Cortese (both Italian varieties), Grenache Blanc, Marsanne (a Rhône Valley variety), Melon (of Muscadet fame), Muscat (used to make sweet wines), Roussanne (another Rhône Valley variety), Sémillon, and Verdelho.

Red grape varieties that you might occasionally see as varietal wines from California include Barbera, Carignan, Dolcetto, Gamay (of Beaujolais fame), Lagrein (from Northern Italy), Mourvedre (also known as Mataro), Petit Verdot, Primitivo, Tempranillo (the main grape of Spain's Rioja wines and many other Spanish wines), and Teroldego (from northern Italy).

Colombard, the other white grape

In all the lists of grape varieties, one major grape in California usually goes unmentioned. That grape is French Colombard. In quantitative terms, it's the state's number two white grape after Chardonnay — and yet we've rarely seen it as a varietal wine (though it did enjoy a period of popularity as a varietal wine several decades ago). It's a grape that originated in France's Cognac region, where it makes a neutral base wine for Cognac brandy production. In California, it grows mainly in the San Joaquin Valley and is used as a blending wine for inexpensive, nonvarietal wines and for the most inexpensive sparkling wines.

Chapter 3

Decoding the Label

. . . .

. . . .

*W*e love looking at the labels on bottles of California wine. As a group, they're more diverse and imaginative than ever. Some wineries still use the same label they adopted 20 or 30 years ago because their labels have become classics. Some brand new wineries use retro labels that give you the impression that the winery is a century old instead of having been born only yesterday. Some wineries use special-interest labels to attract the surfer crowd or the animal-lovers crowd or the crowd that likes to wear dresses in the summertime. Some labels communicate the distinct message that you shouldn't take the wine too seriously — just try it and enjoy it! Other labels communicate such connoisseurship that you might wonder whether you know enough to be entitled to drink that wine.

Despite how different they are, however, labels on bottles of California wine have a lot in common. For one thing, they all contain certain information that's mandatory on wine labels according to Uncle Sam. And they all contain information that can help you understand something about the wine that's inside the bottle, even before you taste the wine. In this chapter, we help you decipher the wine label and introduce you to some of the wine areas listed there.

Label Terms and What They (Sorta) Mean

Imagine a world in which government officials have the specific job of reviewing proposed wine label designs and approving them for use or sending them back to the drawing board. It smacks of Big Brother, but in fact, it's not fiction. Every wine label that enters into commerce in the U.S., whether the wine inside the bottle is a domestically produced wine or an imported one, must first pass muster with the good folks at the TTB — the Alcohol and Tobacco Tax and Trade Bureau of the U.S. Department of the Treasury.

In reviewing the label, the TTB determines

- ✔ Whether it's decent (as in lacking nudity or lewdness, not in artistic merit)

- ✔ Whether it conforms to existing federal regulations for wine labels, which cover a wide range of issues, from the inclusion of mandatory information (such as the wine's alcohol level) and the size of the type displaying that information to the name of the geographic area that's mentioned as the agricultural source of the wine

Regulated wine terms

Much of the information that we check on wine labels when we're buying wine falls into the category of mandatory information that U.S. regulations require to appear on all labels of wine sold in the U.S. On the other hand, some of the mandatory information is so meaningless to us that our eyes glaze over when we see it.

In a nutshell, here's the information that's mandatory on all labels of California (and other) wine sold in the U.S. The wine's main label, known as its *brand* label, must contain the following:

- ✔ A brand name (see the section "Wine names and brand names")

- ✔ An indication of "class or type," a very bureaucratic aspect of the regulations; for nonsparkling wines, a varietal or semigeneric name can satisfy this requirement (Chapter 2 tells you about generic/semigeneric names)

- ✔ The alcohol content of the wine

The main label or another label on the package must contain

- ✔ The name and address of the bottler (see the section "Wine producers, blenders, preparers, and bottlers")

- ✔ The net contents of the bottle (generally 750 milliliters, or 25.36 fluid ounces)

- ✔ The declaration *contains sulfites* if a wine contains more than 10 parts-per-million of sulfur dioxide, which almost all wines do (to prevent the wine from turning to vinegar, among other benefits)

- ✔ The Government Health Warning, which warns against drinking during pregnancy and notes that alcohol impairs the consumer and might cause health problems

Wine names and brand names

Almost every winery makes more than one wine. The name of the wine is the varietal name (name of the dominant grape) or other type of name that distinguishes that specific wine from the winery's other wines. (Chapter 2 has lots of information about varietal names and other names.)

The grape variety that's indicated on the label as the wine name must account for at least 75 percent of what's in the bottle.

The brand name of a wine is usually the name of a winery that presumably produced the wine. What you may be interested to know is that not every brand is a winery name, and not every "winery" is a winery.

Splitting the alcohol bureau

The organization performing the wine label–approval function was once known as the BATF — the Bureau of Alcohol, Tobacco, and Firearms — but effective January 2003, the Homeland Security Act transferred the BATF to the U.S. Department of Justice, where its mission is now to prevent terrorism, reduce violent crime, and protect the nation.

The TTB is the more genteel version of the former BATF, entrusted, in the words of its own mission statement, with "collecting excise taxes on alcohol, tobacco, firearms, and ammunition; ensuring that these products are labeled, advertised, and marketed in accordance with the law; and administering the laws and regulations in a manner that protects the consumer and the revenue. . . ." You won't see any film clips of officers in bulletproof TTB vests raiding any compounds.

Double clarity on labels of blended wines

Some wines are blends of two (or more) varieties and are named for both of them —
for example, a Cabernet-Shiraz. In these cases, the label must state the percentage
of each variety that the wine contains, and these varieties must be the only grapes
used in the wine. Although most varietal labels keep you guessing about the actual
grape variety content in the wine, a dual-varietal label tells you precisely which
grapes you're drinking.

In California today, many wineries have two or more brands —
their main brand, for example, and a secondary brand that usually
sells for less money than the main brand. Wines carrying a secondary brand — or *second label,* as it's often referred to in the wine
trade — can come from the very same winery as the wines selling
under the main brand, and the label might state that. But often,
producers prefer to give the impression that the secondary brand
is a freestanding operation. They do this by stating on the label, in
small print, a name and address that suggests that the secondary
brand is itself a winery. But if you were to drive to that town, you'd
find only the main winery; the secondary winery exists on paper
only. This practice is all perfectly legal, and we don't see any harm
in it except that it aggrandizes relatively minor brands.

Here's another wrinkle on the same theme. These days, wineries
in California and elsewhere create brands overnight to take advantage of what they perceive to be marketing opportunities. These
brands aren't wineries at all: They're just labels slapped on bottles
of wine to sell the stuff. The wine might have been purchased from
another winery ready-made or might have been blended from
wines purchased from several different wineries. The source of
the wine might be different from year to year. But the label usually
states the name of the brand — as if it were a physical winery —
along with the address of the brand owner (which might be just an
office with a few desks in it). This practice bothers us a bit because
we believe that it gives these brands more legitimacy in the eyes of
wine buyers than they really deserve. But it's perfectly legal.

The wine's where and when

Labels of California wine (and other wines) carry a geographic
designation that indicates the area where the grapes for that wine
grew. California wine labels may state that the wine came, simply,

from California, or they can indicate a specific county within California, or they can name a specific *viticultural area* (an officially recognized grape-growing region; see the section "Official Grape-Growing Areas," later in this chapter). If the geographic designation is California or the name of a county, only 75 percent of the wine must have come from that area.

Most California wine labels carry a *vintage year*. This is the year in which the grapes that made that wine were harvested. It's almost always also the year that the grapes grew and the juice was vinified to make that wine. Not 100 percent of the wine need come from that year, however:

- ✔ If the wine's geographic designation is California or a county, 85 percent of the wine must have come from grapes harvested in the year that's indicated on the label.

- ✔ If the wine's geographic designation is a specific viticultural area, 95 percent of the wine must have come from the vintage year indicated on the label.

If a wine doesn't conform to these regulations, then it can't carry a vintage year. It's then known in the wine trade as a *nonvintage* wine. You'll never find the word *nonvintage* on a label, however; you know a nonvintage wine only by the absence of a vintage year on the label. (**Note:** Sometimes the vintage year appears on a separate neck label and sometimes that neck label falls off, leading you to believe that the wine is nonvintage when it's not.)

Why the fudge factors for the geographic designation and vintage year? They're accommodations to producers to enable them to create precisely the wine that they want to make and sell. Producers might use wines from other areas or from other years for the same reasons that they might use grapes other than the named variety in their wine: to fine-tune the wine's taste, to reduce costs, to improve quality, or to use up small lots of wine that would otherwise be wasted.

Alcohol content

We routinely look for the alcohol content information on California wine labels because it can tell us something about the style of the wine. (Generally speaking, the higher the alcohol content, the bigger and more powerful the style of the wine.) You'd think that this would be fairly straightforward information, but it's not. Here's why:

- ✔ If a label states that a wine is a *table wine* (by definition, a wine that's less than 14 percent alcohol), the alcohol content need not appear on the label at all.

- ✔ For wines labeled with 14 percent or less alcohol, the wine's actual alcohol content may be 1.5 percent greater or less than the stated alcohol content, with an upper limit of 14 percent. In other words, if the stated alcohol content is 13 percent, all that you really know is that the wine's alcohol content is somewhere between 11.5 and 14 percent.

- ✔ What if a wine is more than 14 percent alcohol, which many California wines are? In that case, the wine's actual alcohol content may be 1 percent higher or lower than what's stated on the label but not less than 14 percent.

- ✔ The label can state the alcohol content as a range: a 3 percent range for wines of 14 percent or less alcohol ("11 to 14 percent alcohol by volume") and a 2 percent range for wines with more than 14 percent alcohol.

Why the 14 percent cutoff? Once upon a time, yeasts would not ferment juice beyond 14 percent alcohol; the alcohol would kill the yeasts, and the juice would stop fermenting. Therefore, wines with 14 percent alcohol or less were considered products of natural fermentation, and wines with more alcohol were presumed to have gotten that way by the addition of alcohol. Now, heartier yeast strains take juice up to 16.5 percent or so.

Labeling carbs and calories

Regulations governing wine labels have changed fairly little over the past few decades. The sulfite warning, which the Bureau of Alcohol, Tobacco, and Firearms (BATF) mandated in 1987, and the health warning, which Congress passed into law in 1988, are the only two substantial mandatory additions to wine labels in the past 25 years or so.

But the head of the Alcohol and Tobacco Tax and Trade Bureau (TTB) is on record as an ardent supporter of nutrient labeling (requiring wine labels to state calories, carbohydrates, fats, and proteins) as well as ingredient labeling. We're sure that the majority of people who make and sell wine are not in favor of these requirements, mainly because they believe them to be unnecessary. Time will tell what happens.

Considering that the stated alcohol content doesn't have to be true, you might wonder why we bother checking the alcohol content on wines that we drink. Good question. The answer is that the stated alcohol content is true in the relative sense, if not in the absolute. When we find a wine that's 14.8 percent alcohol according to its label, we know that it's considerably higher in alcohol than a wine that admits to 13.5 percent alcohol. We can't take the numbers literally, but they still mean something.

Wine producers, blenders, preparers, and bottlers

If we were to read on a soft drink label that the beverage was "bottled by [company name, city, state]," we'd think nothing of it. We know that soft drinks are churned out on an industrial scale of production in large soft drink factories and that bottling is the last step of this industrial process. But we expect more of wines. We like to think that wines are lovingly produced by passionate winemakers who also grew the grapes and nurtured those grapes to their fullest expression of flavor. To read that a wine was "bottled by so-and-so" somehow detaches the wine from its roots in the vineyard, in our minds, and smacks of cold commercialism.

Because many other wine drinkers also harbor romantic ideas about the grape-growing and winemaking process, wine producers are loathe to use the term *bottled by* and instead find other words to satisfy the requirements of the labeling regulations. Therefore, the regulations regulate the use of these other terms:

✔ **Produced by/made by:** These are the two most specific terms allowed. These phrases mean that the winery or company named on the label fermented at least 75 percent of the wine on the premises indicated on the address. It can also mean that the company

- Conducted a secondary fermentation of a base wine to make it a sparkling wine (read about California's sparkling wines in Chapter 11)

- Added carbonation to a base wine to make it bubbly

- Fortified a base wine with alcohol (see Chapter 11)

- Completed other processes that determined the final nature of a wine

✔ **Blended by:** This term means that the named company mixed wines to create the final wine at the location indicated, but it didn't necessarily produce any of the wines.

✔ **Vinted by/cellared by/prepared by:** These terms mean that the named company "subjected the wine to cellar treatment" at its premises; *cellar treatment* includes blending, oak treatments, and other finishing touches.

Only the terms *produced* and *made* indicate that the named winery actually made the wine in the bottle — or 75 percent of it, anyway — and even then only if the wine is not a sparkling or fortified wine. *Vinted* is a clever way of making wine drinkers think that a wine was actually produced at the named winery when it wasn't.

Of course, even if a wine is "produced by" a certain winery, you still don't know whether that winery also grew the grapes for the wine — whether, in other words, the winery is totally accountable for the quality of the product from grapevine to bottle, as would be the case in our utopian view of wine. But another phrase on the label can tell you that. That phrase is *estate bottled.*

A wine company that also owns vineyards (as opposed to, for example, wineries that purchase and then blend grapes grown or wines made by someone else) is known as a wine *estate.* The phrase *estate bottled* on a wine label means that

✔ **All the wine came from grapes grown on land owned or controlled by the winery named in the *produced by* phrase.** Note that the winery can control the vineyards rather than own them outright; the usual control scenario is that the winery has a long-term lease on the vineyards and farms them as if they were its own.

✔ **The winery and the vineyard are in the same viticultural area.** If, for example, a winery in Napa Valley owns a vineyard across the county line in say, Russian River Valley, the wine from those grapes can't be called *estate bottled.* This provision makes *estate bottled* one of the most highly regulated terms on a wine label. No fudge factor here. (See "Official Grape-Growing Areas" for more on viticultural areas.)

The singular vineyard

Sometimes on a wine label, in addition to the name of the winery, the name of the wine, and the region of production, you can find the name of the specific vineyard where the grapes for that wine grew. In wine circles, wines that come from just one vineyard are known as *single-vineyard wines*.

In some vague way, single-vineyard wines carry a certain prestige. They reflect not just the normal character of grapes grown in that wine region but the more specific characteristics of grapes grown in that specific vineyard. If the vineyard is a particularly fine one, blessed with special soil or very old vines, for example, then the wine can in fact be special. The catch is that not every vineyard is special, and naming the vineyard on the label doesn't make it so.

A variation on the single-vineyard theme is a label that names the overall vineyard property from which the grapes came. The vineyard property mentioned can be very large, and the grapes purchased to make the wine could have come from any or all parts of the property. The point behind such a label is not so much to suggest that the wine is special because it comes from a special vineyard (although that's always a bit of an implication) as to give specific information on the source of the grapes that connoisseurs find useful.

In any case, the use of single-vineyard names and vineyard property names on wine labels is unregulated turf — as is the very definition of what constitutes a specific vineyard.

Unregulated terms intended to influence you

A few years ago, someone at a wine tasting turned to us, pointed to a phrase on a wine label, and asked us, "What does this mean?" The phrase was *estate grown*. We thought about it for a minute because we'd never encountered that term before. Finally, we replied that we had no idea what it means — and we still don't. This term is unregulated: The regulations don't define it, which means that anyone can use it to mean anything. Obviously, the intention behind this term is to make you think that a wine is estate bottled (see the preceding section). But really all it says is that the grapes for that wine grew on some estate somewhere. And any vineyard can be an *estate,* because that, also, is an unregulated term.

Several other unregulated terms adorn wine labels. Take the word *reserve,* for example. On a bottle of California wine, this term means absolutely nothing. But you're supposed to think that somehow the wine is of high quality, because in some parts of the world, the term *is* regulated and *does* imply a higher quality level than a non-reserve wine.

The term *reserve* can have meaning within the context of an individual winery's production. For example, the Clos du Val winery in Napa Valley makes two Cabernet Sauvignon wines, one of which is the Cabernet Sauvignon Reserve; the reserve wine is more expensive (and of higher quality, in the eyes of the producer) than the Clos du Val Cabernet Sauvignon. A reserve wine might be made from the winery's very best grapes, or it might have aged longer than its non-reserve counterpart before being released.

Many inexpensive and mid-priced California wines state *private reserve* or *vintner's reserve* on their labels. These are simply brand terms, and they have no real meaning. Neither do terms such as *private selection* or *special selection.*

Official Grape-Growing Areas

Every wine label must state the origin of the grapes that went into making the wine. Some origins, such as California or Washington, are self-explanatory: The grapes grew somewhere in that state. But other origins are more mysterious. Where on earth are the Sta. Rita Hills, for example, and is that anywhere near Dry Creek Valley? And, you might ask, why does it matter, anyway? What's so important about the origin of the grapes that it must be stated on the label? This section explains officially recognized grape-growing areas and why they matter.

Europe's tradition of viticultural areas

Part of the reason that the origin of the grapes is important is that the place where the grapes grow influences the taste and the quality of the wine. In Chapter 1, we mention a few ways that a locale can influence the grapes grown there.

Another reason is that the origin of the grapes has traditionally (that means, in Europe) been the name of the wine — its very identity. To protect the authenticity of each wine, every European country that produces wine has regulations that spell out the precise territory that each place-name covers. These regulations prevent a wine producer whose grapes come from a vineyard located outside a specific territory, such as Burgundy, from calling his wine by the territory name *Burgundy*.

Most European regulations go way beyond simply defining the territory of wine regions. They also dictate which grape varieties can be used to make the wine of each territory name, as well as other details of the wine's production, such as how long it must age before being released, how much alcohol content it may have, and so forth. These details help create some consistency among the wines that have each place name.

In the European model, the regulations cover only certain specific grape-growing regions — those that authorities of each country consider worthy of defining and protecting. These regions are official *appellations of origin,* or registered place names.

AVAs, America's version of European tradition

Like Europe, the U.S. has registered vineyard areas. These are called *American Viticultural Areas,* commonly abbreviated as AVAs. Because most American wines are named for their grape variety rather than their origin, American regulations defining viticultural areas are less all-encompassing than most European regulations (see the preceding section). They define the boundaries of the territory in question but don't dictate grape varieties that growers can use, how they can grow the grapes, or how the winemakers can make the wine. In the Land of the Free, grape growers and winemakers are free to decide those issues for themselves.

The agency that regulates registered viticultural areas in the U.S. is the TTB (see the section "Label Terms and What They [Sorta] Mean," earlier in this chapter). Right off the bat, the U.S. regulations recognize every state, and every county within every state, as geographic designations that may be used on wine labels. All other areas must go through an approval process with the TTB to become official AVAs.

Here's how the AVA approval process works: The TTB first receives a petition from one or more individuals or companies who want to see a particular area earn status as an AVA. The petition must state the boundaries of the viticultural area, prove that the proposed name of the area is already associated with that territory, provide evidence of geographical features that distinguish the proposed area from surrounding areas (such as climate, soil, elevation, or physical features), and so forth. If the TTB approves the petition, it develops a set of proposed regulations based on the petition, announces these in the Federal Register, and establishes a public comment period. After reviewing any comments received, the TTB can make the proposed regulations effective.

California had 104 AVAs as of the summer of 2008. Some of these are world-famous, but others are still fairly obscure even to wine lovers who live in the U.S. and perhaps even to wine lovers who live in California!

Small, large, and overlapping AVAs

California's AVAs range in size from 150 acres (Cole Ranch AVA) to 4 million acres (Central Coast AVA). Large AVAs usually encompass smaller AVAs within their borders or partially within their borders. Here are some examples:

- ✔ Chalk Hill and Sonoma County Green Valley are small AVAs within the larger Russian River Valley AVA — which itself lies within the territory of the larger Northern Sonoma AVA, which itself lies partially within the Sonoma Coast AVA.

- ✔ Rutherford, Yountville, Oakville, and Howell Mountain — to name just a few — all lie within the larger Napa Valley AVA.

These regions-within-regions are sometimes referred to as *subappellations* or *sub-AVAs*.

When the grapes for a wine come from an AVA that overlaps with other AVAs, the wine producer can decide which name to use on the label of the wine. This decision often has to do with how well-known the AVAs are. Although the smaller AVA is inherently more prestigious because it's more specific and therefore more exclusive, the larger AVA often has more recognition. For example, a winery making a Chardonnay from grapes grown in the prestigious Santa Lucia Highlands might decide to list the wine's origin as Monterey on the label because the larger Monterey AVA has more recognition among wine drinkers. Another example: Wines that come from grapes grown in Rutherford or Oakville — two prestigious AVAs within Napa Valley — often use both the smaller AVA name and the name Napa Valley, because Napa Valley carries far more recognition.

Table 3-1 lists all the AVAs within California and the counties in which they're situated. Don't be surprised if you recognize only a few of them.

Table 3-1	California AVAs and Their Locations		
AVA Name	*County*	*AVA Name*	*County*
Alexander Valley	Sonoma	Mount Harlan	San Benito
Alta Mesa	Sacramento	Mount Veeder	Napa
Anderson Valley	Mendocino	Napa Valley	Napa
Arroyo Grande Valley	San Luis Obispo	North Coast	Lake, Marin, Mendocino, Napa, Solano, Sonoma
Arroyo Seco	Monterey	North Yuba	Yuba
Atlas Peak	Napa	Northern Sonoma	Sonoma
Ben Lomond	Santa Cruz	Oak Knoll District of Napa Valley	Napa
Benmore Valley	Lake	Oakville	Napa
Bennett Valley	Sonoma	Pacheco Pass	San Benito
Borden Ranch	Sacramento, San Joaquin	Paicines	San Benito
California Shenandoah Valley	Amador, El Dorado	Paso Robles	San Luis Obispo
Capay Valley	Yolo	Potter Valley	Mendocino

(continued)

Table 3-1 *(continued)*

AVA Name	County	AVA Name	County
Carmel Valley	Monterey	Ramona Valley	San Diego
Central Coast	Alameda, Contra Costa, Monterey, San Benito, San Francisco, San Luis Obispo, San Mateo, Santa Barbara, Santa Clara, Santa Cruz	Red Hills Lake County	Lake
Chalk Hill	Sonoma	Redwood Valley	Mendocino
Chalone	Monterey, San Benito	River Junction	San Joaquin
Chiles Valley	Napa	Rockpile	Sonoma
Cienega Valley	San Benito	Russian River Valley	Sonoma
Clarksburg	Sacramento, Solano, Yolo	Rutherford	Napa
Clear Lake	Lake	Saint Helena	Napa
Clements Hill	San Joaquin	Salado Creek	Stanislaus
Cole Ranch	Mendocino	San Benito	San Benito
Cosumnes River	Sacramento	San Bernabe	Monterey
Covelo	Mendocino	San Francisco Bay	San Benito, San Francisco, San Mateo, Santa Clara, Santa Cruz
Cucamonga Valley	Riverside, San Bernardino	San Lucas	Monterey
Diablo Grande	Stanislaus	San Pasqual Valley	San Diego

AVA Name	County	AVA Name	County
Diamond Mountain District	Napa	San Ysidro District	Santa Clara
Dos Rios	Mendocino	Santa Clara Valley	Santa Clara
Dry Creek Valley	Sonoma	Santa Cruz Mountains	San Mateo, Santa Clara, Santa Cruz
Dunnigan Hills	Yolo	Santa Lucia Highlands	Monterey
Edna Valley	San Luis Obispo	Santa Maria Valley	San Luis Obispo, Santa Barbara
El Dorado	El Dorado	Sta. Rita Hills	Santa Barbara
Fair Play	El Dorado	Santa Ynez Valley	Santa Barbara
Fiddletown	Amador	Seiad Valley	Siskiyou
Guenoc Valley	Lake	Sierra Foothills	Amador, Calaveras, El Dorado, Mariposa, Nevada, Placer, Tuolumne, Yuba
Hames Valley	Monterey	Sloughhouse	Sacramento
High Valley	Lake	Solano County Green Valley	Solano
Howell Mountain	Napa	Sonoma Coast	Sonoma
Jahant	Sacramento, San Joaquin	Sonoma County Green Valley	Sonoma
Knights Valley	Sonoma	Sonoma Mountain	Sonoma
Lime Kiln Valley	San Benito	Sonoma Valley	Sonoma

(continued)

Table 3-1 *(continued)*

AVA Name	County	AVA Name	County
Livermore Valley	Alameda	South Coast	Riverside, San Diego
Lodi	Sacramento, San Joaquin	Spring Mountain District	Napa
Los Carneros	Napa, Sonoma	Stags Leap District	Napa
Madera	Fresno, Madera	Suisun Valley	Solano
Malibu-Newton Canyon	Los Angeles	Temecula Valley	Riverside
McDowell Valley	Mendocino	Trinity Lakes	Trinity
Mendocino	Mendocino	Wild Horse Valley	Napa, Solano
Mendocino Ridge	Mendocino	Willow Creek	Humboldt, Trinity
Merritt Island	Yolo	York Mountain	San Luis Obispo
Mokelumne River	San Joaquin	Yorkville Highlands	Mendocino
Monterey	Monterey	Yountville	Napa

Chapter 4

California's Major Wine Regions

*W*ine grapes flourish throughout much of California — as far north as Mendocino County in the upper third of the state, as far west as the edge of the Pacific Ocean, and as far east as the city of Fresno. Napa Valley and Sonoma County, north of San Francisco, are of course world-famous wine destinations. But the last 30 years have also witnessed the emergence of Santa Barbara and Monterey along the state's central coast and Anderson Valley in Mendocino County — to mention just a few of the new hot spots for California wine.

In this chapter, we take a good look at the major California wine regions, all of which welcome more and more visitors each year.

Location Matters

Centuries of experience have proven that the place where grapes grow influences their nature and therefore the nature of the wine made from them. In Chapter 1, we describe some of the ways that California's climate, soil, and topography vary from one part of the state to the next. Like the differences in growing conditions, the differences in wines from region to region can be subtle or dramatic.

California's wine producers didn't always take the issue of regional differences, or *terroir,* as seriously as they do today. However, those who make fine wine all over California now have real respect for the individual distinctions that make one vineyard different from the next and that make every wine region unique. Grape growers and wineries in specific regions have banded together, funded research, and shared their experiences to better define and understand the intricate nature of their own region's terroir.

Although plenty of California wines come from the grapes of multiple regions rather than from the grapes of a specific region (the labels of these wines simply state the wines' origin as *California*), a wine's region of production is an increasingly important consideration in buying fine wine from California. Figure 4-1 depicts California's main wine regions.

Figure 4-1: The wine regions of California.

Napa Valley: Wine Country's Hollywood

When someone utters the words *Napa Valley,* the first image that springs to most people's minds is of wine. Napa Valley is by far the best-known, most prestigious wine region in the New World. And yet only about 4 percent of California's wine comes from the very expensive vineyard lands of Napa Valley!

Today, nearly 400 wineries produce wine from about 47,000 acres of vineyards in Napa Valley. The wine boom there is a relatively recent phenomenon: Only 25 wineries existed there in 1960. Most of Napa Valley's wineries are small operations, although a few large wineries, such as Robert Mondavi Winery, Beringer, and Sutter Home, are based in Napa County.

Many Napa Valley wineries own large vineyards, which surround their properties like gorgeous manicured lawns. Other wineries don't own vineyards but instead buy their grapes from independent grape growers or buy juice or bulk wine from other wine producers. And some Napa Valley wine producers (including some winery names that you see on very expensive bottles of wine) surprisingly don't have their own wineries; they bring their grapes to *custom-crush* wine facilities, which they rent — all for the distinction of making "Napa Valley wine."

Reading about Napa Valley and its wines can be confusing at times because the name *Napa* actually applies to three entities:

- ✔ The political entity is Napa County.

- ✔ The city of Napa, situated at the southern end of the county, is the county seat.

- ✔ Napa Valley is the name of the AVA — that is, the official American Viticultural Area within Napa County (see Chapter 3 for more on AVAs).

For all practical purposes, the territory within the Napa Valley AVA is the same as that within Napa County. (The AVA doesn't encompass Lake Berryessa in the eastern part of the county, for example, but no one could grow grapes there, anyway.)

Mapping Napa Valley

Napa Valley is not large: It's about 30 miles long and 5 miles wide at its widest point, around the city of Napa. To put that in an international perspective, it's only about one-eighth the size of France's famous Bordeaux wine region.

In addition to the broad Napa Valley AVA and the even broader (six-county) North Coast AVA, Napa Valley has 14 distinct viticultural areas that are considered subappellations of the Napa Valley AVA itself. An additional subappellation, Calistoga, is pending. The following are the standing Napa Valley AVAs, which you can also see in Figure 4-2:

- Mount Veeder; Spring Mountain District; Diamond Mountain District
- Oak Knoll District; Yountville; Oakville; Rutherford; St. Helena
- Howell Mountain; Stags Leap District; Atlas Peak
- Chiles Valley District
- Wild Horse Valley
- Los Carneros

Although not a large area, Napa Valley has an enviable range of soil types and climatic differences. Mountains surround Napa Valley on both sides — the Mayacamas Mountains to the west and the Vaca Mountains to the east — and the Napa River runs north-south through the valley. Soils vary according to how close to the river a vineyard is or how far into the hills or mountains it is, among other factors.

The climate in Napa Valley is generally warm and dry, but a dominant feature of the region is the combination of cool winds and fog that sweeps up the valley from the San Pablo Bay in the south. Summer weather in the southern part of the valley, in wine districts such as Carneros, Yountville, and Oakville, for example, can be distinctly cooler than that of the Calistoga area at the north end of the valley.

Napa Valley sits next to Sonoma County. The Mayacamas Mountains separate the two counties from each other for most of their length, but in the south, the terrain is open and flatter, and driving from one county to the other is easier (see the nearby sidebar "Sonoma and Napa: Crossing from county to county"). In fact, the two counties share a wine district, Los Carneros, at their southern ends.

Figure 4-2: Napa Valley and its AVAs.

Napa's key wines

Napa Valley certainly benefits from its range of growing conditions. Winemakers of the region produce every major type of wine we discuss in Parts II and III of this book, along with some of the lesser-known whites and reds. Here's how the wines compare in terms of production.

Sonoma and Napa: Crossing from county to county

The easiest way to get from Napa to Sonoma Valley and vice versa is to head to the southern end of either valley (the Carneros district) and cross over along the Sonoma Highway (California 12/121). From Napa to Sonoma, the trip takes about 20 minutes, assuming that there's no traffic. Another option is to take the Oakville Grade (also known as Trinity Rd.) over the Mayacamas Range, which links Oakville in Napa with Glen Ellen in Sonoma. It's an extremely steep and windy road, but it can be a real timesaver if you're headed to the northern end of either valley.

Getting to Northern Sonoma is a snap from Sonoma Valley. Just follow Highway 12, which runs north to south and connects Sonoma Valley's towns, north to get to Santa Rosa. From there, jump on Highway 101 north and exit at the town of your choice.

Frommer's Portable California Wine Country, 5th Edition, by Erika Lenkert; Copyright 2006 Wiley Publishing, Inc.; Reprinted with permission of John Wiley & Sons, Inc.

Cabernets, Napa Valley's top wines

We believe that Napa Valley's best wines are its Cabernet Sauvignons and Cabernet blends. The generally warm, dry climate of Napa Valley suits the Cabernet Sauvignon grape variety just fine. Even though Cabernet Sauvignon wines are produced in many regions throughout the world, only France's Bordeaux region and Napa Valley have achieved world-class status for wines made from this popular variety. In Chapter 6, we name our favorite Cabernet Sauvignons and Cabernet blends from Napa Valley.

Other important reds

Merlot remains Napa Valley's second most produced red wine after Cabernet Sauvignon. When not made as a varietal wine, Merlot is invariably blended into Cabernet Sauvignon (in small quantities, such as 10 percent) or blended into other Napa Valley red wines. We name our favorite Napa Valley Merlots in Chapter 6.

Pinot Noir is Napa Valley's third most produced varietal red wine, and that was true even before the film *Sideways*. Although this award-winning movie definitely increased Pinot Noir wine production in California, the effect in Napa Valley was limited by the land: In Napa Valley, Pinot Noir grows primarily in Carneros, the Valley's coolest district. See Chapter 7 for our recommended Napa Valley Pinot Noirs.

Zinfandel — the original red version — is Napa Valley's fourth largest red varietal wine in production, although as with Pinot Noir, Sonoma is more renowned than Napa Valley for Zinfandel. (*Note:* White Zinfandel, which is really pink, comes primarily from California's inland Central Valley.) See Chapter 8 for our red Zinfandel favorites from Napa Valley.

Blended wines have become increasingly popular in Napa Valley. Three of Napa Valley's elite reds, Opus One, Rubicon, and Dominus, are red wine blends (although all are primarily made from Cabernet Sauvignon). Most Napa Valley blended wines use the grape varieties famous in France's Bordeaux region — Cabernet Sauvignon, Cabernet Franc, Merlot, and sometimes Petit Verdot and/or Malbec. We recommend Napa Valley red blends in Chapter 6.

Napa Valley's whites

Chardonnay continues to be Napa Valley's most popular white wine by a good margin. Sauvignon Blanc (sometimes labeled Fumé Blanc) is Napa Valley's second favorite white. Newcomers such as Pinot Grigio/Gris and Viognier (see Chapter 9) are beginning to make inroads into Chardonnay's dominance, however. Some wine drinkers just want a little more variety in their white wine choices! See Chapter 5 for our recommended Chardonnays and Sauvignon Blancs from Napa Valley.

As with the blended red wines, most Napa Valley blended white wines use grape varieties famous in Bordeaux — in this case, Sauvignon Blanc and Sémillon (pronounced seh-me-yohn).

Getting to and staying in Napa Valley

San Francisco and Oakland are the entry cities via air for Napa Valley, which is about 60 miles northeast of these cities. The drive from both cities over Oakland Bay Bridge or Golden Gate Bridge is about 90 minutes.

For touring Napa Valley, a more luxurious (albeit costlier) alternative to a car rental is limousine service; this is an especially good option if you don't have a designated driver with you and you're splitting the cost among a group of four to six people.

Napa's restaurants, among the best in the nation

When we first visited Napa Valley 30-plus years ago, there were only a couple of restaurants for fine dining. Now Napa Valley is one of the elite dining destinations in the United States. At the top of Napa's list of great restaurants is The French Laundry, one of the finest restaurants in the country, if not the world. The only problem is that reservations are almost impossible to obtain (and most meals will set you back about $240, including the service but not the wine). But don't despair. We name some of our other favorite (and less expensive) Napa Valley restaurants here, in no particular order:

✔ **Auberge du Soleil:** The other great French restaurant in Napa Valley, besides The French Laundry. Great wine list; amazing views.

✔ *étoile:* Domaine Chandon, one of California's original wineries for sparkling wine, is still running a top restaurant in Yountville, 30 years after the winery opened.

✔ **Mustard's Grill:** A Napa Valley classic. California cuisine; great burgers and barbecued ribs. Popular with winemakers. On Highway 29 in Yountville.

✔ **Cindy's Backstreet Kitchen:** Chef/owner Cindy Pawlcyn's other, more casual restaurant in St. Helena (Mustard's and Go Fish are also Cindy's).

✔ **Bouchon and Bistro Jeanty:** Two wonderful, casual French restaurants in Yountville. Moderately priced.

✔ **Brix:** Another casual restaurant on Highway 29 (in Yountville) featuring California cuisine.

✔ **Redd:** Modern, fairly new restaurant in Yountville featuring California cuisine.

✔ **Terra:** Small, homey French restaurant in St. Helena; one of the older places to eat in the Valley; still one of the best.

✔ **Tra Vigne:** One of the two great Italian restaurants in St. Helena; an old favorite.

✔ **Martini House:** The other top Italian St. Helena restaurant. Quite large and beautiful. Excellent wine list!

✔ **Bistro Don Giovanni:** Casual, good value Italian restaurant in Napa; outdoor dining available.

You have tons of places to choose for lodging, ranging from grandiose, posh resorts to chain hotels and motels. You can easily find the hotel or inn to fit your budget online. In this space, we highlight some of our favorite places to stay. Two upscale (over $500 a night) destinations provide luxury accommodations in the Valley:

✔ **Auberge du Soleil:** This "Inn of the Sun" is one of the oldest and still one of the best inns in Napa Valley. A resort that's part of the Relais et Chateaux group, Auberge du Soleil has a wonderful location in the hillsides east of Rutherford village and an outstanding view from its excellent French restaurant.

✔ **Meadowood Resort:** This is a huge facility east of St. Helena, with many private cottages tucked into the woods. It also has a very fine restaurant.

Five comfortable, fine inns extend from the city of Napa in the south part of the Valley northward to the town of St. Helena. Villagio and Harvest Inn are generally over $400 a night, and the other three are less than $300 a night.

✔ **Villagio Inn:** Located in Yountville, close to Domaine Chandon winery, Villagio offers large rooms, top service, and an excellent breakfast. It's one of our favorites.

✔ **Harvest Inn:** Harvest Inn is just off Route 29 as you enter St. Helena from the south. It has modern, well-appointed rooms and cabins, and it's quite luxurious.

✔ **Napa River Inn:** Right in downtown Napa on the Napa River, this inn offers peaceful accommodations at reasonable prices.

✔ **Rancho Caymus:** Rancho Caymus is centrally located and is designed in the Spanish architectural motif. It's in Rutherford on Route 29, close to Beaulieu Vineyard Winery.

✔ **Wine Country Inn:** Here's another one of our old favorites, just north and a bit east of St. Helena. Wine Country Inn is rustic, charming, and bucolic.

Sonoma County: Hardly an Also-ran!

Sonoma County is on California's North Coast, directly north of San Francisco and about an hour's drive from the majestic Golden Gate Bridge. It borders Napa Valley to the east but extends farther north. Sonoma is more than twice as large as Napa, and the wineries are more spread out. You have to allow more driving time when visiting Sonoma's wineries, which now number over 250.

Sonoma (see Figure 4-3) has 3 general American Viticultural Areas (AVAs) and 11 specific AVAs, in addition to being part of the huge North Coast AVA, which takes in six counties north of San Francisco. Here are Sonoma's general AVAs:

✔ Sonoma County AVA

✔ Northern Sonoma AVA (an area that includes Russian River Valley, Alexander Valley, Dry Creek Valley, and Knights Valley, along with other territory)

✔ Sonoma Coast, an elongated area in western Sonoma, along the Pacific coast (*Note:* The Sonoma Coast AVA is particularly known for its Pinot Noir.)

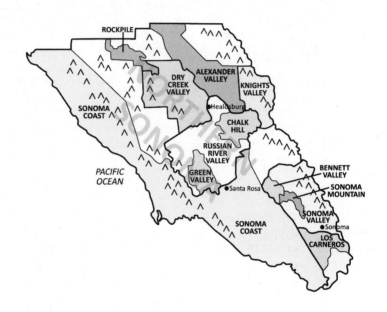

Figure 4-3: Sonoma County and its wine regions.

Sonoma differs from Napa in climate, in the wines that do best, and in attitude:

✔ **Climate:** In general, much of Sonoma is cooler than Napa, especially in Sonoma's coastal areas.

✔ **Top wines:** The cooler areas of Sonoma, such as Russian River Valley, Green Valley, and the Sonoma Coast, produce some of California's finest Pinot Noirs, Chardonnays, Zinfandels, and sparkling wines. Napa's generally warmer climate provides an especially suitable environment for Cabernet Sauvignon, that county's most renowned wine.

✔ **Attitude:** Sonoma doesn't have the glitz and glamour of Napa Valley; it's more laid back. One of the great benefits of this is that fewer tourists visit Sonoma's wineries, and except during rush hour, you don't find the traffic problems that you can find in Napa Valley, especially in the summer.

Sonoma also has more than its share of some of California's largest and most famous wineries, such as Gallo Family Wineries, Kendall-Jackson, Korbel, Simi, Sebastiani, Jordan, and Gloria Ferrer, to name a few. Serious wine lovers could easily spend a week each in both Sonoma and Napa, just visiting some of the top wineries.

An idyllic wine region

In many ways, Sonoma is the most charming wine region in California. It has a little bit of everything, from Old World charm to modern wineries and fine restaurants. Going from the southern part of Sonoma to the north, some of its highlights include the following wineries, cities, and towns:

✔ **Gloria Ferrer Winery:** In windswept, western Carneros, Gloria Ferrer is part of Spain's Freixenet — the largest sparkling wine producer in the world. The winery is an architectural wonder, and its sparkling wines are among the best in California.

✔ **Buena Vista Winery:** Also in Carneros, the dramatically beautiful Buena Vista is California's oldest continually operating winery (since 1857). Guided and self-guided tours are available. Wines are reasonably priced.

✔ **Town of Sonoma:** Dominated by its huge plaza, this fascinating old Spanish mission town is a must-see. Many fine wineries are nearby, including Ravenswood (the great Zinfandel specialist) and Hanzell (one of California's finest Chardonnay producers). Great cheese shops (try the Sonoma Jack) and bread shops offer their wares for picnickers.

✔ **Village of Glen Ellen:** Just north of the town of Sonoma and south of Santa Rosa, this beautiful little village of about 1,000 residents was the home of one of America's great authors, Jack London, and one of its greatest food writers, MFK Fisher. Benziger Family Winery is also in Glen Ellen.

✔ **Santa Rosa:** In the center of the county, Santa Rosa is the largest city in Napa/Sonoma wine country, with lots of hotels and fine restaurants.

✔ **Healdsburg:** In Northern Sonoma, the town of Healdsburg is ideally located for winery visits because it's surrounded by three great Sonoma wine regions: Alexander Valley, Dry Creek Valley, and the Russian River Valley. Simi Winery is also in Healdsburg. The town has great restaurants, such as Cyrus and Bistro Ralph, plus lots of fine hotels and bed and breakfast inns (some of which you can find in the nearby "Staying in Healdsburg" sidebar).

Staying in Healdsburg

The town of Healdsburg is a popular place to stay in Northern Sonoma. Keep in mind that during the high season — between June and November — most hotels charge peak rates and sell out completely on weekends; many have a two-night minimum. Always ask about discounts. For more lodging options, check sonoma.com and winecountry.com.

Les Mars Hôtel
27 North St. (at Healdsb urg Ave.)
Healdsburg, CA 95448
Phone 877-431-1700 or 707-433-4211
Web site www.lesmarshotel.com

One block off Healdsburg Square, the exterior of Northern Sonoma's most luxurious inn is so understated that you're likely to pass it. But inside the three-floor hotel, there's no mistaking the opulence. The lobby alone smacks of old-world French luxury accommodations, and the 16 individually decorated rooms are equally plush. Swathed in creams and warm beiges and furnished with hand-selected 18th and 19th century European antiques, they're equipped with the likes of a canopy bed with Italian linens, a large TV and DVD player, a marble bathroom with a whirlpool soaking tub and walk-in shower, and personal touches at every turn, and they feel more like a rich friend's home than a hotel. Each morning, guests are treated to a continental breakfast in the wood-paneled library, and during evenings they have easy access to the region's finest restaurant, Cyrus, which adjoins the hotel. Without a doubt this is the finest place to stay in the region. *16 units. $495–$995 double. Rate includes continental breakfast. AE, DISC, MC, V.*

Hotel Healdsburg
25 Matheson St. (at the square)
Healdsburg, CA 95448
Phone 800-889-7199 or 707-431-2800
Web site www.hotelhealdsburg.com

This home away from home across the street from the plaza is a visitor favorite because not only does it have spacious, comfortable rooms adorned with country-chic furnishings (You'll find no doilies and lace here!), but it also has amenities associated with a true hotel. Want to spend the day spa-ing it? You're golden. Lounge by a heated pool? No problem. Linger on an oversize couch over the morning paper in front of a roaring fire in the lobby? Sure thing. Dine at a refined restaurant? With Dry Creek Kitchen fronting the hotel, you're already there. Rooms are minimalist-refined (think Pottery Barn) with angular, modern dark-wood furnishings, big fluffy beds, oversized bathrooms with glass walk-in showers (some with soaking tubs), and in many cases, balconies. The region's best shopping is outside your door around Healdsburg's historic plaza. Each floor has a computer with Internet access that's free to use. Yes, it costs a pretty penny to stay here, but you might be able to find a deal on their Web site, where they often post promotions and packages. *55 units. $250–$495 double, $425–790 junior and one-bedroom suites. Rates include a "country harvest" breakfast. AE, MC, V.*

Honor Mansion

14891 Grove St.
Healdsburg, CA 95448
Phone 800-554-4667 or 707-433-4277
Web site www.honormansion.com

Guests who stay at this small luxury inn don't want to leave their rooms — a jaunt to one of the nearby vineyards or a stroll up to the main square of town might be in order, but then it's back to the mansion. Maybe it's the fluffy featherbeds, winter and summer bathrobes, or delicious toiletries. If you are in one of the particularly splendid units boasting a claw-foot tub, cozy gas fireplace, or a private deck with a Jacuzzi, you might only get up to help yourself to the decanter of sherry placed in each room. Be sure to indulge in breakfast, a decadent, two- to three-course affair (think Mexican eggs, baked blintz, or soufflé French toast and espresso chocolate chip muffins) served in the parlor of this 1883 Italianate Victorian or on the redwood deck overlooking the pond. As if this isn't enough, you'll also find bocce and tennis courts, a huge lap pool, a croquet lawn, afternoon wine and cheese, a 24-hour self-serve espresso and cappuccino machine in the main building, and a never-ending supply of cookies. *$190–$325 double; $300–$550 suite. Rates include full breakfast and evening wine and cheese. DISC, MC, V.*

Best Western Dry Creek Inn

198 Dry Creek Rd.
Healdsburg, CA 95448
Phone 800-222-5784 or 707-433-0300
Web site www.drycreekinn.com

It's not exactly a romantic wine country getaway, but anyone looking for a wonder-fully clean and affordable place to crash after a day of wining and dining will be very happy here — especially considering all the extras. Along with basic motel-style rooms, you'll find a complimentary bottle of Sonoma wine upon check-in, a small fridge for chilling your Chardonnay and picnic items, and even a tiny fitness room for working off the pounds you're inevitably putting on. Add to that coffeemak-ers, free high-speed Internet access, and the great promotions featured on their Web site, and you've found one of wine country's best bargains. *103 units. $69 to $239 double. Rates include breakfast. AE, DISC, MC, V.*

Sonoma's signatures: Pinot Noir and Zinfandel

Sonoma County succeeds with many diverse wines, but if we had to name its two most renowned wines, they'd be Pinot Noir and Zinfandel.

Many wine critics believe that the nation's best Pinot Noirs come from Sonoma's Russian River Valley. Other wine regions also have a Pinot following: Carneros and the Sonoma Coast, in Sonoma County (with Carneros extending into Napa Valley); Santa Barbara; Santa Lucia Highlands; Mendocino's Anderson Valley; and Oregon's Willamette Valley, for example. But Russian River Pinot Noirs have a combination of richness, voluptuousness, balance, and elegance that's hard to beat. We name some of our favorite Sonoma Pinot Noirs, including Russian River Valley's, in Chapter 7.

Zinfandel is truly California's wine. Even though the grape's genetic origin has been traced to Croatia, most of the world's Zinfandels, red and pink, are Californian. And most wine experts agree that a majority of the best *Zins* (as they're called for short) hail from Sonoma. Dry Creek Valley is particularly famous for red Zinfandel (the only color of Zin that Zin fanatics recognize). Russian River Valley and other Sonoma AVAs also produce fine Zinfandels, but in Dry Creek Valley, delicious, spicy Zinfandel is a real specialty. In Chapter 8, we recommend some of our favorite Sonoma Zinfandels, including those from Dry Creek Valley.

Sonoma's wines: Something for everyone

Sonoma's vineyards and wineries extend from Carneros in the south to Alexander Valley in the north — a much larger area than Napa Valley's (see the earlier section on Napa). Because Sonoma is so large, and because it has both coastal and interior wine districts, its climate varies from one wine district to another more than Napa's climate does.

In fact, the varied climate and soils of Sonoma offer more different types of wine than any other wine region in California. For example, the vineyard areas of Alexander Valley and Geyserville (in the north) and the Sonoma Mountain area (farther south) can be quite warm and dry, and they're ideal growing regions for Cabernet

Sauvignon. The cooler regions, such as the Russian River Valley, Green Valley, Forestville, and the Sonoma Coast, produce excellent Pinot Noirs, Chardonnays, and sparkling wines. Temperate areas in Sonoma grow Zinfandel, Syrah, Merlot, Sauvignon Blanc, and Petite Sirah, to name a few of the more prominent varieties. But there are many more.

A short drive from one of Sonoma's viticultural areas to another can be a revelation: Each area seems to specialize in different wines. The following are the 11 distinct AVAs in Sonoma County, listed approximately from south to north, and the wines that are most renowned there:

- ✔ **Los Carneros (partly in Napa Valley):** Pinot Noir, Chardonnay, Merlot, sparkling wine

- ✔ **Sonoma Valley:** Chardonnay

- ✔ **Sonoma Mountain:** Cabernet Sauvignon

- ✔ **Bennett Valley:** Chardonnay, Sauvignon Blanc, Merlot

- ✔ **Green Valley (within Russian River Valley):** Sparkling wine, Chardonnay, Pinot Noir

- ✔ **Russian River Valley:** Pinot Noir, Chardonnay, sparkling wine, Zinfandel

- ✔ **Knights Valley:** Cabernet Sauvignon, Sauvignon Blanc

- ✔ **Chalk Hill (within Russian River Valley):** Chardonnay, Sauvignon Blanc

- ✔ **Dry Creek Valley:** Zinfandel, Cabernet Sauvignon

- ✔ **Alexander Valley:** Cabernet Sauvignon, Chardonnay, Sauvignon Blanc

- ✔ **Rockpile:** Zinfandel, Cabernet Sauvignon, Syrah, Petite Sirah

More Key Wine Regions

Napa Valley and Sonoma County might be California's most famous wine regions, but they're only part of today's wine story in the Golden State. North, east, and south of Napa and Sonoma, vineyards grow all sorts of grape varieties for producing all kinds of wines. This section first heads north, to idyllic Mendocino and Lake Counties, before covering the rest of the major wine regions in the state.

Up the North Coast to Mendocino and Lake Counties

California's majestic redwood sequoia trees, some as much as 2,000 years old, are among the oldest living things on Earth. If you follow the giant redwoods — which begin in the Muir Woods just north of San Francisco — up the coastline through Sonoma County, you find forests full of them into Mendocino County and beyond, all the way north to Oregon. For us, California's northern coast is one of the most beautiful parts of the U.S., if not the world. You don't find too many wine tourists in the region, even in the summer, and wineries genuinely welcome visitors up here.

The old town of Mendocino, on the coast, is a fantastic place to stay when visiting the wineries of Mendocino County. The place resembles a New England coastal town in the architectural style of its houses much more than a typical California town. There used to be a standing joke that Mendocino was populated mainly by old beatniks from the '50s and hippies from the '60s. There's still something a bit wild about Mendocino, but nowadays you also find lots of fine little restaurants and interesting places to stay.

If you want an even quainter locale, try the hamlet of Boonville; it's located in the heart of cool Anderson Valley — Mendocino's prime grape-growing district. Anderson Valley is ideal for Pinot Noir, Chardonnay, Gewurztraminer, Riesling, and some of the country's best sparkling wines, including those of the renowned Roederer Estate winery (see Chapter 11).

The other major wine district in Mendocino County lies in the eastern, somewhat warmer part of the county. Redwood Valley is home of Fetzer Vineyards, one of California's largest wineries, with its organic winery affiliate, Bonterra Vineyards. This area of Mendocino is best known for its Syrah, Petite Sirah, and Zinfandel.

Directly north of Napa County lies the smallish, off-the-beaten path Lake County, dominated by Clear Lake, California's largest natural lake. Here you find Lake County's best-known vineyards: Guenoc Vineyards and its sister winery, Langtry Estate. You also find a number of smaller wineries, many of which have sprung up in the past ten years or so. Cabernet Sauvignon is the leading varietal wine in Lake County, and Sauvignon Blanc is Lake County's most important white wine.

Down the Central Coast

California's so-called Central Coast is a huge area that extends from San Francisco to Santa Barbara. This area is actually a collection of separate wine districts, each with its own identity (see Figure 4-4). From north to south, these areas are

- ✔ Livermore Valley and Santa Clara Valley
- ✔ Santa Cruz Mountains
- ✔ Monterey, Carmel, and the Santa Lucia Highlands
- ✔ Paso Robles (San Luis Obispo County)
- ✔ Edna Valley (San Luis Obispo County)
- ✔ The Santa Maria and Santa Ynez Valleys

In this section, we take one area at a time, listing the wines each region does best.

Livermore Valley and Santa Clara Valley

East and south of San Francisco, large tracts of vineyards used to exist. Now urban sprawl, from the cities of Palo Alto to San José (California's Silicon Valley), has usurped most of the vineyards in Livermore Valley, which is east of San Francisco, and Santa Clara Valley, which runs south of San Francisco.

But 39 wineries still exist in Livermore Valley, including two major operations: Wente Family Estates and Concannon Vineyard, both historic wineries. Livermore Valley has always been known for its Sauvignon Blanc and Sémillon, as well as Chardonnay, although Concannon's signature wine is Petite Sirah. Three other popular Livermore Valley wineries are Murrieta's Well, Page Mill, and Tamás Estates, the latter known for its *Cal-Ital varietals* (varietal wines made from native Italian grapes grown in California, such as Sangiovese and Barbera; we discuss these wines in Chapter 10).

Santa Clara Valley includes the Santa Cruz Mountains district, but we regard the Mountains as a separate wine zone because the wines there are so distinct (see the next section). The area of Santa Clara that's east of Santa Cruz Mountains, around San José, still has two major wineries: J. Lohr and Mirassou Vineyards. The latter is now part of the Gallo wine empire. Chardonnay, Cabernet Sauvignon, and Merlot are the three major wines in this part of the Santa Clara Valley.

Figure 4-4: The Central Coast wine regions.

Santa Cruz Mountains

Only an hour's drive south of San Francisco, the rugged, isolated Santa Cruz Mountains seem to be a world apart from urban life. Although Pinot Noir and Chardonnay grow well on the cooler, ocean side of the mountains, most of the wineries — including California stalwarts such as Ridge (with its renowned Monte Bello Vineyard) and Mount Eden Vineyards — are located on the San Francisco Bay side. Magnificent Cabernet Sauvignon grows up here, as does Chardonnay.

Ridge Vineyards, a California icon

Not many wineries in California have been around since the 1950s, and most of those that do date back that far or earlier are in Napa Valley or Sonoma County. Ridge Vineyards is an exception. Situated high up in the Santa Cruz Mountains, this iconoclastic winery has been going its own way from the beginning. Two wine-loving Stanford University professors founded the winery in 1959. In 1969, Paul Draper, a Stanford graduate who majored in philosophy, joined Ridge and became the winemaker. Forty years later, Draper is still at Ridge, now as CEO.

Here's Ridge's approach, which was very unusual back in 1959:

✔ Focus on two grape varieties, Cabernet Sauvignon and Zinfandel.

✔ Produce a Cabernet Sauvignon wine that's capable of aging a long time, as Bordeaux wines are.

✔ Search the state for the best possible vineyards for Zinfandel.

Draper already knew in 1969 that he had an ideal location for Cabernet Sauvignon at Ridge's Monte Bello Vineyard in the Santa Cruz Mountains. Time has proven him right. Ridge Monte Bello continues to shine at international competitions. At a 2006 repeat of the famous Judgment of Paris tasting (see Chapter 1) between California Cabernet Sauvignons and Bordeaux wines, the 1971 Ridge Monte Bello Cabernet Sauvignon was voted the best wine overall.

For Zinfandel, Draper found top vineyards in Sonoma, Napa, and Paso Robles. Ridge's two most acclaimed Zinfandels both come from Sonoma: Geyserville Vineyard (the wine is actually a Zinfandel blend) and Lytton Springs Vineyard.

We count 80 wineries in the Santa Cruz Mountains, but by the time you read this, the number will undoubtedly be higher. These wineries are California's little secret. Even though a number of high-quality wineries such as Bonny Doon, Thomas Fogarty, Kathryn Kennedy, David Bruce, and Cinnabar are here, most wine tourists head north to Napa Valley or Sonoma instead — and lately, they go south to Santa Barbara, since the 2004 film *Sideways* brought celebrity status to that area. If you're considering visiting the Santa Cruz Mountains, you'll be pleased to know that the area isn't actually as isolated as it seems to be when you're in its midst. The city of San José, with its major airport, is less than 15 miles away.

Monterey County

Monterey County has a wealth of attractions, including its beautiful coastline, the Monterey Bay, Pebble Beach golf course, a wildlife refuge, and the very chic town of Carmel. And the rugged beauty of Big Sur, a wilderness area, lies just south of Carmel on Route 1.

Monterey County now has about 85 wineries. But the vineyards of the Monterey peninsula serve an even larger population of wineries. As much as 80 percent of the wine grapes grown in Monterey County are purchased by non-Monterey wineries.

The weather in Monterey County is extremely variable. The northern part, closer to the town of Monterey and the Bay, is quite cool and breezy, with winds blowing in from the Pacific Ocean. As you travel south and farther inland, you can experience warm, even hot days but cool evenings in the summer. Riesling, Pinot Noir, and Chardonnay grow successfully in northern Monterey, especially near the coast, and Cabernet Sauvignon, Syrah, and Zinfandel do well in warmer southern Monterey.

A particularly special part of Monterey wine country is the Santa Lucia Highlands. This remote region, sheltered from the Pacific by the Santa Lucia Mountains, has vineyards up to 1,400 feet in altitude, where they rise into the sunshine above the morning fog line and enjoy cool breezes from Monterey Bay. Most of the wineries up there are small and new, but they're creating considerable fanfare among Pinot Noir lovers for their lush, rich style of wines. We recommend some Santa Lucia Pinot Noirs in Chapter 7.

Monterey's wineries offer something for everyone:

- ✔ **Large wineries:** Estancia Estates and Chateau Julien produce good value wines. Chateau Julien, in the Carmel region, is known for its reasonably priced Merlot.

- ✔ **Mid-sized winery:** Bernardus Winery in Carmel makes mid-priced varietal wines from Cabernet, Merlot, and other varieties. Bernardus offers first-rate lodging as well.

- ✔ **Smaller, more upscale wineries:** These wineries include

  - • Chalone Vineyard, master of Chardonnay and Pinot Blanc

  - • Morgan Winery, renowned for its Pinot Noir and Chardonnay

  - • Robert Talbott Vineyards, known mainly for its Chardonnay and lately for its Pinot Noir (**Note:** This is the same Robert Talbott who designs and produces very classy men's ties.)

- ✔ **Great views:** Smith & Hook/Hahn Estates Winery and Paraiso Vineyards, both in the Santa Lucia Highlands, offer sheer dramatic beauty. You can sip Paraiso's super Pinot Noir in the tasting room while taking in its view of the Pacific Coast from the edge of a cliff.

Monterey County AVAs

Like most California wine regions, Monterey County has been changing rapidly since the 1980s, and now, in addition to the general Monterey County AVA, nine distinct viticultural areas (AVAs) exist here. We list them, approximately from north to south, and include the most renowned wines in each AVA:

AVA	Description/Location	Wines
Monterey	Largest AVA in vineyard acreage	Pinot Noir, Chardonnay, Riesling in the north; Cabernet Sauvignon, Merlot, Syrah, and Chardonnay in the south
Carmel Valley	High in the Santa Lucia Mountains near the coast	Cabernet Sauvignon and Merlot
Santa Lucia Highlands	In the Santa Lucia Mountains close to the Pacific	Pinot Noir and Chardonnay
Chalone	In the Gavilan Mountains, to the east	Chardonnay, Pinot Blanc, Pinot Noir
Arroyo Seco	In the Santa Lucia foothills	Chardonnay, Riesling, and Zinfandel in warmer part
San Bernabe	In central part of the county	Merlot, Syrah, Chardonnay
San Lucas	Warmer AVA south of Salinas Valley	Cabernet Sauvignon, Merlot
San Antonio Valley	Warm AVA south of Santa Lucia Mountains	Cabernet Sauvignon, Petite Sirah, Syrah
Hames Valley	Southernmost tip of the county	Syrah, Rhône varietals

San Luis Obispo: Paso Robles, Edna Valley, and Arroyo Grande

The Big Sur wilderness in the southern part of Monterey County separates the northern districts of the Central Coast from those in the south. The southern part of the Central Coast begins in San Luis Obispo County. San Luis Obispo County resembles Monterey County in that the climate varies a great deal from north to south (see the preceding section on Monterey). In this case, most of the northern part — the hilly Paso Robles region north of the town of

San Luis Obispo — is quite warm, and the southern parts, Edna Valley and Arroyo Grande, both near the coast, are distinctly cooler.

The Paso Robles vineyard area is the true center of the Central Coast, as it's about equidistant from San Francisco and Los Angeles. The sunny, dry Paso Robles climate makes this region primarily red wine country, with Cabernet Sauvignon, Merlot, Syrah, and Zinfandel the leading wines.

Paso Robles is one of California's fastest-growing wine regions; when we wrote *Wine For Dummies*, 4th Edition, in 2006, we reported that the region had more than 90 wineries. Today, Paso Robles has nearly 170 wineries — and probably more by the time you read this. Some of the leading wineries in Paso Robles are Eberle, Justin Vineyards, Meridian Vineyards, Rabbit Ridge Vineyards, Tablas Creek, Treana, and Wild Horse Winery.

Paso Robles has two AVAs: the general Paso Robles AVA and York Mountain AVA. York Mountain is a small area in the southwestern part of the Paso Robles region that specializes in Cabernet Sauvignon. Because York Mountain is only 7 miles from the Pacific Ocean and is 1,500 feet in altitude, it's considerably cooler than the main, eastern part of Paso Robles — thus its need for a separate AVA. That said, the western part of the Paso Robles AVA is itself a fairly cool area.

The cool Edna Valley, south of Paso Robles, and the Arroyo Grande region, farther south, feature Pinot Noir and Chardonnay as their signature wines. But some wineries also grow Rhône varieties, such as Viognier, Syrah, Grenache, and Roussanne; others have Riesling, Pinot Grigio/Gris, Cabernet Sauvignon, and Zinfandel. Paragon Vineyard, one of California's best Pinot Noir vineyards, is in Edna Valley.

Fewer than 20 wineries are located in Edna Valley and Arroyo Grande, most of them in Edna Valley. The leading wineries are Alban Vineyards (Viognier specialists), Claiborne & Churchill (sounds like a law firm, but they make good Riesling), Corbett Canyon, Edna Valley Vineyard (Pinot Noir/Chardonnay specialists), Laetitia (sparkling wine and Pinot Noir), Saucelito Canyon (Zinfandel), and Talley Vineyards (Chardonnay and Pinot Noir).

Santa Barbara County: Santa Maria, Santa Ynez, and Los Alamos Valleys and Sta. Rita Hills

Although Spanish missionaries planted vineyards in what is now Santa Barbara County more than 200 years ago, Firestone Vineyard, the County's first major winery, didn't open until 1975.

Today, more than 110 wineries are operating throughout Santa Barbara. The fact that Santa Barbara County was the setting of the film *Sideways* certainly didn't hurt. Pinot Noir is Santa Barbara's poster child, for sure. But Chardonnay, Sauvignon Blanc, Riesling, and Syrah thrive in Santa Barbara as well.

Santa Barbara has three official AVAs (Santa Maria Valley, Santa Ynez Valley, and Sta. Rita Hills) and one unofficial one (Los Alamos Valley) that's still pending official recognition. All four wine regions are north of the city of Santa Barbara, and all four share a cool, unique climate, thanks to the positions of the Valleys.

Three Valleys (Santa Maria, Santa Ynez, and Los Alamos) run east to west — whereas most of California's coastal valleys run north to south — and are open to the cool breezes of the Pacific Ocean that channel through the Valleys. And so the southern latitude of Santa Barbara matters little; the position of the Valleys is what determines the climate, making all the Santa Barbara wine regions quite cool (the average temperature in Santa Maria Valley during the growing season is 74°F), ideal for Pinot Noir and Chardonnay.

Here's a rundown of the three Santa Barbara Valleys:

- ✔ **Santa Maria:** Santa Maria Valley, the northernmost AVA, is particularly renowned for Pinot Noir; in fact, its Pinot Noir grapes are sought out by many wineries outside of Santa Barbara. Of the Santa Barbara AVAs, the foggy, windswept Santa Maria Valley area is the most influenced by the Pacific Ocean; not only Pinot Noir but also Chardonnay is a true standout here.

- ✔ **Santa Ynez:** Santa Ynez Valley, in the southern part of the County and closest to the city of Santa Barbara, has the largest concentration of wineries. The western part, nearer the Pacific Ocean, grows Pinot Noir; the warmer, eastern end of the Valley features Syrah and other Rhône varieties.

  Sta. Rita Hills AVA, at the western end of Santa Ynez Valley, has a climate quite similar to that of Santa Maria Valley; Chardonnay and Pinot Noir do well here.

- ✔ **Los Alamos:** Los Alamos Valley, which lies between the Santa Maria Valley to the north and the Santa Ynez Valley to the south, uses the general Santa Barbara County AVA for its wines at present. Not as cool as Santa Maria Valley but cooler than Santa Ynez, its most important wines are Chardonnay and Pinot Noir.

Calera Wine Company: Standing alone in San Benito

San Benito County is directly east of Monterey County. San Benito has only one winery of any consequence, but it's quite a winery!

Josh Jensen became hooked on Burgundy wine after a trip to France in 1971. He spent two years going up and down California looking for the same limestone soil that he believed was a key element in the wondrous red and white Burgundies that he loved. Finally, he found it on a mountain 2,200 feet high in the Gavilan Mountain range, near Mount Harlan.

Jensen bought the land in 1974 and founded Calera Wine Company in 1975, planting three different vineyards of Pinot Noir. They're among the highest and coldest vineyards in California. Calera even has its own AVA: Mt. Harlan. Jensen later planted Viognier and Chardonnay, but the Pinot Noir is what established Calera's reputation as one of the elite wineries in California. Jensen took his own path more than 35 years ago and walked into California's wine legend. We recommend Calera's wines in Chapter 5 (Chardonnay), Chapter 7 (Pinot Noir), and Chapter 9 (Viognier).

Santa Barbara wine is typically enjoyable when it's young, within its first five years. The region's Pinot Noir has its own distinctive characteristics: Primarily, it exhibits intense strawberry fruit, with herbal notes.

Santa Barbara has many great wineries. A partial list includes Au Bon Climat, Babcock, Byron, Cambria, Cottonwood Canyon, Daniel Gehrs, Fess Parker, Fiddlehead Cellars, Foxen, Gainey, Hitching Post, Lane Tanner, Qupé, Sanford, Santa Barbara, and Zaca Mesa.

Southern California

Although Southern California saw the very beginnings of California wines, not much wine exists there today. One reason is apparent: Too many people and too many houses occupy the land. Another reason is that vintners found regions more suitable for fine wine farther north, in central California, especially near the coast. But some wineries do still exist in Southern California.

One winery worth noting is actually in the Los Angeles area: Moraga Vineyards. It's located in Moraga Canyon, about 600 to 800 feet in altitude in the Bel Air hills. Tom and Ruth Jones, the proprietors, discovered that the area's soil resembled that of part of France's Bordeaux region: It has gravelly beds, limestone, and fossils — a result of being submerged under the ocean millions of years ago. Tom Jones planted Cabernet Sauvignon, Merlot, and Sauvignon Blanc. He makes about 1,000 bottles a year of Moraga Red (80 percent Cabernet Sauvignon, 20 percent Merlot) and a little bit of Moraga White (all Sauvignon Blanc). The red sells for $125, the white, for $65.

The Temecula Valley, about an hour's drive north of San Diego, near the city of Oceanside, is blessed with cool breezes that funnel in from the Pacific Ocean and create an environment suitable for fine wine grapes. At present, the Temecula Valley has 24 wineries. No one grape variety seems to predominate; Merlot and Syrah are the popular reds, whereas Chardonnay and Sauvignon Blanc are the dominant whites. Many dessert wines come from this area as well, generally from Muscat and late-harvested Zinfandel grapes. The two best-known wineries, both founded in 1969, are Callaway Coastal Winery and Mount Palomar Winery. Both wineries purchase a large part of the grapes for their wine production from Central Coast vineyards, however, partially due to an infestation of the root louse phylloxera that devasted the area in the late 1990s.

Inward and upward

California's coastal regions get the lion's share of critical acclaim, but the state's wine economy owes a debt to the vast, interior vineyard areas. California's largest source of wine production is the huge Central Valley, located smack in the middle of the state. Another interior region, the Sierra Foothills, banks more on charm than on volume of production.

Central Valley

Over 50 percent of all California wine is made in the Central Valley — which is the general name for San Joaquin Valley, Sacramento Valley, and surrounding areas. This huge Valley in the center of the state extends from the city of Bakersfield at its southern end (near coastal Santa Barbara) all the way up and beyond Yuba City at its northern end (at a similar latitude to coastal Mendocino). It encompasses the state capital of Sacramento, the cities of Stockton and Fresno, and the wine towns of Lodi, Woodbridge, Modesto, Madera, and Clarksburg, among others.

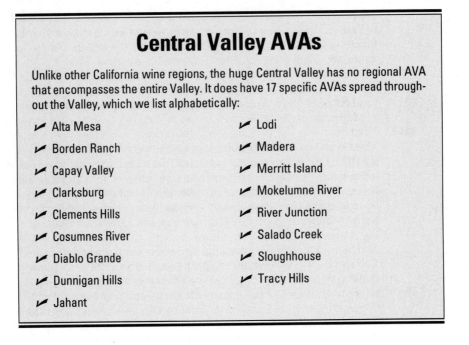

Central Valley AVAs

Unlike other California wine regions, the huge Central Valley has no regional AVA that encompasses the entire Valley. It does have 17 specific AVAs spread throughout the Valley, which we list alphabetically:

- Alta Mesa
- Borden Ranch
- Capay Valley
- Clarksburg
- Clements Hills
- Cosumnes River
- Diablo Grande
- Dunnigan Hills
- Jahant
- Lodi
- Madera
- Merritt Island
- Mokelumne River
- River Junction
- Salado Creek
- Sloughhouse
- Tracy Hills

The largest wine businesses in California have their principal wineries or at least part of their operations in the Central Valley. These include E. & J. Gallo Winery, Constellation Wines, Robert Mondavi-Woodbridge (owned by Constellation), Bronco Wine Company, R.H. Phillips, Cribari, Paul Masson, Mariposa (part of Kendall-Jackson, headquartered in Sonoma), Delicato, Almaden, and Franzia. Three prominent smaller wineries are Bogle Vineyards, Quady, and Ficklin (the latter two are dessert wine specialists).

Climate in the Central Valley is generally warm and dry in the summer and temperate in the winter. Most of the state's grape varieties grow here. Three varieties that thrive in this climate are Zinfandel, Petite Sirah, and Chenin Blanc. The Central Valley specializes in producing inexpensive, large-production wines, helping make it the foundation of the California wine business.

Sierra Foothills

If you want to experience a wine region that has a romantic history and has changed little over time, take a trip into the past and visit the charming wineries in the Sierra Foothills. We love to visit the region. It has a rustic charm that you can't find anywhere else in California. Life is still simple there, so don't expect to find any fancy restaurants. But the people are real and friendly, and the wines are good — and reasonably priced!

 One of the most memorable events in California's history was the Gold Rush of 1849. With the discovery of gold in Sutter Creek, in the foothills of the Sierra Nevada Mountains, this previously isolated area was forever changed. Besides prospectors and miners, others arrived there, and some of them decided to plant vineyards. By 1870, the Sierra Foothills boasted 100-plus wineries, more than Napa and Sonoma combined at the time! One of the vines planted there, Zinfandel, eventually gave the region its most renowned wine. Most of the oldest grapevines in the United States — some even over 100 years old — are in the Sierra Foothills.

The Sierra Foothills is a rather large region east and southeast of Sacramento (which is a good entry point). Most of the wineries are in Amador, El Dorado, or Calaveras Counties or a little north or south of them. The Shenandoah Valley and Fiddletown are the two major viticultural areas, and many of the wineries are located in one of these two areas. Some major wine towns (where you can find accommodations) are Plymouth, Placerville, Sutter Creek, and Amador City.

In addition to the general Sierra Foothills AVA, five specific AVAs exist:

- California Shenandoah Valley (**Note:** There's also a Virginia Shenandoah Valley AVA)
- El Dorado
- Fiddletown
- Fair Play
- North Yuba

 Most of the vineyards in the Sierra Foothills are about 1,500 to 2,000 feet in altitude, some even higher. Much of the soil is decomposed granite or crushed volcanic rock, both very good for growing wine grapes.

Besides red Zinfandel, which dominates the region, other leading grape varieties in the Sierra Foothills include Syrah, Cabernet Sauvignon, Barbera, Petite Sirah, and Sauvignon Blanc.

After being practically wiped out by Prohibition in the 1930s, more than 100 wineries are in business today. Some of the leading wineries are Monteviña (now known as Terra d'Oro), Renwood, Shenandoah Vineyards, Amador Foothill, Boeger, Sierra Vista, Karly, Renaissance Vineyard, and Sobon Estate. Just about every winery here specializes in Zinfandel (and many produce true Old Vines Zinfandels), but many wineries also make Syrah and Barbera.

Part II
The Headliners

The 5th Wave · By Rich Tennant

"I'm trying to remember the type of California white wine I like, but my mind keeps drawing a blanc."

In this part...

Does reading about wine make you thirsty for a nice, cool glass of Chardonnay or Sauvignon Blanc? Cabernet or Merlot might be your pleasure instead — or California's suddenly fashionable Pinot Noir, or maybe its ever-classic red Zinfandel. These are the varietal wines that California is best-known for, the major types of wine from California that you can find in just about every wine shop and on every restaurant wine list, all across the U.S. And these are the wines that we profile in this part of the book. For each type of wine, we discuss where the grapes grow, how the wines differ from region to region, what the wines taste like, what they cost, and which brands to trust. That's enough to make us thirsty, for sure!

Chapter 5

Chardonnay and Sauvignon Blanc

*O*ver the years, we've loved California Chardonnays — except for the times when we've been disappointed in them. Chardonnay has been a staple of California wine production since the very first days when producers began naming wines after their dominant grape variety, and the style of California's Chardonnays has varied quite a lot over those 40 or so years. But stylistic changes haven't dampened California Chardonnay's popularity. It's the single best-selling type of wine that California has — red or white (or pink).

Sauvignon Blanc is Chardonnay's perpetual sidekick in California. Its production is much smaller than Chardonnay's, and its appeal is much less universal among wine drinkers. Nonetheless, Sauvignon Blanc is California's number two white varietal wine and for many good reasons.

In this chapter, we describe the taste of these two wines, discuss the regions where Chardonnay and Sauvignon Blanc grow best in California, and recommend some of our favorite examples of these varietal wines.

Chardonnay: The Wine That California Made Famous

If you were born less than 50 years ago, what we're about to tell you might seem preposterous: Back in the 1960s, wines named *Chardonnay* for all practical purposes did not exist! California had a few of them, but practically nobody knew the wines. Chardonnay's trajectory from unknown entity to the biggest-selling wine in the United States is truly spectacular. In this section, we explain some of the history and talk about the taste of Chardonnay.

The Chardonnay grape traces its origins back to the Burgundy region in eastern France, where it was cultivated as early as the 1100s. It's the primary — and practically the only — variety used in making Chablis and the other iconic white wines of Burgundy. Also, Chardonnay is one of the major varieties in Champagne and in other sparkling wines. Today, Chardonnay is the second most planted grape variety in the world; only Airén — a minor Spanish variety used for making brandy and inexpensive white wines — occupies more acreage than Chardonnay. Chardonnay is planted in more wine regions of the world than any other variety, even more than the ubiquitous Cabernet Sauvignon!

A brief history of California Chardonnay

The honor of producing California's first varietal Chardonnay went to Wente Vineyards, which made Chardonnay in 1936. Carl Wente, a German immigrant working for the Charles Krug Winery in Napa Valley, founded his own winery in Livermore Valley in 1883 (see Chapter 1 for details). In 1912, a Wente descendant visited the University of Montpellier's Agriculture Department in France and returned with Chardonnay vine cuttings. Grape growers planted these cuttings throughout California in the 1940s, after Prohibition, and vines descended from these cuttings are now known as the *Wente clone* of Chardonnay (a *clone* is a subdivision of a grape variety).

Besides the Wente family, three Californians stand out as true pioneers for producing Chardonnay as a varietal wine:

> ✔ **Martin Ray:** A man who always went his own way, Martin Ray was a protégé of the legendary Paul Masson (see Chapter 1). In the early 1940s, Ray planted three noble grape varieties — Cabernet Sauvignon, Chardonnay, and Pinot Noir — on the

steep hillsides of the Santa Cruz Mountains in an area called Mount Eden. Ray used French methods of vinification to make his wines, including fermenting and aging the wines in French oak.

He sold his wines under the Martin Ray label, and the few wine critics that existed then praised Ray's wines as masterpieces. Although all three wines were special, the Chardonnay proved to be the finest and longest-lived. Ray charged the unheard-of price of $50 for his 1970 Chardonnay, at a time when almost all California wines cost well under $10. Not a good businessman, Ray lost his winery; it was renamed Mount Eden Vineyards — and is still renowned for its Estate Chardonnay today.

✔ **Fred McCrea:** San Francisco advertising executive Fred McCrea and his wife Eleanor bought a property on the west slope of Napa Valley, north of St. Helena, in 1943. They planted Chardonnay and four other varieties in 1947, harvested their first grapes in 1952, named the property Stony Hill Vineyard, and sold their first Chardonnay in 1954. Stony Hill Vineyard was one of the first Chardonnay specialists — about 60 percent of the few thousand cases a year that the winery produces is Chardonnay.

Stony Hill's Chardonnay is different from most other California Chardonnays: The winery uses minimal oak (only old barrels, which impart no oak flavor), and the wines are lean, racy, intense, and minerally. Only two winemakers have ever made Stony Hill wines: Fred McCrea from 1952 to 1973 and Mike Chelini for the past 35 years. Now that's continuity! The McCreas' son and daughter-in-law run Stony Hill today.

✔ **James Zellerbach:** Once the U.S. Ambassador to Rome, Zellerbach became enamored of Burgundy wines in his travels to France. In 1948, Zellerbach purchased 200 acres in the Mayacamas Mountains, north of the town of Sonoma; he planted Chardonnay and Pinot Noir in 1953, named his winery Hanzell, and sold the first vintage of the two wines in 1957. Today, three-quarters of Hanzell's production is Chardonnay. Hanzell Chardonnay remains one of the great white wines made in California to this day.

But as we mention in Chapter 1, Robert Mondavi is the one who truly brought fame to the wine named Chardonnay. He opened Robert Mondavi Winery in 1966 and started producing premium varietal wines, such as Chardonnay and Cabernet Sauvignon (and later, Sauvignon Blanc, Merlot, and Pinot Noir). The wines were good, received fine reviews, and sold well. And then most other wine producers in California jumped on the varietal wine bandwagon.

California Chardonnay reached its peak of popularity in the late 1980s and the 1990s. The wine went through various stylistic evolutions, from very rich and exotic wines to leaner, cleaner (and some said anemic) "food wines" to the style of today, which is somewhere in between.

The taste of California Chardonnay

The Chardonnay grape variety brings little aroma or flavor to its wines. In cooler regions, its wines often have hints of apple aromas and flavors; in warmer regions, they suggest tropical fruits, particularly pineapple. In some regions (such as Chablis, France), the wines have a distinctive mineral character, such as flintiness. These characteristics hold true in California's cooler and warmer wine regions. But because California has more warm wine regions than cool ones, California Chardonnays tend to gravitate toward tropical fruit flavors, as well as ripe lemon.

Because of the wine's fairly limited aromas and flavors — and because Chardonnay juice is particularly compatible with oak — winemakers in California and elsewhere ferment and/or age most of their better Chardonnays in oak barrels. Lower-priced Chardonnays typically obtain oaky aromas and flavors from oak planks, oak chips, or oak powder that soaks in the wine while the wine is in stainless steel vats (because oak barrels are expensive!).

California Chardonnays made using any form of oak can smell and taste toasty, spicy, and/or smoky, with aromas and flavors of vanilla or butterscotch. All these aromas and flavors come from oak, not from the grape. Oaked Chardonnays can also have some tannin that comes from the oak. If the wine is actually fermented in oak barrels, which is common practice for pricier Chardonnays, it can have a special richness of texture as a result. But many California Chardonnays today, even cheap brands, have a thick, viscous texture not from oak but as the result of very high alcohol content; this characteristic is positive, unless (like one of us) you have a low threshold for alcohol and therefore taste a hard, burning character along with the rich texture.

Some critics, including us, have taken issue with the way California Chardonnay is made. We can sum up their complaints in two words: *too much.* Too many Chardonnays have been too high in alcohol, too sweet, and too oaky. A few California producers make Chardonnays without using any oak, or even more commonly, with few or no new oak barrels. (Used barrels, depending on their age, give little or no oaky flavor to the wine.) The trend in California seems to be moving slowly away from heavily oaked Chardonnays toward more lightly oaked styles, and we, for two, say, "Hallelujah!" We would still like the wines to be less sweet and more restrained in their alcohol levels, however.

For richer or for value

Some wine drinkers believe that California Chardonnays are too expensive. In fact, some of the most celebrated brands cost upwards of $100 a bottle. But California Chardonnays exist at all price levels: You can even find California Chardonnay for $3 a bottle.

However, the taste of the wine does vary according to price:

✔ In our experience, the least expensive wines are quite sweet. You can sense their sweetness — a combination of residual sugar in the wines, in some cases, and the sweetness of high alcohol levels — as soon as you put the wine in your mouth. In a way, this sweetness is good because it counterbalances the edgy, sharp burn that overly high alcohol brings to a wine.

✔ Mid-priced wines, especially those that cost about $15 to $20 a bottle, seem a bit less overtly sweet.

✔ The highest priced wines vary a lot from brand to brand. In the best wines, you can sense a real concentration of flavor, and those flavors remain along the whole length of your tongue instead of stopping short midway.

We recommend some Chardonnays at each price level in the later section titled "Some Top Chardonnay Producers."

Where Chardonnay Grows in California

Chardonnay is somewhat of a workhorse variety: It can grow productively in all kinds of climates. But as California wine producers discovered in the last decades of the 20th century, Chardonnay does best in cool, coastal regions — such as Carneros, Russian River Valley, and the Sonoma Coast — where the soil is usually quite poor and the vines don't grow prolifically. Figure 5-1 shows Russian River Valley, a key Chardonnay region.

Chardonnays produced in the cool, coastal places can be quite expensive, but if you want to pay $15 or less, rest assured that lots of Chardonnay is made in this price range. The majority of inexpensive Chardonnays come from California's warmer regions, such as the Central Valley, where the soil is more fertile and grape-growing is more bounteous. Instead of having specific regional names on their labels, most of these wines simply carry the wider geographic designation of California.

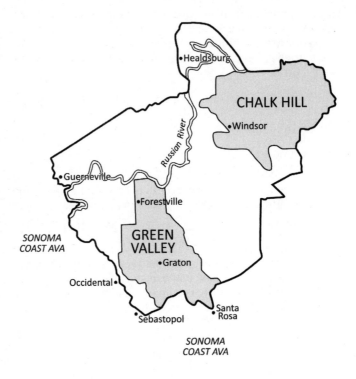

Figure 5-1: Russian River Valley.

Cool, coastal classic regions

Most of California's best Chardonnays come from its coolest growing areas, which are near its coastline and/or located at high altitudes. Many of these regions are in the coastal and northern parts of Sonoma County, such as Russian River Valley and its even cooler subregion, Green Valley. The newest area that's gaining acclaim for Chardonnay is the Sonoma Coast, which is really pushing the envelope with its marginal growing conditions: It's a very cool area with poor soil, and both of these factors challenge the grapevines to perform.

FROMMERS TRAVEL TIP

Napa versus Sonoma: Which area is right for you?

Determining whether to spend your wine country vacation in Napa Valley, Sonoma Valley, or Northern Sonoma — or some combination of two or three — depends on what kind of vacation you're looking for and how much time you have to spend. If you have only a long weekend, it's better to choose one destination and make the most of it rather than spend a good portion of your vacation driving and checking in and out of hotels or B&Bs.

Sonoma Valley and Northern Sonoma maintain backcountry ambience. Though Sonoma County is home to more than 250 wineries, it seems far less commercial than Napa, primarily because the attractions are scattered over a far greater area, so there's a lower density of wineries, restaurants, hotels, and manmade structures in general (vineyards aside). However, though both the Valley and the environs to the north are technically in Sonoma, they offer dramatically different experiences.

A current favorite destination is Northern Sonoma's Healdsburg area. In the last few years, this area has seen the addition of truly exceptional dining and accommodations. Consider its offerings: You can cruise vast vine-trellised countryside and wind down tiny dirt roads to discover small gem wineries often manned by the winemakers; feast on excellent cuisine in chic new restaurants and longstanding casual local haunts; shop or people-watch at Healdsburg's historic square; and even float down a lazy river on an inner tube if you want. It has the best of both Napa and Sonoma Valleys. It certainly feels the least commercial.

If you have the luxury of time, don't visit just one destination: Tour two so you can compare and contrast these very different — and very wonderful — worlds of winemaking.

Carneros, a region that's partly in Napa and partly in Sonoma, is another classic Chardonnay region. Although Carneros is in the southern part of both counties, the cool ocean breezes coming through San Pablo Bay in the south create ideal growing conditions for Chardonnay.

Santa Barbara County, although quite southerly, has valleys open to Pacific Ocean breezes and is generally an excellent region for Chardonnay. In particular, Santa Maria Valley, in the northwest part of Santa Barbara County, is one of Santa Barbara's coolest districts because of its ocean breezes, and it's a fine area for growing Chardonnay.

Other cool regions that are perfect for Chardonnay include coastal Monterey County and the Chalone region in Monterey's Gavilan Mountains. Monterey County makes lots of Chardonnay, and most of it is fairly inexpensive. Mendocino County's Anderson Valley, along California's North Coast, is another cool location suited to making top-flight Chardonnays.

Warm regions for everyday Chardonnays

California's gigantic Central Valley produces most of the state's inexpensive Chardonnays. You find some of these wines carrying appellations of origin such as Lodi, Woodbridge, Modesto, and Madera — but most of them simply carry the California designation. Growing conditions such as warm, sunny days, fertile soil, and irrigation enable grape growers here to produce huge crops of Chardonnay that find their way into many of the mass-market, value-priced brands.

Top Chardonnay Producers

California is the largest producer of varietal Chardonnay wines in the world. We estimate that at least 2,000 different brands of California Chardonnay exist. Our intention in this section is to name just a few of these brands to guide you toward what we consider to be some of the best Chardonnays available at various price levels.

Most, but not all, of the top-rank California Chardonnay producers harvest their Chardonnay grapes from vineyards located in cool-climate areas, as you can see from the vineyard locations that appear in parentheses in our lists.

We place our top Chardonnay producers' wines into three price categories, based on the average retail price of the wine across the U.S.:

- ✔ **Moderately priced Chardonnays:** About $12 to $20

- ✔ **Moderate-plus Chardonnays:** Between $20 and $50

- ✔ **High-end Chardonnays:** Mainly between $50 and $100, with a few over $100

But if your budget doesn't stretch that far, you can still find decent Chardonnays. Check out our sidebar titled "Six top-value California Chardonnays" for a few recommended Chardonnays that sell for $12 or less.

Moderately Priced Chardonnays, $12–$20

Alma Rosa Winery (Santa Barbara County)

Bernardus Winery (Monterey County)

Cambria Winery, Katherine's Vineyard (Santa Maria Valley)

Franciscan Oakville Estate (Napa Valley)

Freemark Abbey (Napa Valley)

Gainey Vineyard (Sta. Rita Hills)

Kendall-Jackson, Grand Reserve (Monterey/Santa Barbara Counties)

Markham (Napa Valley)

Sebastiani Vineyards (Sonoma County)

Wente Vineyards, Riva Ranch Reserve (Arroyo Seco, Monterey)

Moderate-Plus Chardonnays, $20–$50

Anderson's Conn Valley Vineyards, Fournier Vineyard (Carneros, Napa Valley)

Arrowood Vineyards (Sonoma County)

Au Bon Climat, "Nuits-Blanchesau Bouge," Bien Nacido Vineyard (Santa Maria Valley)

Beringer Vineyards Private Reserve (Napa Valley)

Byron Vineyard (Santa Maria Valley)

Chalk Hill Estate (Chalk Hill)

Chalone Vineyard (Chalone, Monterey County)

Chappellet (Napa Valley)

Chasseur Wines (both in Sonoma Coast and Russian River Valley)

Chateau Montelena (Napa Valley)

Dehlinger (Russian River Valley)

Domaine Alfred, Chamisal Vineyards, "Califa" (Edna Valley)

Ferrari-Carano, "Tre Terre" (Russian River Valley)

Foley Estate (Sta. Rita Hills)

Forman Vineyard (Napa Valley)

Gallo Family Vineyards, Laguna Ranch (Russian River Valley)

Gary Farrell Vineyards, Russian River (Russian River Valley)

Grgich Hills Estate (Napa Valley)

The Hess Collection, Su'skol Vineyard (Napa Valley)

Jordan Vineyard (Russian River Valley)

Long Vineyards (Napa Valley)

Lynmar Winery, Quail Hill Vineyard (Russian River Valley)

Marimar Torres, Don Miguel Vineyard (Green Valley, Russian River Valley)

Mayacamas (Mt. Veeder, Napa Valley)

Morgan, "Metallico" (Monterey)

Nickel & Nickel, Searby Vineyard (Russian River Valley)

Patz & Hall, Dutton Ranch (Russian River Valley)

Ramey Wine Cellars, Russian River Valley, or Sonoma Coast (Sonoma)

Ridge Vineyards, Estate (Santa Cruz Mountains)

Robert Talbott Vineyards, Sleepy Hollow Vineyard (Monterey)

Saintsbury, Carneros Estate (Carneros, Napa Valley)

Sonoma-Cutrer (Russian River Ranches and Sonoma Coast)

Stag's Leap Wine Cellars, Karia Vineyard (Stags Leap District, Napa Valley)

Stony Hill Vineyard, Estate (Napa Valley)

Talley Vineyards, Rincon Vineyard (Arroyo Grande)

Trefethen Vineyards, Estate (Oak Knoll District, Napa Valley)

Six top-value California Chardonnays

These six Chardonnays, all selling for about $12 or less, are consistently reliable, and they're our picks as top values for the money:

✔ Acacia Winery, A by Acacia (California)

✔ Chateau Julien, Barrel Select (Monterey County)

✔ Chateau St. Jean (Sonoma County)

✔ Estancia, Pinnacles Ranches (Monterey County)

✔ Guenoc Winery (Lake County)

✔ J. Lohr, Riverstone (Arroyo Seco, Monterey County)

On the high end of the spectrum, we recommend about 20 Chardonnays. Our list includes a few Chardonnays from Kistler, Marcassin, and Aubert (all small production wines) that cost over $100. And yet the rest of the wines, which fall into the $50 to $100 range, include some of the very best Chardonnays in the world — producers such as Mount Eden Estate, Hanzell, and Peter Michael. We believe that these excellent Chardonnays do offer top value and warrant their price tags.

High-End Chardonnays, Mostly $50–$100

Aubert Wines, Ritchie, Lauren, or Quarry Vineyard (Sonoma Coast); *over $100*

Brewer-Clifton, Seasmoke Vineyard (Sta. Rita Hills)

Dumol (Russian River Valley)

Far Niente (Napa Valley)

Fisher Vineyards, Whitney's Vineyard (Sonoma)

Flowers Vineyard (Sonoma Coast)

Hanzell Vineyards (Sonoma Valley)

Hyde De Villaine (HDV) Los Carneros (Carneros, Napa Valley)

Kistler Vineyards, Dutton Ranch (Russian River Valley); *over $100*

Kistler Vineyards, Kistler Vineyard (Sonoma Valley); *over $100*

Marcassin Vineyard, Zio Tony Ranch (Sonoma Coast); *over $200*

Marcassin, Marcassin Vineyard (Sonoma Coast); *over $200*

Mount Eden Estate (Santa Cruz Mountains)

Newton, "Unfiltered" (Carneros, Napa Valley)

Pahlmeyer (Napa Valley)

Paul Hobbs (Russian River Valley)

Peter Michael, Ma Belle-Fille (Knights Valley, Sonoma)

J. Rochioli Vineyards, Estate (Russian River Valley)

Rudd Estate, Bacigalupi Vineyard (Russian River Valley)

Williams Selyem, Allen Vineyard (Russian River Valley)

Chardonnay stars: The Establishment and the new guys

Two wineries that first began making Chardonnay in the 1950s, Stony Hill Vineyards in Napa Valley and Hanzell Vineyards in Sonoma Valley, remain two of California Chardonnay's brightest stars today.

The 1970s and 1980s were golden years for California as many great new wineries opened. In 1972, Napa Valley's renowned Chateau Montelena was born; this property still makes world-class Chardonnays and Cabernet Sauvignons. Other California wineries born in the 1970s and acclaimed for their Chardonnays include Grgich Hills, Forman Vineyard, Long Vineyards, and Far Niente, all in Napa Valley. (Actually, Far Niente was founded in 1885 but was reborn in 1979 when it made its first Chardonnay.) A great 1970s-era Sonoma winery is Kistler Vineyards, which makes single-vineyard Sonoma Chardonnays; Kistler is one of the true superstars of California Chardonnay, and consequently, its wines are almost impossible to find except in a few high-end restaurants — or if you're lucky enough to be on Kistler's mailing list.

The 1980s ushered in a few noteworthy California Chardonnay producers, including Au Bon Climat in Santa Barbara, Patz & Hall in Napa (but most of its Chardonnays come from Sonoma), and Peter Michael and Marcassin in Sonoma. Marcassin, like Kistler, produces small amounts of expensive Chardonnays that are prized by wine collectors. Williams Selyem in Russian River Valley, renowned for its prized Pinot Noirs, also just happens to make darn good Chardonnays as well.

Newer wineries that are making excellent Chardonnays include Ramey Wine Cellars and Lynmar Winery, both of whom make quite affordable Chardonnays from Russian River Valley vineyards. Really hot new Chardonnays include Aubert from the Sonoma Coast and Brewer-Clifton from the Sta. Rita Hills in Santa Barbara.

Sauvignon Blanc: Always a Bridesmaid, Never a Bride

Sauvignon Blanc is California's second most popular white wine, but it's far behind Chardonnay in production and sales. In fact, Italian Pinot Grigio outsells California Sauvignon Blanc in the United States. Although some California winemakers have been passionate about Sauvignon Blanc, quite a few wineries, particularly in Napa Valley, gave up on Sauvignon Blanc — either because their winemakers weren't satisfied with their version of the wine or because the wine didn't sell well enough.

Sémillon as a secret style-maker

Sémillon (seh-mee-yohn) gets our vote as the least-known important white wine grape variety in the world. It plays a crucial role in the makeup of many wines — but usually in a supporting role, seldom as the lead. One region in which Sémillon is a star is in the Graves (*grahv*) district of Bordeaux, where it's an important component of dry white Bordeaux wines, together with Sauvignon Blanc. In the same district, Sémillon is the major variety of Sauternes, which is arguably the world's finest dessert wine.

Although a few varietal Sémillon wines do exist, Sémillon invariably finds itself blended with Sauvignon Blanc, for many good reasons. Whereas Sauvignon Blanc makes wines that are very aromatic and herbaceous with high acidity and light to medium body, Sémillon wines have subtler aromas, lower acidity, and fuller body. Sémillon has a thick, almost oily texture, with aromas of figs and sometimes lanolin; its texture complements the leaner structure of Sauvignon Blanc.

Another major reason this blend works so well is how the two wines age: Sauvignon Blanc makes its presence felt early in the life of a Sauvignon Blanc–Sémillon blended wine, but the characteristics of the longer-lived Sémillon take a while to emerge and continue developing with time.

For the many California winemakers who add Sémillon to their Sauvignon Blanc wines, Sémillon plays the crucial role of toning down the sometimes too-aggressive aromas and flavors of Sauvignon Blanc and also adding years to the life of the wine.

One of the main reasons for Sauvignon Blanc's failure to compete with Chardonnay is that in the early days of its history in California, Sauvignon Blanc didn't have a distinct identity. During the 1970s and part of the 1980s, producers often planted Sauvignon Blanc grapes in areas similar to where they planted Chardonnay and gave Sauvignon Blanc wine the same oak treatment as Chardonnay. And guess what? It tasted like Chardonnay.

But within the last decade, things have been changing in California for Sauvignon Blanc. Producers have been identifying the best regions to plant the grape, and many winemakers are now using little or no oak in the fermentation and aging process. As a result, California Sauvignon Blanc is slowly gaining a distinct identity and, in some cases, new respect among wine drinkers.

Many wine critics believe, however, that Sauvignon Blanc still hasn't hit its stride in California. Common complaints are that the high alcohol of many Sauvignon Blanc wines (sometimes combined with residual sugar in the wines) creates a sweetness that's discordant with the raw, bitter flavors that high alcohol can extract from the grapes. We've tasted many Sauvignon Blancs like that ourselves, and we hope that when California producers get over their high-alcohol fixation, the wines will become more balanced and appealing.

Some history on Sauvignon Blanc

Sauvignon Blanc, as far as anyone can determine, originated in Bordeaux, France, in the 1600s. It's a major variety in most Bordeaux Blanc wines and also in many wines from France's Loire Valley, such as Sancerre and Pouilly Fumé.

Although Sauvignon Blanc came to California from France in the late 1870s (and was first planted in the Livermore Valley, east of San Francisco), Robert Mondavi in Napa Valley was the first California wine producer to truly popularize Sauvignon Blanc.

In the 1960s, sales were slow for all California Sauvignon Blancs. In 1968, when Robert Mondavi made his first Sauvignon Blanc wine, he named it *Fumé Blanc* (as a tribute to the Loire Valley's Pouilly Fumé, perhaps; maybe French names are sexier). Lo and behold, it was a big hit. A few producers followed Mondavi's lead and also called their wines Fumé Blanc. Today, the two names, Sauvignon Blanc and Fumé Blanc, coexist in California, but most producers call the wine Sauvignon Blanc. However, a few of California's top Sauvignon Blanc brands, such as Dry Creek Vineyard and Grgich Hills (pronounced *ger*-gich), prefer the name Fumé Blanc.

One of us believes that Sauvignon Blanc will become one of the next hot white wines in the United States, along with Riesling. Sauvignon Blanc is already New Zealand's most popular white, is well-established in France, Northeast Italy, and South Africa, and is becoming a chic white wine in Chile.

The other one of us believes that California producers need to decide which style of Sauvignon Blanc to make and work harder at perfecting that style. In an effort to emulate New Zealand's wines from this variety, producers are picking their grapes later and later to avoid the so-called *green* (raw herbal and vegetal) flavors that come from underripeness; but in the process, they're harvesting grapes with so much sugar that the wines' alcohol levels are ridiculously high for what should be a zesty, refreshing wine.

Three styles of California Sauvignon Blanc

The Sauvignon Blanc grape variety has always made wines of different styles in different wine regions. Depending on how ripe the grape gets, it can express herbal and vegetal aromas and flavors (when it's less ripe) or fruity aromas and flavors (when the grapes are riper). In some regions, particularly the Loire Valley in France, the wines can have a distinct mineral flavor.

The grape typically brings high acidity to its wines, which results in a freshness and vibrancy in the wine unless a winemaker masks these characteristics with oak or by blending with another variety, typically Sémillon (see our nearby sidebar titled "Sémillon as a secret style-maker").

One of Sauvignon Blanc's identity problems in California is that the wines don't exhibit any one style. Often, you don't know what to expect when you buy a bottle. In this sense, Sauvignon Blanc is the antithesis of Chardonnay: Each brand is as different from the next as each brand of Chardonnay is similar to the next.

Today, California Sauvignon Blanc seems to fall into three main styles:

- **Grassy, herbaceous:** Sauvignon Blanc wines in this style have aromas and flavors that suggest freshly mown grass, fresh herbs, and/or green vegetables such as asparagus and bell peppers; these aromas can be more or less intense, depending on the wine. These wines are generally crisp and vibrant, with high acidity, but lately some of them are soft rather than crisp in texture. Sauvignon Blancs made in the grassy, herbaceous style usually ferment and age in stainless steel tanks, with little or no use of oak, which would diminish the vivid flavors of the grape.

- **Fruity:** Sauvignon Blancs in this style emphasize fruity aromas and flavors — melon, fig, citrus, passion fruit, and/or pear. These wines, generally crisp and lively but sometimes soft, are fermented and aged mainly or totally in stainless steel tanks, with little or no use of oak — just like wines in the herbaceous style. To tone down Sauvignon Blanc's grassy, herbal tendencies, winemakers either blend in other varieties, particularly Sémillon, or ensure that their grapes are ripe enough to prevent any underripe herbaceous or vegetal notes.

✔ **Oak-influenced:** This style, formerly the predominant type of Sauvignon Blanc in California, is closest to the style in which Chardonnays are made — although these days, most wines in this style have much less overt oakiness than most Chardonnays do. Typically, winemakers barrel-ferment and barrel-age these Sauvignon Blancs, which results in a more richly textured, somewhat fuller-bodied wine with toned-down aromas and flavors from the grape and gentle vanilla notes from the oak. Oak-influenced Sauvignon Blancs usually have Sémillon in the blend. The closest model for the oak-influenced style is white Bordeaux from the Graves and Pessac-Léognan districts in France.

Today in California, the grassy, herbaceous style and the fruity style have overtaken the oak-influenced style in popularity. But you can still find all three styles of Sauvignon Blanc. What is hard to find, however, is a truly dry Sauvignon Blanc. Whether from high alcohol or from actual residual sugar in the wines, almost every Sauvignon Blanc tastes a bit sweet.

Sauvignon Blanc complements many foods, such as fish, shellfish, many chicken entrees, and Asian cuisine. And most California Sauvignon Blancs are ready to drink when you buy them; they don't need extra aging. We do recommend, however, that you drink these wines well-chilled, because a low temperature enhances their vibrancy and diminishes the perception of any sweetness in the wine.

Taste trumps price

One of the great aspects of California Sauvignon Blanc is that most cost less than $20. Some retail in the $20 to $30 range, and just a handful sell for more than $30. Sauvignon Blanc wines from California are much more affordable than California Chardonnays for two reasons:

✔ Chardonnay is still in much more demand, and therefore the grapes themselves, as well as the wines, cost more.

✔ Most Sauvignon Blanc producers use little or no expensive new French oak barrels for fermenting and aging their wines.

We personally tend to buy the Sauvignon Blanc wines that we enjoy, without regard to price, because price isn't a huge differentiating factor.

Regions for Sauvignon Blanc

Nowadays, many of the best Sauvignon Blancs come from California's cooler American Viticultural Areas (AVAs), especially sites in Sonoma and Santa Barbara but also in Napa Valley's cooler regions, such as Carneros and mountainous regions within Napa County.

Napa Valley made sense as a region for producing Sauvignon Blanc because Cabernet Sauvignon shone in Napa Valley, and Sauvignon Blanc performs well in Bordeaux where Cabernet Sauvignon also excels. In fact, Sauvignon Blanc is genetically one of the parents of the Cabernet Sauvignon grape, along with Cabernet Franc.

Many of the early fine examples of Sauvignon Blanc wines did come out of the Napa Valley. Although these Napa Valley wineries still produce good Sauvignon Blancs, we sense that today's epicenter for California Sauvignon Blanc might be switching to cooler Sonoma County and, to a lesser extent, Santa Barbara.

In this section, we focus on the main wine regions in California producing Sauvignon Blanc wines, and we name some of our favorite California Sauvignon Blancs.

Napa originals

After the success of Robert Mondavi's Fumé Blanc in 1968 (see the earlier section "Some history on Sauvignon Blanc"), other Napa Valley wineries began to make Sauvignon Blanc a part of their portfolio of wines. Three Napa wineries that continue to be standard bearers for Sauvignon Blanc today are Frog's Leap, St. Supéry, and Voss Vineyards:

- ✔ **Frog's Leap:** This was one of the first California wineries to specialize in Sauvignon Blanc; today, Sauvignon Blanc comprises half of the winery's 50,000-case Rutherford AVA production.

- ✔ **St. Supéry:** Here's another one of the rare Napa Valley wineries that feature Sauvignon Blanc, not Chardonnay, as the primary white wine. In fact, St. Supéry makes two Sauvignon Blancs: its standard Sauvignon Blanc, which sells for less than $20, and an excellent single-vineyard Sauvignon Blanc, Dollarhide Ranch, which costs $30 to $35.

✔ **Voss Vineyards:** This winery, which grows its Sauvignon Blanc grapes in Napa Valley's Rutherford district, champions the grassy, herbaceous style of Sauvignon Blanc. Voss is also one of the few California producers using a screwcap rather than a cork on its Sauvignon Blanc bottles (although other California wineries are switching over to screwcaps as fast as they can). Voss Vineyards' Sauvignon Blanc retails for about $16.

Seven other Napa Valley wineries known for their Sauvignon Blancs are Flora Springs, which calls its wine Soliloquy, Selene (whose grapes come from Carneros's Hyde Vineyard), Cakebread Cellars, Grgich Hills, Honig, Rudd Estate, and Mayacamas. Spottswoode is another Napa Valley winery making a fine Sauvignon Blanc, but production is small and the wine is difficult to find.

Mayacamas Vineyards is an old-time (for California) mountain winery known for its long-lasting wines. Mayacamas's history dates back to 1889. Its present owner, Bob Travers (along with his son, Chris), produces only 600 cases or so of Sauvignon Blanc every year in a style that we love: crisp, lively, assertive, and with excellent citrus and mineral notes. Mayacamas Sauvignon Blanc is one of the truly long-lived Sauvignons made in California; in a good vintage, it will age for ten years or more. The current vintage sells for $30.

Another iconic Sauvignon Blanc that we love — and wish we could get our hands on more of — is the "I Block" Fumé Blanc Reserve of Robert Mondavi Winery. This limited production wine, from the To-Kalon Vineyard, costs about $75 a bottle. If that sounds pricey for a Sauvignon Blanc, well, it can seem like a bargain when you taste how complex and compelling the wine is after several years of age. We also love the Robert Mondavi Winery Fumé Blanc Reserve, which also comes from the To-Kalon Vineyard but costs a lot less — only about $35 to $40.

A positive sign for Sauvignon Blanc in California is that a few wineries have begun making varietal Sauvignon Blanc for the first time. For example, Napa Valley's prestigious Franciscan Estate has released its first Sauvignon Blanc ever with its 2007 vintage. And it's a good one, made in a combined fruity and herbal style with a bit of ingratiating sweetness. It sells for $16 to $17.

Sonoma takes on Sauvignon

With the stylistic preference for California Sauvignon Blancs gradually switching from oak-influenced to grassy, herbaceous, and fruity styles, the cooler American Viticultural Areas (AVAs) in Sonoma County are now producing many of California's most sought-after Sauvignon Blancs. Russian River Valley, in particular, and the cooler parts of Dry Creek Valley — the district's western vineyards, near Russian River Valley — excel with Sauvignon Blanc today.

Russian River Valley

Sonoma's cool Russian River Valley (refer back to Figure 5-1) has already proven to be an excellent location for Pinot Noir and Chardonnay wines, but lately it's become known as a fine source of Sauvignon Blancs as well.

Leading the way for Sauvignon Blancs in the Russian River Valley is J. Rochioli, a winery known for its Pinot Noirs. Rochioli's Sauvignon Blanc is a lively, crisp wine made in the fruity style, with lots of citrus notes; a small amount of oak fermentation rounds out the wine's texture and gives the wine weight. At $33 to $34, it's a bit pricey for a Sauvignon Blanc, but we believe it's worth the price.

Another Russian River Valley winery, Sauvignon Republic, is (as its name suggests) devoted exclusively to Sauvignon Blanc. Sauvignon Republic's Russian River Valley Sauvignon Blanc, made in the grassy, herbaceous style, sells for $15 to $16.

Hanna Winery also makes its Russian River Sauvignon Blanc ($14 to $16) in the grassy style. Other top Russian River Valley Sauvignon Blancs include Adler Fels, Chateau St. Jean, Dutton Estate, Gary Farrell, Paradise Ridge, and Rodney Strong.

Dry Creek Valley

Although Dry Creek Valley is best known for its terrific Zinfandels and its Cabernet Sauvignons, we now add Sauvignon Blanc to its list of very good varietal wines. At Dry Creek Vineyard, in fact, Sauvignon Blanc is the flagship white. Dry Creek Vineyard produces three Fumé Blancs, as they're called at this winery. Its Sonoma County Fumé Blanc, about $14, is in a restrained grassy, herbaceous style. Dry Creek Vineyards' two fine single-vineyard Fumé Blancs — its Estate DCV 3 and its Taylor's Vineyard Musqué, both about $25 — are in the fruity style. Dry Creek Vineyard formerly made an oak-influenced Reserve Fumé Blanc, but the owners dropped the Reserve from the winery's portfolio. Now all its Fumé Blancs are oak-free.

Fritz Winery is also a champion of Sauvignon Blanc in Dry Creek Valley. Its Estate Sauvignon Blanc, about $20, is crisp and lively, with pronounced fruity flavors but also with a touch of grassiness.

Other fine Dry Creek Valley Sauvignon Blancs include those of Adobe Road, a small, new winery producing two Sauvignons (one from Dry Creek Valley and one from Russian River Valley); Dutcher Crossing; Handley Cellars; Lambert Bridge; Mill Creek; and Quivira Vineyards.

Top Sauvignon Blanc wines from other regions

Two important Sauvignon Blanc producers are in Santa Barbara County:

- ✔ **Babcock Winery and Vineyards:** Babcock is in the Sta. Rita Hills, an AVA known for its Chardonnay and Pinot Noir. Although Babcock produces good examples of these other wines, it has become well-known for its assertive Sauvignon Blanc, made in the grassy style, which sells for about $20.

- ✔ **Brander Vineyard:** In the Santa Ynez Valley AVA, this winery is arguably the greatest Sauvignon Blanc specialist of any winery in California — no, make that the entire U.S. Although Brander does make other wines, its most important wine is Sauvignon Blanc. Brander produces an amazing five different Sauvignon Blancs — in all styles and with prices ranging from $15 to $30. Brander ferments and ages most of its Sauvignons in stainless steel tanks and avoids new oak at all costs.

The Santa Ynez Valley, an inland area of Santa Barbara County, is in fact a prime source for Sauvignon Blancs, despite the fact that it's warmer than other parts of Santa Barbara County. Besides Brander, some top Santa Ynez Valley producers of Sauvignon Blanc include the Ojai Vineyard, Fiddlehead Cellars, Lincroft Vineyards, Firestone Vineyard, and Gainey Vineyard.

Other California Sauvignon Blancs we enjoy are Greenwood Ridge Vineyards in Anderson Valley (Mendocino) and Bernardus in Monterey County.

Dining in Healdsburg in Sonoma

Russian River Valley, Dry Creek Valley, and Alexander Valley come together around Healdsburg, the main wine town in Northern Sonoma. Even before the true destination dining rooms arrived, Healdsburg was still a fantastic place to dine — thanks to sweet little country restaurants and a few more contemporary staples. But now you have even more options.

Cyrus: Without question, this is Sonoma County's finest fine-dining restaurant. Run by veteran San Francisco maitre d' Nick Peyton and heralded chef Douglas Keane, it's truly a gastronome's dream destination: Romantic Burgundy, France–inspired interior, an intimate and friendly yet somewhat formal atmosphere, and to-die-for seasonal "contemporary luxury" cuisine (read: French-inspired with seasonal and global influences). An evening appropriately starts, if your heart desires, with selections from carts showcasing caviar (measured to order on a scale against tiny gold bars) and Champagne. It continues with a menu of build-your-own fixed-price three-, four-, or five-course options, which might include heavenly seared foie gras with fig compote, crispy potato, and balsamic reduction; roasted quail with black mission figs and mushrooms, and glazed pork belly with braised lettuce and fried green tomato. If there's any question this restaurant wants to perfect the dining experience, consider this: The chef's personal line is listed on the Web site for those who want to discuss special dietary requests. *29 North St. (at Healdsburg Ave.); phone 707-433-3311; Web site www.cyrusrestaurant.com. Reservations required. 3 courses $58; 4 courses $69; 5 courses $80.*

Bistro Ralph (California): Located on the square and looking rather industrial-chic amidst its country-town environs, this longtime standby is a prime pick for a fresh, tasty meal in an upbeat and casual environment. Whether in the narrow dining room with high ceilings, concrete floors, and stainless steel embellishments around the open kitchen and bar or on the small sidewalk patio, diners have come to feast on chef/owner Ralph Tingle's deliciously simple fare showcasing local ingredients. Though the menu changes weekly, with seasonal dishes such as sautéed mahi mahi with hedgehog mushrooms, there are some standards that would inspire protest if taken off the list — osso buco (veal shanks) with saffron risotto, for example. Lunch goes lighter with upscale salads and sandwiches. *109 Plaza St. (at Healdsburg Ave.); phone 707-433-1380. Web site www.bistroralph.com. Reservations recommended. Main courses $9.50–$15 lunch, $17–$25 dinner.*

Willi's Seafood & Raw Bar (seafood/Latin-inspired American): This relative newcomer underscores Healdsburg's evolution from down-home dining rooms to festive, modern restaurants with city-slick bars and menus. With urban-Caribbean decor, an exotic selection of international small plates (think ceviches, skewers, New England-style "rolls," and a crazy-good array of other options), and 40 mostly local wines (all of which are available by the glass, carafe, and full bottle), Willi's slick but relaxed surroundings and unconventional fare are a far cry from the area's traditional joints. But that's a good thing — especially if you're in the mood for delicate flash-fried calamari appetizer with orange chili gremolata (a parsley-based condiment), outstanding sliced hanger steak drizzled with chimichurri sauce atop a bed of cucumber salad, or caramelized eggplant and French green beans with roasted garlic vinaigrette. Add to that heated sidewalk seating and a fun and friendly bar scene (with a full bar) and reasonable prices, and you have one of downtown's hottest attractions. *403 Healdsburg Ave., (at North St.); phone 707-433-9191; Web site www.willisseafood.net. Reservations recommended for parties of 8 or more. Small plates $4–$14.*

Costeaux French Bakery (bakery/café): Swing by this simple, quaint bakery in the heart of Healdsburg for breakfast, lunch, or a coffee and pastry. Owned by Karl and Nancy Seppi for over 25 years, this family-operated gem churns out sandwiches made with homemade artisan bread, hearty soups (the French onion is to die for), imaginative salads (daily specials include pistachio pasta and cherry tomato with fresh herbs), and insane cakes to satisfy any sweet tooth. (The caramel macadamia nut tart is crowned with Belgian chocolate; the pink Champagne unites rum custard, whipped cream, and chocolate.) Wash it all down with glass of local Fumé Blanc, a Pabst Blue Ribbon, or root beer, and contemplate which winery to hit next. *417 Healdsburg Ave.; phone 707-433-1913; Web site www.costeaux.com. Main courses $4.25–7.95 breakfast, $4.95–$8.50 lunch.*

Healdsburg Downtown Bakery & Creamery (bakery): If you want a local experience along with your morning jolt of caffeine, head to the pastry party happening every morning fronting Healdsburg's plaza. Inside crowds form to mingle over the baked goods by Kathleen Stewart, who used to work at Berkeley's famed restaurant Chez Panisse. Along with your standard lattes and the like, you can load up on outstanding breads, focaccia, legendary cinnamon rolls, cakes, and during summer, homemade ice cream and sherbets. A bonus for anyone who previously visited and experienced the inevitable standing-room-only, in 2005 they added 20 closely packed family-style seats, breakfast items ranging from eggs to pancakes, and soups and salads for lunchtime. *308 A Center St. (at Matheson St.); phone 707-431-2719; Web site www.downtownbakery.net. Pastries and breads $1.35–$5.50; breakfast and lunch main courses $7–$10.*

Jimtown Store (deli): Full of wine country character, this retro-hip country store is a Sonoma County landmark. Stop by and grab a seat at the counter for a cup of strong coffee and check out their seasonal menu — it focuses on local farm fare — or take your order to go as a boxed lunch. The store, owned by cookbook author and chef Carrie Brown, sells its own brand of condiments. (Try artichoke, caper, or fig and olive spreads.) In addition, bottles of local wine share shelf space with candy, antiques, and an assortment of wares they describe as "Gifts that are Different." Putter through aisles of patterned oilcloth (sold by the yard), metal lunchboxes, vintage Coca-Cola signs, and gift boxes teeming with homemade crostini and local cheeses. *6706 State Hwy. 128; phone 707-433-1212; Web site www.jimtown.com. Box lunches $11–$13.*

Frommer's Portable California Wine Country, 5th Edition, by Erika Lenkert; Copyright 2006 Wiley Publishing, Inc.; Reprinted with permission of John Wiley & Sons, Inc.

Names to Trust in Sauvignon Blanc

Many producers make two Sauvignon Blanc wines, a mid-priced Sauvignon that ferments and ages in stainless steel and a more expensive Sauvignon that often — but not always — ferments and/ or ages at least partially in French oak. Sometimes the costlier Sauvignon simply comes from a better vineyard site, sometimes a specific single vineyard, and has been produced without oak.

Generally, if we like one Sauvignon Blanc wine from a particular producer, we also like the other Sauvignon Blancs from that producer. In our lists of recommended Sauvignon Blancs, we usually name each recommended winery without naming specific wines from each winery.

We place our top Sauvignon Blanc producers' wines into two price categories:

- ✔ **Moderately priced Sauvignon Blancs:** Between $12 and $25
- ✔ **Moderate-plus Sauvignon Blancs:** Between $25 and $50

Top-value California Sauvignon Blancs

These 12 Sauvignon Blancs, all available for $12 and under at nationwide average retail prices, are consistently reliable, and they're our picks as top values for the money:

- ✔ Benziger Family Winery (Sonoma Mountain)
- ✔ Estancia Estates (Monterey County)
- ✔ Firestone Vineyard (Santa Ynez Valley, Santa Barbara)
- ✔ Geyser Peak (California)
- ✔ Guenoc (Lake County)
- ✔ Kendall Jackson (California)
- ✔ Kenwood Vineyards (Sonoma County)
- ✔ Murphy-Goode (Alexander Valley, Sonoma)
- ✔ Robert Pepi Winery (Napa County)
- ✔ Pedroncelli, East Side Vineyards (Dry Creek Valley, Sonoma)
- ✔ Simi (Sonoma County)
- ✔ Wente Vineyards (Livermore Valley)

Unlike Chardonnay, our Sauvignon Blanc recommendations don't warrant a high-end listing. Only one Sauvignon Blanc on our list, Araujo Estate, retails for more than $40.

Note: A few Sauvignon Blancs on our lists include the term *Musqué* in their names; the word refers to a variant of the Sauvignon Blanc grape variety that produces particularly rich, aromatic wines. Also, when the producer calls its wine *Fumé Blanc,* we include the name in the list.

Moderately Priced Sauvignon Blancs, $12–$25

Adler Fels (Russian River Valley)

Babcock Vineyards (Sta. Rita Hills)

Bernardus Winery (Monterey)

The Brander Vineyard (Santa Ynez Valley)

Cain Cellars, Musqué (Monterey)

Chateau Potelle (Napa Valley)

Chateau Souverain (Alexander Valley, Sonoma)

Chateau St. Jean Fumé Blanc, "La Petite Etoile" (Russian River Valley)

Dry Creek Vineyard Fumé Blanc (Sonoma County)

Duckhorn Vineyards (Napa Valley)

Dutcher Crossing Winery (Dry Creek Valley)

Dutton Estate (Russian River Valley)

EOS Estate (Paso Robles)

Ferrari-Carano Fumé Blanc (Sonoma County)

Flora Springs "Soliloquy" (Napa Valley)

Franciscan Estate (Napa Valley)

Fritz Winery (Dry Creek Valley and Russian River Valley)

Frog's Leap (Napa Valley)

Gainey Vineyard (Santa Ynez Valley)

Gary Farrell (Russian River Valley)

Greenwood Ridge Vineyards (Anderson Valley)

Groth Vineyards (Napa Valley)

Handley Cellars (Dry Creek Valley)

Hanna Winery, Slusser Road (Russian River Valley)

Honig Vineyard (Napa Valley)

Justin Vineyards (Paso Robles)

Kunde Estate, "Magnolia Lane" (Sonoma Valley)

Mason Cellars (Napa Valley)

Matanzas Creek (Sonoma County)

Mill Creek Vineyards (Dry Creek Valley)

Quivira Vineyards, "Fig Tree Vineyard" (Dry Creek Valley)

Robert Mondavi Winery, Fumé Blanc (Napa Valley)

Robert Pecota Winery, "L'Artiste" (Napa Valley)

Rodney Strong Vineyards, Charlotte's Home (Sonoma County)

Silverado Vineyards, Miller Ranch (Napa Valley)

St. Supéry (Napa Valley)

Stag's Leap Wine Cellars (Napa Valley)

Voss Vineyards (Napa Valley)

Whitehall Lane (Napa Valley)

Wildhurst Vineyards Reserve (Lake County)

Moderate-Plus Sauvignon Blancs, mostly $25–$50

Adobe Road (Russian River Valley, and Dry Creek Valley)

Araujo Estate (Eisele Vineyard, Napa Valley); *$75 to $90; very scarce*

The Brander Vineyard, "Au Naturel" (Santa Ynez Valley)

Cakebread Cellars (Napa Valley)

Chalk Hill Estate (Chalk Hill, Sonoma)

Dry Creek Vineyard Fumé Blanc, "DCV3," and "Taylor's Musqué" (Dry Creek Valley)

Fiddlehead Cellars, "Goosebury," (Santa Ynez Valley)

Grgich Hills Fumé Blanc (Napa Valley)

Mayacamas Vineyards (Napa Valley)

The Ojai Vineyard, Westerly Vineyard (Santa Barbara County)

Robert Mondavi Winery, Fumé Blanc Reserve (Napa Valley)

J. Rochioli Vineyards (Russian River Valley)

Rudd Estate (Napa Valley)

Selene Wines, Hyde Vineyard (Carneros)

St. Supéry, Dollarhide Ranch (Napa Valley)

Spottswoode Winery (Napa Valley)

Sonoma Coast Vineyards, Hummingbird Hill Vineyard (Sonoma Coast)

Chapter 6

Cabernet Sauvignon, Merlot, and Their Blends

- -

In This Chapter

▶ Cabernet, the star of Napa Valley

▶ The value end and the elite of California's Cabernet wines

▶ Merlot's rise to popularity

▶ Red blends venturing beyond varietal naming

- -

*N*ot long ago, a proposed ruling to declare Zinfandel the official wine of California made its way around legislative circles in Sacramento, the state capital. Although Zinfandel has impressive family ties to the soil and the people of California — as you can read in Chapter 8 — we personally would have voted for Cabernet Sauvignon as California's official wine. Over the past few decades, most of our memorable California wines have been Cabernets. And Cabernet Sauvignon is the wine that proved to the world California's stellar standing in the red wine universe.

Where there's Cabernet, there's Merlot — often coexisting in the bottle, regardless of which grape gets official billing on the label. California's Merlot wines have a shorter history than the state's Cabernets, and they've had a tougher time establishing a reputation for greatness. But from the right vineyard, they are indeed great.

When the two grapes come together, is the whole greater than the sum of the parts? In other words, do California's nonvarietal Cabernet-Merlot blends outshine varietal Cabernets and Merlots? Sometimes yes, sometimes no. At least we're sure of this: California Cabernet, Merlot, and their blends together offer terrific drinking. In this chapter, we discuss these wines and provide our top recommendations in various price categories.

Hailing the California Cab, a World-Class Red

Cabernet Sauvignon is California's leading red grape variety in terms of quantity produced. This is a fairly recent occurrence. For many years, Zinfandel topped the statistics (although, of course, most of the wine made from those Zinfandel grapes was pink rather than red). Now that Cabernet is number one, it can probably expect to have a long reign as the king of California's reds, because except for Zinfandel, nothing else is close. This section gives you the history of Cabernet and describes the taste that brought Cabernet Sauvignon its place at the top.

A brief history of Cabernet

As grape varieties go, Cabernet Sauvignon is quite young; it was born in southwestern France in the 1600s, the product of a crossing between Cabernet Franc and Sauvignon Blanc, both much older varieties. In fact, the first recorded reference to Cabernet Sauvignon dates back only to the 1700s, in a history of Bordeaux's Château Mouton (now Château Mouton-Rothschild). Bordeaux's legendary wines have made the grape famous since the 1800s.

The Cabernet Sauvignon grape probably came to California in the late 1850s or early 1860s, when Agoston Haraszthy introduced several hundred European grape varieties to the state (see Chapter 1 for more on this founder of the California wine industry).

Perhaps the most renowned early California Cabernet Sauvignon was Beaulieu Vineyard's Georges de Latour Private Reserve, which made its debut with the 1936 vintage. (*Note:* We tasted that 1936 just eight years ago, and it was still very much alive — although 1951 and 1968 are Beaulieu Vineyard's true all-time standout Cabernet Sauvignon vintages.) More great early California Cabernet Sauvignons include Simi's 1935 and Inglenook's 1941 Reserve Cask. The 1943, 1949, 1955, and 1968 are also fine Inglenook Reserve Cask Cabernets.

Those wines and other superb early wines helped establish California Cabernet Sauvignon as one of the world's classic wines. Notable contributors to California's reputation for Cabernet greatness include the following:

- ✔ Heitz Martha's Vineyard 1968, 1969, and 1974
- ✔ Louis Martini 1968
- ✔ Robert Mondavi 1968, 1969, and 1974
- ✔ Ridge Vineyard Monte Bello 1970, 1971, and 1974
- ✔ Mayacamas Vineyards 1970 and 1974

Robert Mondavi helped popularize Napa Valley Cabernet Sauvignons, as did the great Joe Heitz, who released his first single-vineyard Martha's Vineyard Cabernet Sauvignon, the 1965, in the late 1960s.

A landmark event for California Cabernet Sauvignon was the so-called Judgment of Paris tasting in 1976. In a blind tasting with top Bordeaux wines, California Cabernets had the highest average ratings, and the 1973 Stag's Leap Wine Cellars Cabernet placed first. Thirty years later, at a repeat tasting in California with the same wines, the 1971 Ridge Monte Bello Cabernet Sauvignon ranked first. The second tasting did much to refute the argument that the Bordeaux wines merely needed time to develop and would rank higher in the future.

The taste of California Cabernet

Cabernet grapes (like all grapes) grow differently and develop different taste characteristics in different wine regions. For instance, when Cabernet Sauvignon grapes grow in very cool climates, the flavor of the wine can run toward vegetal notes, such as green bell peppers. In very warm climates, the wine's flavors can suggest baked fruit rather than fresh fruit.

In general, however, wines from the Cabernet Sauvignon grape are deep in color and medium- to full-bodied, with firm tannin, lean structure, and a relatively simple aroma/flavor profile that includes black currant, mint, tobacco, and cedar. Some Cabernets are slightly sweet, with flavors that suggest candied fruit, and others are dry, with flavors of dark fruits and sometimes earthy notes.

Given California's fairly warm climate, the Cabernet wines produced there tend to be rather full-bodied and high in alcohol, with many containing 14 percent alcohol and upward. The richest wines have dense, velvety texture as well as a considerable amount of tannin that shows itself in the back of your mouth as you taste the wine. The lightest wines are fairly smooth in texture with a medium to small amount of tannin.

The majority of California's Cabernets are dry wines and do have noticeable tannin. That tannin is just a fact of life for Cabernet, although today's winemakers are adept at softening the tannin so that it doesn't taste bitter. And frankly, a meal with meat or cheese generally mellows that tannin right out of the wine's taste. (For tips on pairing wine and foods, flip to Chapter 12.)

We've overheard many wine drinkers tell clerks in wine shops that they prefer Merlot to Cabernet because Cabernet is "too dry." In fact, most Merlots and Cabernets are equally dry, in the sense of lacking residual sugar (natural grape sugar that fails to ferment into alcohol). But Cabernet wines are often dryer in *texture* than Merlot because the grape has more aggressive tannin.

California's winemakers make Cabernet wines to suit different consumer tastes, and those wines taste different depending on the price tier. Elite Cabernets, costing $50 a bottle or double (and sometimes more than quadruple), for example, are powerful red wines with a serious amount of firm tannin from aging in small, new barrels of French oak. In contrast, Cabernets that sell for about $10 or less are often medium-bodied, easy-to-drink, very fruity red wines with a bit of sweetness and very little tannin to speak of.

Making a California original from a Bordeaux grape

In describing the taste of California Cabernets, we feel compelled to compare them to red Bordeaux wines. The Bordeaux region of western France produces the world's most legendary wines based on the Cabernet Sauvignon grape.

The red wines of a particular part of Bordeaux, known as the Left Bank, are the most Cabernet Sauvignon–dominant Bordeaux wines; they typically contain about 60 to 65 percent Cabernet Sauvignon. Connoisseurs and collectors revere some Left Bank Bordeaux wines that have maintained the highest standards of quality over decades and sometimes centuries. The best Left Bank Bordeaux wines can age for many decades, developing complex, compelling aromas and flavors of leather, tobacco, and cedar and becoming soft in texture and nearly sweet from their aged tannins.

California's Cabernets are different from Cabernet-based Bordeaux reds, even comparing the best wines from each region. California's Cabs tend to

✔ Be fruitier and therefore more enjoyable when they're young

✔ Be fuller in body

✔ Have sweeter, riper fruit flavors and less earthy flavor

✔ Have higher alcohol content

✔ Have softer, denser texture

In our experience, they also retain their youthfulness longer, so at 20 years of age, for example, many taste fresher and more youthful than 20-year-old Bordeaux wines of comparable quality.

Most of Bordeaux's least expensive wines are heavily based on Merlot rather than Cabernet, which makes comparisons at the lowest price levels meaningless. At mid-price levels, however — say about $25 a bottle — the general differences between Bordeaux and California Cabs do ring true: California's wines are fruitier and fuller-bodied, with riper fruit flavors, less earthiness, and less vegetal suggestion in their flavor than Bordeaux wines.

The California style of Cabernet Sauvignon (we're talking mid-priced and higher here) is so unique, in fact, that it has redefined Cabernet Sauvignon wine. California's top Cabernets have become role models for winemakers all over the world, who emulate their ripe fruit character, relatively soft tannins, and rich texture.

TIP

When in doubt, reach for a Cabernet

When we choose a California Cabernet, we have various reasons for doing so. Sometimes we want a powerhouse wine with ripe, fruity flavor to accompany rare steak. Sometimes in restaurants, when all the affordable options are fairly young wines (the older vintages cost almost as much as our monthly mortgage!), we opt for California Cabernet because we know it will be enjoyable even when it's really too young.

But other times, we choose Cabernet because it's the safest choice. On an airplane (in coach)? At a wedding that features no-name wines chosen by a frugal caterer? Buying a boxed wine for a weekend outdoors? In all these situations, we choose Cabernet, because our experience has proven that Cabernet is the most reliable wine. It holds up to poor storage better than other red wines, and it's more consistent in quality from one brand to the next than Pinot Noir is. Also, a cheap Cabernet is usually better quality than a cheap white wine or a cheap Merlot.

Where the Cabernet Grows: Our Cabernet Recommendations

Cabernet Sauvignon needs a warm, dry climate with a fairly long growing season because it's a late-ripening grape. In terms of quality, the three most important regions for Cabernet Sauvignon wines and Cabernet-based blended wines are Napa Valley, Sonoma County, and the Santa Cruz Mountains.

Cabernet is king in Napa Valley, where it arguably grows best. Parts of Sonoma County do very well with Cabernet, especially Alexander Valley, Dry Creek Valley, and Sonoma Mountain. Cabernet Sauvignon is, together with Pinot Noir, the main red variety in the Santa Cruz Mountains. It has a strong presence in southern Monterey County (Arroyo Seco), San Luis Obispo's Paso Robles region, and in the Lodi-Woodbridge region of the San Joaquin (Central) Valley.

Although Cabernet Sauvignon is a reliable grape variety that can grow well in many regions, it doesn't thrive everywhere. Early attempts to grow Cabernet Sauvignon in northern Monterey County and other cool Central Coast regions ended in failure because the grapes were underripe and gave the wines overpowering aromas of bell peppers (caused by a chemical compound called *pyrazine*). Eventually, these vines had to be pulled out.

In this section, we characterize the Cabernet Sauvignons of the major Cabernet regions and list our recommended wines in four price categories.

Napa Valley Cabernet Sauvignons

Napa Valley has the most Cabernet Sauvignon acreage in the state and clearly the largest number of wineries producing Cabernet Sauvignon wines. Probably about two-thirds of California's best Cabernets come from Napa Valley grapes.

Even though Napa Valley is quite small, it has 14 distinct American Viticultural Areas (AVAs; see Chapter 4 for the listing), all of which — even cool, windy Carneros — grow Cabernet Sauvignon. Cabernet grows on the valley floor and the benchlands leading up to the mountains, as well as in the mountains themselves: the Mayacamas Mountains to the west and Vaca Mountains to the east.

This diversity of growing areas leads to interesting comparisons between mountain Cabernets (which are generally more tannic and have more acidity and concentrated fruit character) and valley floor Cabernets (which are usually broader in structure, with riper, more generous fruit character).

Eleven of Napa Valley's 14 AVAs are most important for Cabernet Sauvignon. Here they are, listed from south to north within each bullet point:

- ✔ **Valley floor/benchland:** Oak Knoll District, Yountville, Oakville, Rutherford, and St. Helena

- ✔ **Mayacamas Mountains:** Mt. Veeder, Spring Mountain District, and Diamond Mountain District

- ✔ **Vaca Mountains:** Atlas Peak, Stags Leap District (hillside), and Howell Mountain

Los Carneros is certainly an important AVA in Napa (and Sonoma), but only a few wineries make Cabernet Sauvignon in that cool region.

Each AVA produces distinctly different Cabernet Sauvignons. For example, Stags Leap District and Oak Knoll District (typified by the Cabernets of Stag's Leap Wine Cellars, Clos du Val, and Trefethen Vineyards) are known for their elegant, finesseful wines, whereas Diamond Mountain and Howell Mountain (typified by the Cabernets of Diamond Creek and Dunn Vineyards) are known for powerful, tannic, full-bodied wines requiring considerable aging before they're ready to drink.

Napa Valley Cabernet Sauvignons are by far the most expensive wines in California. Witness our recommendations, which include only one moderately priced ($12 to $20) wine and, at the opposite extreme, 40 high-end ($50 to $100) Cabs. And we had to create a fourth category, luxury Cabernets, for the many over-$100, well-regarded Napa Valley Cabernet Sauvignons.

However, a quick perusal of our moderate-plus ($20 to $50) rec-ommendations reveals many excellent Napa Valley Cabernet Sauvignons, including favorites of ours that stylistically stand out from the mainstream. These include Clos du Val, Dyer Vineyard, Frog's Leap, Mount Veeder Winery, Trefethen, and Truchard Vineyards, all elegantly styled, restrained Cabernets that are great dinner companions.

SNOB ALERT

Paying for cult Cabernets

Just as people make cult heroes out of celebrities in the U.S., they also give certain California red wines cult status. These cult wines include, in particular, small-production, hard-to-find Napa Valley Cabernet Sauvignons and Cabernet blends that receive high ratings from a few influential wine critics. How else can anyone explain $1,800 as an average per-bottle price for a recent-vintage Screaming Eagle Cabernet Sauvignon? It's a fine Cabernet, no doubt, but worth ten times as much as other fine California Cabernets? Or worth more than elite Bordeaux wines with 200-year histories and proven longevity?

Other really expensive Napa Cabernets and Cabernet blends include Harlan Estate Proprietary Red Blend ($750 for the latest vintage and over $1,000 for older vintages); Bryant Family Cabernet Sauvignon ($600); Colgin Cellars Cabernet Sauvignons (up to $500); and Araujo Estate Eisele Vineyard Cabernet Sauvignon (over $300). These prices are immaterial for most people because all these wines are very difficult to find.

And yet ironically, too many Napa Valley Cabernets, including the expensive ones, lack distinctiveness: They are powerful, fleshy wines with soft tannins and aromas and flavors redolent of overripe fruit and new oak barrels. Generally, these wines are too powerful to complement food. In short, if you want to own Napa Valley cult Cabernets, you can find them. But if you simply want a good-drinking Napa Cabernet with dinner, check out our less-expensive recommended Cabernet Sauvignon wines.

Moderately Priced Napa Valley Cabernet Sauvignon, $12–$20
Joseph Carr Cellars (Napa Valley)

Moderate-Plus Napa Valley Cabernet Sauvignons, $20–$50
Anderson's Conn Valley, "Prologue" (Napa Valley)
Beaulieu Vineyard, "Rutherford" (Napa Valley)
Charles Krug, "Yountville" (Napa Valley)
Clos du Val (Napa Valley)
Chappellet, "Signature" (Napa Valley)
Chimney Rock, "Stags Leap" (Napa Valley)
Cuvaison, "Mt. Veeder" (Napa Valley)

Dyer Vineyard, "Estate" (Diamond Mountain, Napa Valley)
Flora Springs Vineyards (Napa Valley)
Franciscan, "Oakville Estate" (Napa Valley)
Frog's Leap, "Napa Valley" and "Rutherford" (Napa Valley)
Heitz Wine Cellars (Napa Valley)
Hess Collection, "Estate" (Mt. Veeder, Napa Valley)
Joseph Phelps (Napa Valley)
La Jota Vineyard (Howell Mountain, Napa Valley)
Mount Veeder Winery (Mount Veeder, Napa Valley)

Newton Vineyard, "Unfiltered" (Napa Valley)

Pine Ridge (Rutherford, Napa Valley)

Ramey Wine Cellars (Napa Valley)

Robert Mondavi (Napa Valley)

Silverado Vineyards (Napa Valley)

Snowden Vineyards, "The Ranch" (Napa Valley)

Smith-Madrone (Spring Mountain, Napa Valley)

St. Clement (Napa Valley)

Swanson Vineyards, "Alexis" (Oakville, Napa Valley)

Terra Valentine (Spring Mountain, Napa Valley)

Tom Eddy, "Elodian" (Napa Valley)

Trefethen Vineyards (Oak Knoll District, Napa Valley)

Truchard Vineyards (Carneros, Napa Valley)

Turnbull Cellars (Oakville, Napa Valley)

Vineyard 29, "Cru" (Napa Valley)

Whitehall Lane (Napa Valley)

High-End Napa Valley Cabernet Sauvignons, $50–$100

Altamura Winery (Napa Valley)

Anderson's Conn Valley, "Estate Reserve" (Napa Valley)

Beaulieu Vineyard, "Georges de Latour Private Reserve" (Napa Valley)

Bennett Lane (Napa Valley)

Beringer Vineyards, "Private Reserve" (Napa Valley)

Cakebread Cellars (Napa Valley)

Caymus Vineyard (Napa Valley)

Charles Krug, "Vintage Selection" (Napa Valley)

Chateau Montelena (Napa Valley)

Clark-Claudon Vineyards (Napa Valley)

Clos du Val, "Stags Leap" (Napa Valley)

Corison Winery (Napa Valley)

Duckhorn, Estate (Napa Valley)

Dunn Vineyards, "Napa Valley" and "Howell Mountain" (Napa Valley)

Etude (Napa Valley)

Fisher Vineyards, "Coach Insignia" (Napa Valley)

Forman Vineyard (Napa Valley)

Freemark Abbey, Bosché and Sycamore Vineyards (Napa Valley)

Grgich Hills (Napa Valley)

Groth Vineyards (Napa Valley)

Hartwell Vineyards (Stags Leap District, Napa Valley)

Heitz Wine Cellars, Bella Oaks and Trailside Vineyard (Napa Valley)

Hoopes Vineyard (Oakville, Napa Valley)

J. Davies (Diamond Mountain, Napa Valley)

Jarvis Winery (Napa Valley)

Kuleto Estate (Napa Valley)

Mayacamas Vineyards (Mt. Veeder, Napa Valley)

Nickel & Nickel, all single-vineyard Cabernet Sauvignons (Napa Valley)

Palmaz Vineyards (Napa Valley)

Paradigm (Oakville, Napa Valley)

Pine Ridge, "Oakville" and "Stags Leap District" (Napa Valley)

Pride Mountain (Napa Valley)

Ramey Wine Cellars, Larkmead Vineyard (Napa Valley)

Robert Craig Winery, "Mt. Veeder" and "Howell Mountain" (Napa Valley)

Saddleback Cellars (Napa Valley)

Shafer Vineyards, "One Point Five" (Napa Valley)

Silver Oak Cellars "Napa Valley" (Napa Valley)

Silverado Vineyards, "Solo" (Stags Leap, Napa Valley)

Stag's Leap Wine Cellars, S.L.V. and Fay Vineyard (Stags Leap District, Napa Valley)

Tom Eddy (Napa Valley)

The Mondavi legacy

When Constellation Brands, the world's largest wine company, purchased Robert Mondavi Corporation and all its brands in 2004, many Mondavi fans wondered what would become of the family. Four years later, all seems to be going well with Robert Mondavi Winery, judging by its latest vintages. And Robert Mondavi's two sons and daughter — Michael, Tim, and Marcia — now have Napa Valley Cabernet Sauvignon–based wines of their own. The two wines (Tim and Marcia are partners in producing one of them) are different, but both are exceptional.

In 2005, the families of Tim Mondavi, Marcia Mondavi, and the late Robert Mondavi joined forces to produce a wine, appropriately named Continuum, from grapes grown in Oakville vineyards and vineyards in the Stags Leap District that the Robert Mondavi family had cultivated for decades. The 2005 Continuum is a Bordeaux-style blend: 58 percent Cabernet Sauvignon, 23 percent Cabernet Franc, and 19 percent Petit Verdot. The blend can change with each vintage, according to what Tim Mondavi and his winemaking team deem best. The 2005 Continuum (about $150) really impressed us. It's a cross between fine Bordeaux and elegantly-styled Napa Cabernet, with firm acidity and lots of finesse. Tim made just 1,500 cases of this wine.

Even at this early stage, 2005 Continuum tastes as if it will be one of the great Mondavi family wines. Production will increase a bit, but Tim wants to keep it small and high-quality, not more than several thousand cases a year.

The impressive 2005 M by Michael Mondavi (about $200) is entirely Cabernet Sauvignon, sourced from an Atlas Peak vineyard owned by Michael and his wife Isabel. M is more typical of a top Napa Valley Cabernet Sauvignon than Continuum is; it's richer and fleshier but with the restraint and balance that typifies the Mondavi Cabernet style. Still a baby now, the 2005 M will join the ranks of California's finest red wines. Only 600 cases of the 2005 exist, and Michael says that no more than 1,200 cases will be produced in future vintages. The wine will sell primarily in fine restaurants and resorts.

With these two impressive wines, the Mondavi family's legacy is in good shape.

Luxury Napa Valley Cabernet Sauvignons, over $100

Araujo Estate, Eisele Vineyard (Napa Valley); *$300+*

Chappellet, Pritchard Hill (Napa Valley); *$120/$130*

Chateau Montelena, "Estate" (Napa Valley); *$100-plus*

Diamond Creek, Gravelly Meadow, Red Rock Terrace, and Volcanic Hill Vineyards (Napa Valley); *$160*

Far Niente, "Oakville" (Napa Valley); *$115*

Fisher Vineyards, Lamb Vineyard (Napa Valley); *$125*

Heitz Wine Cellars, Martha's Vineyard (Napa Valley); *$150*

Joseph Phelps, Backus Vineyard
(Napa Valley); *$250*

M by Michael Mondavi (Napa Valley);
$200

Nickel & Nickel, Martin Stelling
Vineyard (Oakville, Napa Valley);
$125

Ramey Wine Cellars, Pedregal
Vineyard (Oakville, Napa Valley);
$150

Robert Mondavi "Reserve" (Napa
Valley); *$125*

Spottswoode Estate (Napa Valley);
$130

Staglin Family Vineyard, Estate
(Rutherford, Napa Valley); *$155*

Sonoma Cabernets

When we think of wines from Sonoma County, Pinot Noir, Chardonnay, and Zinfandel usually come to mind because Sonoma does so well with these three grape varieties. But Cabernet Sauvignon is actually the second most planted grape variety in Sonoma (after Chardonnay). Sonoma is also second only to Napa Valley in all of California in its Cabernet Sauvignon acreage.

About twice as large as Napa Valley, Sonoma County has more-diverse microclimates (see Chapter 1 for more on microclimate); only the warmer areas of Sonoma — such as Alexander Valley, parts of Dry Creek Valley, and smaller areas such as Sonoma Mountain and parts of Sonoma Valley — are known for their Cabernet Sauvignon wines.

Most of Sonoma's Cabernet Sauvignons come from five AVAs:

- **Alexander Valley:** Cabernet Sauvignon is the leading variety in this huge valley in Northern Sonoma.

- **Dry Creek Valley:** This AVA is just west of Alexander Valley. Cabernet Sauvignon is the leading variety, followed by Zinfandel.

- **Knights Valley:** The warmest Sonoma AVA, Knights Valley is bordered by Alexander Valley in the west and Napa County in the east. Cabernet Sauvignon reigns supreme here.

- **Sonoma Mountain:** Cabernet Sauvignon is the dominant grape variety in this AVA, which is situated within the larger Sonoma Valley AVA.

- **Sonoma Valley:** Sonoma Valley is a huge AVA in southern Sonoma. Among red wines, Cabernet rules here, followed by Zinfandel and Syrah.

We list our recommended Sonoma Cabernet Sauvignons in three price categories: moderately priced, moderate-plus, and high-end.

Moderately Priced Sonoma Cabernet Sauvignons, $12–$20

B. R. Cohn, "Silver Label" (Sonoma County)

Benziger Family Winery (Sonoma County)

Souverain (Alexander Valley)

Foppiano Vineyards (Russian River Valley)

Frei Brothers, "Reserve" (Alexander Valley)

Louis M. Martini (Sonoma County)

Ravenswood (Sonoma County)

St. Francis (Sonoma County)

Sebastiani Vineyards (Sonoma County)

Moderate-Plus Sonoma Cabernet Sauvignons, $20–$50

Arrowood Vineyards (Sonoma County)

B. R. Cohn, Olive Hill Estate (Sonoma Valley)

Beringer Vineyards (Knights Valley)

Chalk Hill Estate (Chalk Hill)

Clos Du Bois, "Briarcrest" (Alexander Valley)

Dry Creek Vineyard (Dry Creek Valley)

Ferrari-Carano (Alexander Valley)

Gundlach Bundschu, Rhinefarm Vineyard (Sonoma Valley)

Hanna Winery (Alexander Valley)

Jordan Vineyard (Alexander Valley)

Kendall-Jackson Highland Estates, "Hawkeye Mountain" (Alexander Valley)

Kenwood Vineyards, Jack London Vineyard (Sonoma Valley)

Laurel Glen, "Counterpoint" (Sonoma Mountain)

Louis M. Martini (Alexander Valley)

Martin Ray Winery (Sonoma Mountain)

Rodney Strong Vineyards, "Alexander Valley" and Alexander's Crown Vineyard (Alexander Valley)

Sbragia Family Vineyards, Monte Rosso Vineyard (Sonoma Valley)

Schrader Cellars, Double Diamond Mayacamas Range Estate Vineyard (Sonoma County)

Scherrer Winery (Alexander Valley)

Schug Carneros Estate (Sonoma Valley)

Sebastiani Vineyards (Alexander Valley)

Simi Winery (Alexander Valley)

Stonestreet (Alexander Valley)

Stuhlmuller Vineyards (Alexander Valley)

Trentadue Winery, "Estate" (Alexander Valley)

High-End Sonoma Cabernet Sauvignons, $50–$100

Kendall-Jackson Highland Estates, "Trace Ridge" (Knights Valley)

Kenwood Vineyards, "Artist Series" (Sonoma County)

Laurel Glen, "Estate" (Sonoma Mountain)

Louis M. Martini, Monte Rosso Vineyard (Sonoma Valley)

A. Rafanelli (Dry Creek Valley)

Sebastiani Vineyards, "Cherryblock" (Sonoma Valley)

Silver Oak (Alexander Valley)

REAL DEAL

Laurel Glen Estate, a Sonoma star

One of California's consistently finest Cabernet Sauvignons comes not from Napa Valley but from Sonoma, and it costs but a mere $55! We're talking about owner-winemaker Patrick Campbell's Laurel Glen Estate Cabernet, from grapes sourced high on Sonoma Mountain, above the fog line.

What is Patrick Campbell's secret (besides a great site for Cabernet Sauvignon)? First of all, he chooses only the best vineyard blocks for his Laurel Glen Estate Cabernet Sauvignon; the remainder goes into a second Cabernet called "Counterpoint" (about $30). Second, Campbell's winemaking philosophy favors balanced, complex Cabernet Sauvignon that ages well; he's not interested in producing the sort of ripe, jammy, powerful Cabs that attract big scores from some wine critics. And he insists on charging what he considers to be a fair price for his wines. Wouldn't it be nice if there were more people in the wine business like Patrick Campbell?

For fun, Campbell makes an everyday red called "Reds" — usually a blend of 60 percent 70-year-old-vine Zinfandel, 30 percent Carignan, and 10 percent Petite Sirah — which sells for about $9 to $11. It happens to be one of the best under-$12 red wines in California.

Santa Cruz Mountain Cabernet Sauvignons

The rugged terrain of the Santa Cruz Mountains AVA, about an hour's drive south of San Francisco, spreads out over Santa Clara, Santa Cruz, and San Mateo Counties. The isolation, lack of modern conveniences, and thin mountain soil are just some of the challenges that face grape growers and wineries there, and yet the AVA has more than 80 wineries, including some of the best in the state. Even though the Santa Cruz Mountains area seems large, it encompasses fewer than 1,500 acres of vines.

Microclimates vary widely, depending on which side of the mountain range a vineyard is situated on (Pacific Ocean or San Francisco Bay) and what its elevation is. The three leading varietal wines produced in the Santa Cruz Mountains are Chardonnay, Pinot Noir, and Cabernet Sauvignon, in that order. Most of the wineries specializing in Cabernet Sauvignon are on the warmer San Francisco Bay side of the mountain range, but they're high enough in elevation to avoid coastal fog.

Ridge Vineyards is undoubtedly the most renowned winery in the Santa Cruz Mountains. Ridge's acclaimed Monte Bello Cabernet Sauvignon is certainly one of the finest Cabernets produced anywhere in the world.

Here are our recommended Santa Cruz Mountain Cabernet Sauvignons in four price categories.

Moderately Priced Santa Cruz Mountain Cabernet Sauvignon, $12–$20

Clos La Chance, "Ruby Throated" (Santa Cruz Mountains)

Moderate-Plus Santa Cruz Mountain Cabernet Sauvignons, $20–$50

Cinnabar Vineyard (Santa Cruz Mountains)

Martin Ray Winery (Santa Cruz Mountains)

Mount Eden Vineyards, "Saratoga Cuvée" and Estate (Santa Cruz Mountains)

Ridge Vineyards, Santa Cruz Mountains Estate (Santa Cruz Mountains)

High-End Santa Cruz Mountain Cabernet Sauvignon, $50–$100

Kathryn Kennedy Winery, "Small Lot" (Santa Cruz Mountains)

Luxury Santa Cruz Mountain Cabernet Sauvignons, over $100

Kathryn Kennedy Winery, Estate (Santa Cruz Mountains); *$140*

Ridge Vineyards, "Monte Bello" (Santa Cruz Mountains); *$145*

Seventeen top-value Cabernet Sauvignons

These 17 Cabernet Sauvignons, all under $15, are consistently reliable, and they're our picks as top values for the money:

- ✔ Blackstone, California (California)
- ✔ Chateau Julien (Monterey)
- ✔ Chateau St. Jean (California)
- ✔ De Loach, California (California)
- ✔ Edna Valley Vineyard (San Luis Obispo)
- ✔ Esser Vineyards (California)
- ✔ Estancia (Paso Robles)
- ✔ Fetzer Vineyards, Valley Oaks (California)
- ✔ Gallo of Sonoma, Estate (Sonoma County)
- ✔ Hahn Estates (Central Coast)
- ✔ Hawk Crest (California)
- ✔ Hess (California)
- ✔ J. Lohr Vineyards, Seven Oaks (Paso Robles)
- ✔ Jekel Vineyards (Central Coast)
- ✔ Lockwood Vineyard (Monterey)
- ✔ Kenwood Vineyards (Sonoma County)
- ✔ Red Truck (California)

Other California Cabernets

Although Napa Valley and Sonoma County are the prime regions for Cabernet Sauvignon (with a nod to Santa Cruz Mountains as a small but excellent source), the state's leading red varietal wine comes from many other regions. Paso Robles in San Luis Obispo County, for example, is known for its Cabernet Sauvignons. On the other hand, very few wineries in Santa Barbara County produce Cabernet Sauvignons; it's just not warm enough for Cabernet, a variety that needs a long, warm growing season.

In this section, we list our recommended Cabernet Sauvignons from other regions throughout California in two price categories: moderately priced and moderate-plus. Make sure you also check out the nearby sidebar for some reliable California Cabs that retail for $15 or less.

Other Moderately Priced Cabernet Sauvignons, $12–$20

Bonterra Vineyards, "Organically Grown" (North Coast)

Clayhouse Vineyard (Paso Robles, San Luis Obispo County)

Eberle Winery (Paso Robles, San Luis Obispo County)

Guenoc Winery, "Lake County" (Lake County)

Lolonis Vineyards (Redwood Valley, Mendocino County)

Rabbit Ridge Vineyards (Paso Robles, San Luis Obispo)

Shannon Ridge (Lake County)

Wild Horse Winery (Paso Robles, San Luis Obispo County)

Other Moderate-Plus Cabernet Sauvignons, $20–$50

Beckmen Vineyards (Santa Ynez Valley, Santa Barbara)

Justin Vineyards (Paso Robles, San Luis Obispo County)

Langtry Estate, Tephra Ridge Vineyard (Lake County)

Lava Cap Winery, "Reserve" and "Stromberg" (Sierra Foothills)

Paul Dolan Vineyards, "Organically Grown" (Mendocino County)

Renaissance Vineyard (Sierra Foothills); *vintages back to 1995 are available from* www. renaissancewinery.com

Merlot, Sometimes a Contender

The Merlot grape, like Cabernet Sauvignon, hails from the Bordeaux region of France. Genetic testing has proved that Merlot is the offspring of Cabernet Franc and therefore is related to Cabernet Sauvignon, which also originated from Cabernet Franc. Today, Cabernet Sauvignon plantings worldwide exceed those of Merlot but not by much. In California, however, a big gap exists: Cabernet Sauvignon claims 62 percent more acreage than Merlot does.

In this section, we introduce you to Merlot wine and characterize its style.

Merlot's up, down, and Sideways reputation

Merlot in California is a bundle of contradictions. Merlot grapes are fairly easy to grow and therefore are very popular with grape growers, and yet only in a few places in California do the grapes grow well enough to make seriously good wine. California's Merlot wines have mass appeal with wine drinkers, and yet many connoisseurs dismiss them. (You might recall the sentiments toward "[expletive deleted] Merlot" expressed by Miles Raymond, the main character in the film *Sideways*.) And yet some excellent California Merlots do exist.

As a varietal wine, Merlot got off to a late start in California. The very first varietal Merlot wines were those of Sterling Vineyards and Louis M. Martini Winery, which both produced varietal Merlot from the 1968 vintage.

Merlot today is the number three red grape variety in the state in terms of tons harvested, after Cabernet Sauvignon and Zinfandel. Merlot wine began an impressive ascent in popularity in the mid-1990s, racking up sales growth of almost 35 percent each year, on the average, from 1995 to 1999. That was a period when many wine drinkers were shifting to red wines from white and blush wines, and Merlot became a popular choice. Since then, growth in Merlot sales has slowed to more reasonable levels — particularly in 2005, as the impact of *Sideways* made itself felt. Still, Americans drank 21.4 million cases of California Merlot in 2006, proving that Merlot is alive and well in California.

One of California's top Merlot producers, Swanson Vineyards (in Napa Valley) promoted Merlot heavily with wine journalists and restaurant wine buyers in the wake of the *Sideways* backlash against Merlot. The reason Merlot is so popular with some wine drinkers and yet so scorned by others, the winery representatives theorized, is that Merlot vines need certain vineyard conditions — a relatively cool climate; well-drained soils, generally clay; and sites conducive to slow, even growth and ripening — to produce grapes capable of making great wine. When grown in less-than-optimal conditions, the grapes produce wines that are thin and lack concentration of flavor. Such wine can be appealing to those who want an easy-to-drink red wine whose tannins are soft, but they fall short of Merlot's potential.

The taste of California Merlot

Imagine a deeply colored red wine — a full-bodied, dry wine with soft, velvety tannin and aromas and flavors of ripe, dark plums, a hint of chocolate, and a slight toasty note of oak. It fills your mouth with its fleshy texture and its plump, fruity flavors, yet it's not too soft; it has enough firmness to give it definition. If you had to associate it with a shape, you'd say it tastes "round." That's the experience of California Merlot at its best. And who wouldn't love such a wine? Its plumpness, richness, and softness are the reason that Merlot became popular in the first place.

To capture the experience of a plump, rich, and soft Merlot, you should expect to pay at least $20 a bottle in a wine shop. When you pay less than $20 for Merlot, you get less plump-fruit impression, and you might find aromas and flavors of tea or other herbal notes, as well as a thinner, less velvety texture. You still get the deep color, full body, and soft tannin, however.

Either way, you find that Merlot's *intensity* of aroma and flavor (how pronounced the aromas and flavors are) is fairly low key, especially compared to a wine such as Pinot Noir (Chapter 7 tells all about California Pinot Noir). Merlot has that characteristic in common with Cabernet Sauvignon; what's appealing about these types of wine is their structure (their mouthfeel, body, texture, and depth) at least as much as their flavors.

Because Merlot is not an intensely flavorful wine, it's a good accompaniment to food. It lets the food's flavors take center stage and doesn't compete with them. (Read more about pairing California wine with food in Chapter 12.)

Just as Cabernet producers often blend in a bit of Merlot to give their wine softness, Merlot producers often take advantage of their "25 percent other-grapes allowed" option to blend in some Cabernet Sauvignon. (See Chapter 2 for info on varietal wine regulations.) The more Cabernet that a Merlot wine has, the firmer and less "round" the wine will be. Some winemakers say that Merlot can taste a bit hollow — or they describe it as seeming to have a hole in the middle of its taste — unless the wine includes some Cabernet. Unfortunately, the label rarely tells you whether the wine contains any Cabernet Sauvignon.

Regions That Excel with Merlot

About one-third of California's Merlot vineyards is in the very warm Central Valley, where conditions aren't optimal for this variety. Another one-third, approximately, is in Napa Valley and Sonoma County together, and most of California's best Merlots hail from these areas.

Eighteen top-value California Merlots

These 18 Merlots, all under $15, are consistently reliable, and they're our picks as top values for the money:

- Beringer, Third Century (North Coast)
- Blackstone (California)
- Bonterra Vineyards (Mendocino)
- Chateau Julien (Monterey)
- De Loach (California)
- Esser Vineyards (California)
- Estancia (Paso Robles)
- Fetzer Vineyards, Valley Oaks (California)
- Foppiano Vineyards (Russian River Valley)
- Gallo of Sonoma, Estate (Sonoma County)
- Hawk Crest (California)
- J. Lohr Vineyards, Los Osos (Paso Robles)
- Jekel Vineyards (Central Coast)
- Kenwood Vineyards (Sonoma County)
- Raymond Vineyard, R Collection (California)
- Red Truck (California)
- Sebastiani Vineyards (Sonoma County)
- Taft Street Winery (Sonoma County)

Just as for Cabernet Sauvignon, Napa Valley is the leading region for varietal Merlots. One main difference from Cabernet Sauvignon, however, is that the cool Carneros AVA, which extends from Napa into Sonoma County, is a prime region for Merlot in Napa Valley. Merlot grows quite well in fairly cool microclimates such as Carneros because it ripens earlier than Cabernet Sauvignon.

Paso Robles AVA in San Luis Obispo boasts the third-largest production of Merlot, apart from Napa and the statewide California AVA itself. Sonoma County is also a prime region for Merlot: Sonoma's microclimates vary so widely that Merlot finds many areas throughout the county in which to thrive. Other important regions in California for Merlot are Monterey and Santa Barbara Counties.

In this section, we recommend some reliable wines from California's main Merlot regions.

Reliable Napa Valley Merlots

Napa Valley has the largest contingent of renowned Merlot producers. Unlike Napa Cabernet Sauvignons, varietal Napa Valley Merlots haven't developed cult followings; this is fortunate for wine drinkers, because it means that there are no $100-plus Merlots! We list our recommended Napa Valley Merlots in three price categories, from moderate to high-end.

Moderately Priced Napa Valley Merlots, $12–$20
Beringer Vineyards (Napa Valley)

Franciscan, "Oakville Estate" (Napa Valley)

Joseph Carr Cellars (Napa Valley)

Markham Vineyards (Napa Valley)

Moderate-Plus Napa Valley Merlots, $20–$50
Chappellet Winery, Estate (Napa Valley)

Charles Krug Winery (Napa Valley)

Clos du Val (Napa Valley)

Duckhorn Vineyards (Napa Valley)

Flora Springs Winery (Napa Valley)

Frog's Leap Winery (Napa Valley)

Grgich Hills (Napa Valley)

Havens, "Napa Valley" and "Reserve Carneros" (Napa Valley)

MacRostie Winery (Carneros, Napa Valley)

Merryvale, Beckstoffer, Las Amigas Vineyard (Carneros, Napa Valley)

Newton Vineyards, "Unfiltered" (Napa Valley)

Neyers, Neyers Ranch, Conn Valley (Napa Valley)

Paradigm, Estate (Oakville, Napa Valley)

Pine Ridge, "Crimson Creek" (Napa Valley)

Robert Mondavi (Napa Valley)

Rubicon Estate (Napa Valley)

Selene, Frediani Vineyard (Napa Valley)

Shafer Vineyards (Napa Valley)

Silverado Vineyards (Napa Valley)

Stag's Leap Wine Cellars (Napa Valley)

Swanson Vineyards (Oakville, Napa Valley)

Trefethen Family Vineyards, "Estate" (Oak Knoll District, Napa Valley)

Turnbull Wine Cellars (Oakville, Napa Valley)

High-End Napa Valley Merlots, over $50
Cakebread Cellars (Napa Valley)

Duckhorn Vineyards, Three Palms Vineyard (Napa Valley)

Nickel & Nickel, Suscol Ranch and Harris Vineyard-Oakville (Napa Valley)

Pahlmeyer (Napa Valley)

Other California Merlots

Most of our Merlot recommendations other than Napa Valley wines hail from various AVAs in Sonoma County. We list our recommended "other California" Merlots in two price categories, with no high-end wines.

Other Moderately Priced Merlots, $12–$20

Benziger Family Winery (Sonoma County)
Clos du Bois (Sonoma County)
Dry Creek Vineyard (Dry Creek Valley)
Lolonis Winery, Redwood Valley (Mendocino County)
Murphy Goode (Alexander Valley)
Ravenswood (Sonoma County)
St. Francis Winery (Sonoma County)
Wild Horse Winery (Paso Robles)

Other Moderate-Plus Merlots, $20–$50

Arrowood (Sonoma County)
Bargetto Winery, Reserve (Santa Cruz Mountains)
Ferrari Carano (Sonoma County)
Matanzas Creek (Bennett Valley, Sonoma)
Schug Carneros Estate, "Sonoma Valley" and "Carneros Estate" (Sonoma)
Thomas Fogarty Winery, Razorback Vineyard (Santa Cruz Mountains)

The Secret's in the Bordeaux Blend

The wines of France's Bordeaux region are the role models for most of the world's Cabernet Sauvignon and Merlot wines, and yet most of those wines themselves rarely contain 75 percent of either grape variety — the minimum amount required to make a varietal wine in the U.S. Some California producers have decided to follow the Bordeaux model more closely and forego a varietal name for their wine in order to have more leverage in blending Cabernet Sauvignon and Merlot. While they're at it, they might throw in other so-called Bordeaux grape varieties, such as Cabernet Franc, Petit Verdot, or Malbec. In this section, we introduce you to these red wines, which are loosely called California's *Bordeaux blends*.

Some of these blended wines might be named *Meritage* or be described on their labels as Meritage wines. As we mention in Chapter 2, The Meritage Association (www.meritagewine.org) permits its members to call a red wine Meritage if no single variety makes up more than 90 percent of the blend and if the grapes include at least two of eight permitted grape varieties. (Besides the five classic Bordeaux varieties — Merlot, Cabernet Sauvignon, Cabernet Franc, Petit Verdot, and Malbec — the others are St. Macaire, Gros Verdot, and Carmenère, which are minor varieties in the Bordeaux region.) But not every winery that makes a so-called Bordeaux blend is a member of the Meritage Association, and therefore you don't always find this term on wine labels.

Combining strengths

The point behind blending Cabernet Sauvignon, Merlot, and other Bordeaux varieties is not to change the nature of the dominant grape but to create a harmonic whole that goes beyond the sum of its parts. This is possible because of the similarities among the various grape varieties rather than their differences.

Cabernet Sauvignon, Cabernet Franc, and Merlot are all genetically related. All three red varieties make wines that have fairly subtle aromas and flavors and strong structural character — meaning that the experience of tasting them is more about how they feel in your mouth than it is about specific flavors that you can perceive. (However, Cabernet Franc is the fruitiest and most flavorful of the three, especially in California.) All three varieties have aromas and flavors of dark fruits and a tendency toward herbal or vegetal notes, especially when the grapes aren't fully ripe. All three can develop tobacco notes with age.

Petit Verdot — a minor variety compared to the other three but one that's becoming increasingly popular with winemakers around the world, especially in California — has the characteristics of a darker, more concentrated and more tannic Cabernet Sauvignon. Malbec to some extent suggests a more rustic Merlot.

In a blend incorporating some or all of these varieties, you ideally can't recognize any one variety. The Merlot rounds out the linear structure of the Cabernet Sauvignon, for example, the Petit Verdot (usually only a small part of the blend, if used at all) contributes some color and spiciness, and the Cabernet Franc brings a bit of fruitiness. Each variety completes the others, for a harmonious whole.

Many wines that are Bordeaux-style blends mention the grape varieties and the percentage of each on the bottle's back label, but some wines don't reveal the blend on the label — frustrating, we know!

Sometimes, you find a wine that could be labeled as a varietal Cabernet Sauvignon or a varietal Merlot because one of those varieties accounts for at least 75 percent of the wine. But the percentages of each variety can and do change from one vintage to the next, and the winemaker chooses a nonvarietal name for the wine so that he or she has the flexibility to use less than 75 percent of a dominant variety in the future if desired.

Key brands of Bordeaux-style blends

Many California wine producers who make varietal Cabernet Sauvignon also produce at least one blended red wine. In most of these blends, Cabernet Sauvignon is the dominant variety, although Merlot or even Cabernet Franc occasionally plays a primary role. For example, the prestige blend of HdV Wines is mainly Merlot, and Dalla Valle's prestige blend called Maya is often more Cabernet Franc than Cabernet Sauvignon.

California's Bordeaux-style blended wines vary widely: Some utilize only Cabernet Sauvignon and Merlot or Cabernet Franc; some use all three of these varieties; and a few — such as the wines called Cain Five and Cinq Cépages — utilize all five of the major Bordeaux varieties, including Petit Verdot and Malbec. The percentage of each variety usually varies each year, depending on the nature of the vintage and/or the tastes of the winemaking team.

Here are two recent trends that we've noted in Bordeaux-style red blends:

- ✔ **Petit Verdot is becoming an increasingly important part of many wines.** This late-ripening variety adds color, tannin, and blueberry and violet aromas and flavors to the blend. Petit Verdot generally grows better in many parts of California than it does in Bordeaux. The wine called V from Viader Winery is a Bordeaux blend that's primarily Petit Verdot, with a bit of Cabernet Sauvignon and Cabernet Franc.

- ✔ **Carmenère and especially Syrah are showing up more and more in California's Bordeaux-style red wine blends.** The late-ripening Carmenère, an almost-forgotten Bordeaux variety that's achieving new fame in Chilean wines, brings texture and berry-like aromas and flavor, especially blueberries, to blends.

   Syrah — a classic Rhône variety — adds color, tannin, and its own spicy aromas and flavors. (Read about Syrah wines in Chapter 10.) As long as the blended wine doesn't call itself Meritage, Syrah is a perfectly permissible addition to California blends.

Frequently, the producer's blended red wine is its top wine. It can often be the winery's most expensive wine and is sometimes made in small quantities, especially in vintages when the weather has been difficult.

The origins of blending

The origins of blending grape varieties in Bordeaux have less to do with the taste of the wine and more to do with practicality. Merlot vines bud earlier than Cabernet Sauvignon vines, and the grapes ripen earlier. In years when autumn rains came early, Cabernet Sauvignon wouldn't ripen fully, its growing season cut short by the rains, but the Merlot grapes got ripe. In years when there was a late spring frost, the Merlot crop could be wiped out because the vines had budded (a very vulnerable stage), but the Cabernet vines, not yet budded, endured. Each of the two grape varieties was an insurance policy against catastrophe with the other variety. Like Merlot, Cabernet Franc ripens earlier than Cabernet Sauvignon.

California usually doesn't have such issues with the weather. When California producers blend Merlot, Cabernet Sauvignon, and other varieties, it's more for taste than agricultural expediency.

The following lists name some of our picks for red California blends based on the Bordeaux grape varieties.

Moderate-Plus Bordeaux-Style Blends, $20–$50

Alexander Valley Vineyards, "Cyrus" (Alexander Valley)

Archipel (Sonoma/Napa Valley)

Bernardus, "Marinus" (Carmel Valley)

Chateau St. Jean, "Cinq Cépages" (Sonoma County)

Clos du Bois, "Marlstone" (Alexander Valley)

Dry Creek Vineyard, "Meritage" and "The Mariner" (Dry Creek Valley)

Murrieta's Well, "Meritage" (Livermore Valley)

Ramey Wine Cellars, "Claret" (Napa Valley)

Ravenswood, Pickberry Vineyard (Sonoma Mountain)

High-End Bordeaux-Style Blends, $50–$100

Anderson's Conn Valley Vineyards, "Eloge" (Napa Valley)

Benziger Family Winery, "Tribute" (Sonoma Mountain)

Flora Springs, "Trilogy" (Napa Valley)

HdV Vineyards, "HdV Red" (Carneros, Napa Valley)

Justin Vineyards, "Isosceles" (Paso Robles)

Mount Veeder Winery, "Reserve Red" (Napa Valley)

St. Supéry, "Élu" (Napa Valley)

Stonestreet, "Legacy" (Alexander Valley)

Turnbull Cellars, "Black Label" (Oakville, Napa Valley)

Viader Vineyards, "Viader Red" (Howell Mountain) and "V" (Napa Valley)

Luxury Bordeaux-Style Blends, over $100

Cain Cellars, "Cain Five" (Napa Valley); *$125*

Continuum (Oakville); *$150*

Dalla Valle, "Maya" (Oakville, Napa Valley); *$400*

Dominus Estate, "Dominus" (Napa Valley); *$110*

Harlan Estate (Napa Valley); *$700 to $900*

Joseph Phelps, "Insignia" (Napa Valley); *$200*

Moraga Vineyards, "Bel Air Estate Red" (California); *$125*

Opus One (Napa Valley); *$190*

Pahlmeyer, Red (Napa Valley); *$120*

Peter Michael, "Les Pavots" (Knights Valley); *$175*

Quintessa Estate, "Quintessa" (Rutherford, Napa Valley); *$130*

Rubicon Estate, "Rubicon" (Rutherford, Napa Valley); *$115*

Rudd Estate, "Oakville Estate" (Oakville); *$125*

Stag's Leap Wine Cellars, "Cask 23" (Napa Valley); *$180*

Vérité Winery, "La Joie," "La Muse," and "Le Désir" (Sonoma County); *$150 each*

Chapter 7

Pinot Noir

. . . .

. . . .

*M*any of the best wines that we've ever tasted have been red Burgundies from France (made entirely from Pinot Noir grapes) or Pinot Noir wines from various New World regions. This isn't surprising, because Pinot Noir is one of the world's noble grape varieties, capable of making great, complex, truly exciting red wines. But this grape is also one of the most temperamental varieties. So many winemakers we've met over the years have devoted a good part of their lives to making great wine from this extremely challenging grape, only occasionally succeeding. Pinot Noir has the nickname "The Heartbreak Grape" for good reason.

What's so difficult about making a great Pinot Noir wine? First of all, finding the best places to plant Pinot Noir vines is tricky. And the best locations often have erratic weather that's great in some years and poor in others. The winemakers of the Burgundy region in France might seem to have a handle on this grape, but it took them hundreds of years, and they still don't always succeed in making great wine. For every superb red Burgundy we've tasted, we've had just as many that were merely okay or worse.

We confess that we have mixed feelings about Pinot Noir. Some of the very best wines we've enjoyed have been made from Pinot Noir. But like our largest male cat, Max (who is so lovable and yet drives us crazy most of the time), Pinot Noir wines often frustrate us. In this chapter, we explain how Pinot Noir became an overnight star in California. Then we point out the regions where Pinot Noir grows best in the state and finish up by listing our recommended California Pinot Noirs.

From Obscurity to Overnight Fame

 Pinot Noir is one of the world's oldest major grape varieties. It probably originated in eastern France nearly 2,000 years ago, or even earlier. Pinot Noir first became renowned as the great red grape variety of Burgundy. Later, the Champagne region adopted it as its most important red variety (by the nature of its structure, Pinot Noir is ideal for use in sparkling wines).

In California, Pinot Noir has had a fitful history. Some evidence exists that Buena Vista Winery in Sonoma grew this variety as early as 1858. But before the 1970s, not many Pinot Noir vineyards existed in California — and many of those were in the wrong location, such as warm sites in Napa Valley, which can be fine for Cabernet Sauvignon but not for the more delicate Pinot. (We remember some of these Napa Valley Pinot Noir wines from vintages such as 1978; they had roasted flavors and really didn't resemble Pinot Noir at all, nor did they age well.)

The new age of Pinot Noir in California began when producers started identifying regions suitable for growing Pinot Noir grapes. Josh Jensen searched all of California before founding his winery, Calera Wine Company, in 1975, in a place he believed to be ideal: Mount Harlan in the Gavilan Mountains of San Benito County, just east of Monterey County (see the map in Chapter 4). From his first Calera Pinot Noirs in 1978, Jensen's wines were superior to what was being produced at the time.

Besides Josh Jensen at Calera, other Pinot Noir specialists of the time included Dick Graff at Chalone, Merry Edwards at Mount Eden, Francis Mahoney at Carneros Creek, Brad Webb and Bob Sessions at Hanzell, Richard Sanford at Sanford & Benedict, and the great Joe Swan of Joseph Swan Vineyards in Russian River Valley.

Pinot Noir regrets

The late, great André Tchelistcheff, California's legendary winemaker who devoted his life to producing outstanding Cabernet Sauvignons for Beaulieu Vineyard and other wineries, once told us that if he could do it all over again, he'd make Pinot Noir instead of Cabernet Sauvignon. The wine he was most proud of was his 1946 Beaulieu Vineyard Pinot Noir, one of only two outstanding wines he made from this variety (the other was Beaulieu Vineyards' 1947 Pinot Noir).

By the 1980s, a small Pinot Noir movement was in full swing, with Jim Clendenon of Au Bon Climat in Santa Barbara, Richard Ward and David Graves of Saintsbury in Carneros, and a group of great wineries in Russian River Valley — Williams Selyem, Rochioli, Dehlinger, and Gary Farrell — all producing their own, very fine, unique versions of California Pinot Noir.

Consumer interest in Pinot Noir started growing slowly in the late 1990s as the quality of the wines improved and new wineries began to specialize in Pinot Noir. But it took a popular 2004 Hollywood film, *Sideways*, to give Pinot Noir wines the shot in the arm they needed. *Sideways*, set primarily in the Santa Barbara wine country, aroused the interest of thousands of wine drinkers, some of whom had never tasted Pinot Noir. With the film's success, all Pinot Noir, but especially California Pinot, became the *in* wine, almost over-night. California Pinot Noir sales grew 70 percent in 2005 from the previous year.

Pinot Noir is now a hot commodity in California and throughout the world. Wine producers in California have been planting Pinot Noir at a frenzied pace since the successful film — often pulling out Merlot at the same time. (Poor Merlot was slammed — unfairly, we think — in *Sideways*.) Today, well over 200 wineries in California make Pinot Noir wine.

Unfortunately, many of the Pinot Noirs rushed to the market haven't been of very high quality. Wine drinkers have had to be more careful than ever selecting Pinots. The quest continues.

California-Style Pinot Noir

Pinot Noir wines can vary tremendously according to their vine-yard site and the winemaking techniques used to make the wine. In this section, we discuss the general styles of California Pinot Noir and then point out the specific styles of the major California Pinot Noir wine regions.

The general style

Pinot Noir wines can be light to deep ruby red in color. Most California Pinot Noirs tend to be darker rather than paler; how-ever, because of the grape's light pigmentation, Pinot Noir wines are generally lighter in color than other popular red wines.

Structurewise, Pinot Noir can range from medium-bodied to full and rich. The fuller-bodied examples are typically deeper in color and riper in flavor than the lighter-bodied Pinot Noirs. In general, Pinot Noir wines are high in alcohol (most of today's California Pinot Noirs contain over 14 percent alcohol). They have medium to high acidity and a low to medium amount of tannin — although wines aged in new oak barrels have more tannin. At its best, the texture of Pinot Noir wines feels silky or satiny.

Pinot Noir's aromas and flavors are definitely a strong point: They can range from an assortment of berries — mainly raspberries and/or strawberries and cherries — to earthy, woodsy, and mushroomy. In some wines, the aromas and flavors can give the impression of very pure fruit. The richest, darkest wines tend to be oaky in aroma and flavor. Most California Pinot Noirs express fruity rather than earthy, woodsy aromas and flavors.

The delicacy of aroma and flavor in Pinot Noir wines allows variations in vintages and in vineyard sites to become evident, much more so than in other wines. This transparency to site accounts for wide differences in Pinot Noir wines between one producer and another. Because of the wine's delicate, pure aromas, Pinot Noir is, in its classic examples, rarely blended with other grapes.

Some of California's Pinot Noirs have real finesse: They're fragrant, elegant, and well balanced, with great purity of fruit expression. But too many Pinot Noir wines suggest excessive ripeness of the grapes: They're too sweet, rather clumsy, and too high in alcohol. These heavy-handed excesses blur the delicacy and elegance that we believe Pinot Noirs should possess. Other Pinot Noirs, especially many of the inexpensive (under $15) ones, are just too light, with candied fruit aromas and flavors as well as perceptible sweetness.

Local styles

California's unique climate and soil situations have spawned styles of Pinot Noir wine distinctly different from those of Burgundy, New Zealand, Chile, and even nearby Oregon; however, no such thing as "the typical California Pinot Noir" exists. If you were to line up, say, an Au Bon Climat Pinot Noir from Santa Barbara County, a Calera from Mount Harlan in San Benito County, a Saintsbury from Napa Valley's Carneros, and a Williams Selyem from Sonoma's Russian River Valley — all iconic California Pinot Noirs — you might be able to recognize all of them as Pinot Noirs, but they would be four very different wines.

A new trend in California Pinot Noirs

The distressing trend we've seen in other California red wines — darker color, fuller body, higher alcohol — is occurring among Pinot Noirs as well. The fleshier, richer, darker Pinot Noirs certainly have a following, but this style tends to blur regional characteristics. Wines made in this new style often taste similar to each other, regardless of their region of origin.

Here are some probable reasons for this evolution in style:

✔ The darker, more powerful Pinot Noirs seem to obtain higher ratings from some wine critics.

✔ Most wineries are now growing different *clones* (genetic variants) of Pinot Noir vines — particularly the so-called *Dijon* clones from the Burgundy region — rather than the Martini, Swan, and Pommard clones formerly grown. The grapes from these new-for-California clones make wines with more color, weight, and alcohol.

✔ Some producers are allegedly adding Merlot and/or Syrah to their Pinot Noirs, which certainly would make the wines darker in color and fleshier in texture (although no respectable producer will admit to such a practice).

In the following list, we make some generalizations about Pinot Noir styles from various regions of California (for more on these regions and specific wine recommendations, please see the next section):

✔ **Carneros:** Carneros Pinot Noirs are renowned for their tight structure, herbal aroma nuances, and spicy berry flavors, mainly strawberry and black cherry. Some Carneros wineries are maintaining an elegant, herbal style that put them on the Pinot Noir map in the first place; however, many winemakers are now making darker, weightier Pinot Noirs, in keeping with the general California trend toward bigger, riper, fruitier, and higher-alcohol Pinot Noirs.

✔ **Santa Maria Valley:** The classic Pinot Noir style of Santa Maria Valley encompasses aromas and flavors of cherries, plums, spices, and sometimes a tomato-like character. High acidity and purity of fruit expression also characterize these wines.

✔ **Russian River Valley:** Classic Russian River Valley Pinot Noirs have always emphasized cherry and berry fruit — primarily raspberry and strawberry — in their aromas and flavors, which are concentrated and focused. They typically have been medium-bodied and medium to dark ruby in color, with a good amount of acidity and a reputation for aging 10 years or more. This classic style still exists (in such wineries as Hartford Court, Littorai, Mueller Winery, Rochioli Vineyards, and Williams Selyem), although the newer, bigger style has been making serious inroads.

✔ **Anderson Valley:** Classic Anderson Valley Pinot Noirs are characterized by crispness and natural acidity. As a group, they tend to be somewhat leaner in style and exhibit more earthiness than the plusher, fruitier Russian River Valley Pinots. Some critics talk about a *red-fruit style* of Anderson Valley Pinot Noir — medium-bodied, with aromas and flavors of red berries and cherries — and a *black-fruit style* — fuller-bodied, with aromas and flavors of black cherries, plums, and black berries.

✔ **Sta. Rita Hills:** It's difficult to generalize about a Sta. Rita Pinot Noir style because the region is so new. Many of the Sta. Rita Pinot Noirs that we've tasted from new wineries have been very dark in color and quite full-bodied, with lots of ripe, concentrated black cherry and other black-fruit flavors.

✔ **Santa Lucia Highlands:** These Pinot Noirs are typically rich and full-bodied rather than elegant, with rich, black cherry aromas and flavors.

✔ **Sonoma Coast:** In style, Sonoma Coast Pinot Noir wines somewhat resemble Pinot Noirs from their neighbor, Russian River Valley. They sport lush red and black fruit aromas and flavors, especially black cherry but sometimes also red cherry, along with forest and mushroom aromas and a spiciness typical of cool-climate wines. They also tend to have higher acidity than Pinot Noirs from other regions.

California's Pinot Noir Regions

Over the years, through trial and error, California wine producers have found their best areas for growing Pinot Noir — or at least the best areas so far. One characteristic that all these regions have in common is a relatively cool climate.

In the following sections, we cover first the classic California Pinot Noir regions and our recommended producers from those regions, and then we look at the new, trendy California regions and their recommended producers. We then cover Pinot Noirs from other areas, such as Santa Cruz Mountains and Edna Valley.

What's cool about cool climates

Every Pinot Noir region we describe in this chapter has a cool climate, which slows the ripening of the grapes, thanks to one or more of the following factors:

✔ Fog that blocks out otherwise warming sun

✔ Winds that cool daytime temperatures

✔ Nighttime temperatures that fall dramatically

Why is that so important? Generally speaking, the more slowly that grapes ripen, the fresher, purer, more focused, and more delicate their aromas and flavors will be. Also, the more slowly grapes ripen, the less likely that they'll be extremely high in sugar and low in acid when they're harvested. (A high sugar level and low acidity in the grapes generally results in huge, full-bodied, high-alcohol wines that are less refreshing to drink.)

Because the Pinot Noir grape has a delicate disposition, it tends to favor cool climates that enable it to ripen slowly but adequately — and we tend to favor the Pinot Noir wines that have the delicacy of aroma and flavor and the balanced structure that such cool climates foster.

Note: Some of the Pinot Noirs we recommend in this chapter are small-production wines that have only limited national distribution. Check www.wine-searcher.com to find retail stores where the wine is available and to comparison shop for the lowest prices.

The classic regions

California has five classic Pinot Noir regions, which emerged in the 1970s and early 1980s:

✔ Mount Harlan in San Benito County

✔ Carneros in Napa Valley and Sonoma County

✔ Santa Barbara County (including Santa Maria Valley and Santa Ynez Valley)

✔ Russian River Valley (including its subregion, Green Valley)

✔ Anderson Valley in Mendocino County

Read on for a brief history of each region's relationship with Pinot Noir, along with some of our wine recommendations.

Mount Harlan, San Benito County

Mount Harlan, a rugged, remote region in the Gavilan Mountains, has very few producers. It looks like a cool, barren desert — where morning fog and afternoon winds protect the grapes from the heat. The nearest town, Hollister, is the place you go for electricity, telephones, paved roads, and other modern conveniences. Only a true believer would go through all the hardships to establish a winery in a place as remote as Mount Harlan.

But the region does have limestone in the soil — one of the only places in California that has it. According to Josh Jensen, many other California regions where Pinot Noir grows contain too much clay in their soil, which produces dull wines. Jensen, who believed limestone soil to be essential for Pinot Noir, founded the Calera Wine Company there in 1975, planting three distinct vineyards — Selleck, Jensen, and Reed. In 1984, Jensen added a fourth, Mills Vineyard, and in 1998, he added a fifth, Ryan Vineyard. (*Note:* Chalone AVA, 20 miles south of Calera Wine Company and in the same Gavilan Mountain range, also has limestone, but that region is more renowned for its Chardonnays.)

Calera Wine Company's single-vineyard Pinot Noirs, especially Selleck, Jensen, and Reed, are known for their ability to age and improve with age. In a good vintage, they need at least 10 years of aging to reach their peak of development. (We've enjoyed some of Calera's single-vineyard Pinot Noirs from the 1978 through 1984 vintages — which were 20 years old when we drank them — and they still were very fine.)

Besides the single-vineyard wines, Jensen makes a moderately priced Mt. Harlan Cuvée Pinot Noir, which contains grapes from his various estate vineyards. He also makes a Central Coast AVA Pinot Noir, from purchased grapes, which retails for $21 to $24. (Mount Harlan is one small part of the much larger Central Coast AVA.)

In brief, here are our recommended Mount Harlan AVA Pinot Noirs, all from Calera Wine Company:

- ✔ Calera Mills Vineyard and Ryan Vineyard (Mount Harlan, San Benito County); $37 to $40

- ✔ Calera Mt. Harlan Cuvée (Mount Harlan, San Benito County); $29 to $30

- ✔ Calera Selleck Vineyard, Jensen Vineyard, and Reed Vineyard (Mount Harlan); $50 to $70

Los Carneros

The Los Carneros AVA, commonly known simply as Carneros, is a cool, windy area that stretches from southern Napa Valley to the southern Sonoma Coast (see Chapter 4 for a map). Winemakers Louis Martini and André Tchelistcheff stirred interest in Carneros in the 1930s when they planted Pinot Noir there.

When Carneros became an AVA in 1983, it was the first California AVA established on the basis of climate rather than political boundaries. Pacific breezes move in from San Pablo Bay, to the region's south, making Carneros not only the coolest area in Napa Valley and one of the coolest regions in Sonoma but also the windiest area in both counties by far. Fog rolls into Carneros in the early afternoon, moderating the heat and tempering the grapes' sugar levels, thereby fostering crisp acidity in the grapes. The territory also has thin soils and little rainfall, two prime ingredients for good Pinot Noir.

Carneros Creek Winery, founded by Francis Mahoney in 1973, was Carneros's first winery focusing on Pinot Noir. Mike Richmond opened Acacia Winery and Kent Rasmussen began his self-named winery in Carneros in 1979. The Carneros Pinot Noir movement was spurred further by Dick Ward and David Graves in 1981, when they started Saintsbury, perhaps the iconic Carneros winery specializing in Pinot Noir today.

Currently, 37 wineries are in Carneros (almost all of which make Pinot Noir), and lots of wineries in other regions use Pinot Noir grapes from Carneros for their wines. Of the 37 wineries, over a dozen have earned national acclaim for their Pinot Noirs. A few of these — such as Domaine Carneros, Artesa (formerly Codorniu Napa), and Gloria Ferrer — began as sparkling wine houses.

Bouchaine Vineyards, with a long history in Carneros, is experiencing a revival with its Pinot Noir, now under the direction of winemaker/general manager Mike Richmond, formerly of Acacia. And Buena Vista Carneros Estate, the oldest continually operating winery in California (founded in 1857 by Hungarian emigrant Count Agoston Haraszthy), is still going strong with its Pinot Noir and other wines.

We're not recommending any high-end (over $50) Carneros Pinot Noirs, because they're invariably darker, richer, oakier wines rather than the lighter, more elegantly styled Carneros Pinot Noirs we prefer. However, we do have some picks in the moderately priced and moderate-plus price ranges. Here are three recommended Carneros Pinot Noirs for under $20:

✔ **Acacia Winery, "A by Acacia" (California):** This is the reliable second wine of the prestigious Acacia Pinot Noir of Carneros. "A by Acacia" is widely distributed throughout the U.S., and it's a real value at $17 to $18.

✔ **Saintsbury "Garnet" (Carneros):** This wine has been an old friend since its first vintage, 1983. Anytime we see it on a restaurant wine list, we order it. It's light, fresh, fragrant, and totally delicious, with lots of berry and cherry flavor. Unfortunately, "Garnet," which retails for $16 to $18, sells out quickly each year after it's released. Your best bet might be to order it directly from the winery if your state allows it (see Chapter 13 for more on wine shipping regulations).

✔ **Jacuzzi Family Vineyards (Carneros):** Jacuzzi Family Vineyards (of the same family that invented the Jacuzzi whirlpool bathtub) is less well known than Saintsbury — and is therefore more readily available. We had our first Jacuzzi Pinot Noir just recently and were pleasantly surprised at how good it is for its price ($17 to $19); it has herbal and cherry aromas and flavors, and it's quite elegant and well balanced. A winner!

And here are our recommendations for moderate-plus Pinot Noirs.

Moderate-Plus Carneros Pinot Noirs, $20–$50

Acacia Winery, Carneros (Carneros)

Artesa Winery, Carneros (Carneros)

Bouchaine Vineyards, Carneros (Carneros)

Buena Vista Carneros Estate (Carneros)

Cuvaison Winery, Estate Selection (Carneros)

Domaine Carneros, Estate (Carneros)

Domaine Chandon, Carneros (Carneros)

Gloria Ferrer, Carneros (Carneros)

Kent Rasmussen, Carneros (Carneros)

MacRostie Winery, Carneros (Carneros)

Mahoney Vineyards, Estate (Carneros)

Robert Mondavi Carneros (Carneros)

Saintsbury Carneros (Carneros)

Schug Carneros Estate, Carneros, and "Heritage Reserve" Carneros (Carneros)

Toad Hall Cellars, Lavender Hill Vineyard and Willow Pond Vineyard (Carneros)

Truchard Vineyards (Carneros)

Santa Barbara County

Wine production in Santa Barbara County really didn't get going commercially until 1975, when Firestone Vineyards opened. By the early 1980s, Santa Barbara County had 13 operating wineries. From the beginning, Pinot Noir was a major player, especially in the northwest part of the county, where Santa Maria Valley is situated. Over 30 wineries are located within Santa Maria Valley, and another 50 wineries source grapes from this region.

Saintsbury: Classic Carneros Pinot Noir

Saintsbury Winery has been foremost in establishing Carneros as a fine region for Pinot Noir. Currently, Saintsbury is trying to bring Carneros back into the public eye in the face of stiff competition from places such as Sta. Rita Hills in Santa Barbara and Monterey's Santa Lucia Highlands.

Saintsbury's Pinot Noirs will never be like the powerful blockbusters coming out of the newer regions, and we're grateful for that. Not that Saintsbury's Pinots are wimpy — except for their least expensive Pinot Noir (the lighter-bodied "Garnet"), Saintsbury's six other Pinot Noirs range from medium-bodied to quite full-bodied. But they're well-balanced, elegant, and consistently Carneros in style, and they don't approach the 15-percent-plus alcohol of many newer California Pinots.

Saintsbury's flagship wine, its Carneros Estate, is the quintessential Carneros Pinot Noir: crisp and lively, medium-bodied, with aromas and flavors of tart cherries. It retails in the $28 to $32 range.

Santa Maria Valley runs east-west, which is a great advantage because the cool Pacific breezes have a clear path to funnel their way into the Valley. Santa Maria Valley, in fact, has the coolest average temperature during growing season of all California wine regions. Because it's so cool, the Valley's growing season is on the average four weeks longer than other regions', allowing slower maturation and longer hangtime for the Pinot Noir grapes.

Santa Maria Valley is the home of a great Pinot Noir site, the renowned Bien Nacido Vineyard. Many of Santa Barbara's best producers buy Pinot Noir grapes from Bien Nacido's owners (and you can find a number of them in our recommended wine lists).

Southeast of Santa Maria Valley, Los Alamos Valley is on the average 10 degrees warmer. Many different varieties, including Pinot Noir, grow in Los Alamos.

In the southern part of Santa Barbara County, just north of the city of Santa Barbara, lies the huge Santa Ynez Valley, which runs east-west. Many varieties do well in the eastern end, which is the warmest part of the Santa Barbara wine region. The western end of Santa Ynez Valley, nearer the Pacific, is much cooler. Because of its obvious climatic differences from the eastern end, this part of Santa Ynez Valley became a separate AVA in 2001: Sta. Rita Hills. (We cover the Pinot Noirs of Sta. Rita Hills in our section "Hot new Pinot Noir regions," later in this chapter.)

We have no Santa Barbara County wines under $20 to recommend and only one high-end wine.

Moderate-Plus Santa Barbara Pinot Noirs, $20–$50

Alta Maria Vineyards, Bien Nacido Vineyards (Santa Maria Valley)

Au Bon Climat (Santa Barbara County)

Au Bon Climat, "La Bauge Au-Dessus" (Santa Maria Valley)

Byron Vineyard, Santa Maria Valley, Nielson Vineyard and Bien Nacido Vineyard (Santa Maria Valley)

Cambria Winery, Julia'a Vineyard and Bench Break Vineyard (Santa Maria Valley)

Foley Estate, Santa Maria Hills Vineyard (Santa Maria Valley)

Foxen Winery (Santa Maria Valley)

Hartley-Ostini Hitching Post Winery, "Cork Dancer" (Santa Barbara County)

Kenneth Volk Vineyards, Santa Maria Cuvée (Santa Barbara County)

Lane Tanner Winery, Santa Barbara County and Bien Nacido Vineyard (Santa Maria Valley)

Summerland Winery, Bien Nacido Vineyard (Santa Maria Valley)

Tantara Winery, Bien Nacido and Solomon Hills Vineyards (Santa Maria Valley)

Whitcraft Winery, Bien Nacido Vineyard–N Block (Santa Maria Valley)

High-End Santa Barbara Pinot Noir, $50–$75

Foxen Winery, Bien Nacido Vineyard–Block Eight (Santa Maria Valley)

Russian River Valley

The huge Russian River Valley AVA, about 198 square miles, is in the central part of Sonoma County and encompasses two smaller AVAs, Green Valley and Chalk Hill. However, Chalk Hill, in the extreme northeast part of Russian River Valley, is too warm for Pinot Noir. Russian River Valley's largest city is Santa Rosa, at its southeastern end, about 55 miles north of San Francisco; however, its wine center is the rapidly growing town of Healdsburg, in the northern part of the Valley.

Climate defines the region, particularly cooling fog from the Pacific Ocean, which churns through the Petaluma Wind Gap up the Russian River Valley. Fog typically arrives in the evening, dropping temperatures 35 to 40 degrees from their daytime highs. The fog dissipates in the morning, allowing warm, sunny days during the growing season. The natural air-conditioning at night creates an extended growing season, up to 20 percent longer than that of neighboring regions, allowing the Pinot Noir grapes to develop full-flavor maturity while retaining their natural acidity.

Depending on the location of their vineyards, Russian River Valley Pinot Noirs can carry either Russian River Valley or Green Valley AVAs on their labels. Although many of the wines we recommend actually come from Green Valley grapes, the producer often chooses to use the better-known Russian River Valley AVA on the wine's label.

We recommend Russian River Valley Pinot Noirs in three price categories: moderately priced, moderate-plus, and high-end.

Moderately Priced Russian River Valley Pinot Noirs, under $20

De Loach Vineyards, Estate (Russian River Valley)

Kenwood Vineyards (Russian River Valley)

Rodney Strong Vineyards (Russian River Valley)

In our picks for moderate-plus Pinot Noirs, you'll notice that Dutton Ranch vineyard appears three times. Warren Dutton planted Pinot Noir in 1964, and today Dutton Ranch is one of California's celebrated vineyards for Chardonnay and Pinot Noir, selling its grapes to many elite wineries as well as making its own wines. As for other notable names, the family of the legendary late Joseph Swan — perhaps the first person to make great, long-lived Russian River Valley Pinot Noirs (and Zinfandels) — makes a couple of wines on this list.

Moderate-Plus Russian River Valley Pinot Noirs, $20–$50

Chasseur (Russian River Valley)

Davis Bynum Winery, Moshin Vineyards (Russian River Valley)

De Loach Vineyards, Green Valley and "O. F. S." (Russian River Valley)

Dutton-Goldfield Winery, Dutton Ranch (Russian River Valley)

Freeman Vineyard (Russian River Valley)

Frei Brothers (Russian River Valley)

Gary Farrell Vineyards (Russian River Valley)

Inman Family Wines, Olivet Grange Vineyard (Russian River Valley)

Iron Horse Vineyards, Estate (Green Valley)

"J" Vineyards (Russian River Valley)

Joseph Swan, Great Oak and Trenton Estate Vineyards (Russian River Valley)

La Crema Winery (Russian River Valley)

Lynmar Winery (Russian River Valley)

MacMurray Ranch (Russian River Valley)

Marimar Estate, Don Miguel Vineyard (Russian River Valley)

Moshin Vineyards, Estate and Lot 4 (Russian River Valley)

Mueller Winery, Emily's Cuvée (Russian River Valley)

Orogeny Vineyards (Green Valley)

Papapietro Perry Winery (Russian River Valley)

Paul Hobbs Wines (Russian River Valley)

Porter Creek Vineyards (Russian River Valley)

Roessler Cellars, Dutton Ranch (Russian River Valley)

Russian Hill Estate (Russian River Valley)

Rutz Cellars, Dutton Ranch (Russian River Valley)

Siduri Wines, Sapphire Hill Vineyard (Russian River Valley)

A big name in our high-end Russian River Valley Pinot Noirs is Joe Rochioli, who planted Pinot Noir and Chardonnay in 1966. He started his own winery, Rochioli Vineyards, in 1982 but also sold his grapes to two then-new wineries, Williams Selyem Winery and Gary Farrell Vineyards. Today, all three are still among Russian River Valley's brightest Pinot Noir stars, with loyal followings. Dehlinger Winery and Kistler Vineyards, which also appear in the high-end list, are two other major Russian River wineries focusing on Pinot Noir; they started in the 1980s.

High-End Russian River Valley Pinot Noirs, Mostly $50–$75

Arista Winery, Mononi Vineyard and Toboni Vineyard (Russian River Valley)

Davis Bynum Winery, Allen Vineyard (Russian River Valley)

Dehlinger Winery, Estate and Goldridge Vineyard (Russian River Valley)

DuMOL, Russian River Valley and Aidan, Finn, or Ryan Vineyards (Russian River Valley)

Dutton Estate, Jewell Block and Thomas Road Vineyards (Russian River Valley)

Failla, Keefer Ranch (Russian River Valley)

Freeman Vineyard, Keefer Ranch (Russian River Valley)

Hartford Court, Arrendell Vineyard (Russian River Valley)

Hartford Court, Fog Dance Vineyard (Green Valley)

"J" Vineyards, Nicole's and Robert Thomas Vineyards (Russian River Valley)

Kistler Vineyards, Kistler Vineyard (Russian River Valley); *over $100*

Lynmar Winery, Quail Hill Vineyard (Russian River Valley)

Merry Edwards, Olivet Lane (Russian River Valley); *over $75*

Rochioli Vineyards, Estate (Russian River Valley)

Williams Selyem Winery, "Westside Road Neighbors" (Russian River Valley)

Williams Selyem Winery, Allen Vineyard (Russian River Valley); *over $75*

Anderson Valley

Anderson Valley is in Mendocino County, about 115 miles north of San Francisco. The Valley is in the western part of the county, just 10 to 15 miles from the Pacific and southeast of the coastal town of Mendocino. Steep mountains surround the 15 mile–long Valley, and the Navarro River runs through it.

Anderson Valley has the coolest year-round temperatures of any wine region in California. Amazingly, temperatures can fall 40 to 50 degrees at night. This temperature range enables Pinot Noir grapes to retain their acidity throughout the long, warm summer and autumn. Grapes ripen slowly and develop intense flavors. The westernmost part of Anderson Valley, closest to the Mendocino Coast, has the coolest climate, and that's where many Pinot Noir vineyards are situated — close to the majestic, coastal Redwoods.

Williams Selyem: The essence of Russian River Valley

No California winery has won more acclaim for its Pinot Noirs than Williams Selyem Winery. Burt Williams and Ed Selyem were friends who shared a passion for Pinot Noir, and they became weekend winemakers in 1979, using a local garage as their first winery. They made their first commercial wine under the Hacienda del Rio label in 1981 and changed the name to Williams Selyem in 1983. Their 1985 Rochioli Vineyard Pinot Noir won top prize at the 1987 California State Fair, and Williams Selyem Pinot Noirs attained cult status. As time went by, Williams Selyem Pinot Noirs helped to establish Russian River Valley as the prime region for California Pinot Noir.

Burt Williams and Ed Selyem retired in 1998, selling their winery to John Dyson, who hired veteran winemaker Bob Cabral to handle winemaking duties. Dyson's greater financial resources have allowed somewhat more Pinot Noir to be produced. Williams Selyem's Pinot Noirs are still limited in production, but now you can find them in some retail stores and in restaurants. Still, the best way to get your hands on these wines is to get on Williams Selyem's mailing list.

At present, Williams Selyem produces as many as 16 different Pinot Noirs, 11 of them single-vineyard wines, all made in small lots. The five relatively larger-production Pinot Noirs are the winery's "Central Coast," "Sonoma County," "Sonoma Coast," "Russian River Valley," and "Westside Road Neighbors" (a blend from several top vineyards) Pinot Noirs. The 11 single-vineyard Pinot Noirs, including such notable wines as "Allen Vineyard," "Hirsch Vineyard," and "Rochioli Riverblock," are mainly in Russian River Valley and the Sonoma Coast, with two sourced from Mendocino County.

The modern era in Anderson Valley started in 1964 when Edmeades Vineyards opened, followed two years later by Husch Vineyards. In the 1970s, three other small wineries — Navarro Vineyards, Lazy Creek Vineyards, and Greenwood Ridge Vineyards — opened. But what really put Anderson Valley on the California wine map was the arrival of Champagne Louis Roederer in 1982; this great Champagne house decided that Anderson Valley was the ideal location to plant Chardonnay and Pinot Noir vineyards for its new sparkling wine operation, Roederer Estate (see Chapter 11 for more on sparkling wines). In 1983, Anderson Valley became an official AVA.

We classify Anderson Valley as a classic Pinot Noir region because wineries have been making Pinot Noir there for more than 25 years; however, you could argue that Anderson Valley is a hot new region because most of the Pinot Noir action there has taken place over the past decade or so. In 1994, only 300 acres of

Pinot Noir existed in Anderson Valley; by 2005, that number had quadrupled to 1,200 acres. What happened was that many of the top Pinot Noir producers — particularly from Sonoma County but also from Napa Valley — discovered the ideal growing conditions of Anderson Valley. Some leading Pinot Noir producers that are now using Anderson Valley grapes include Williams Selyem, Littorai, Siduri, Duckhorn's Goldeneye, La Crema, Adrian Fog, Roessler, and Copain.

About 25 Anderson Valley wineries make Pinot Noir, and another 17 wineries outside of the Valley use Anderson Valley grapes for one or more of their Pinot Noirs. We name our recommended Anderson Valley Pinot Noirs in two price categories: moderate-plus and high-end. We found no under-$20 Pinot Noirs to recommend.

Moderate-Plus Anderson Valley Pinot Noirs, $20–$50

Black Kite Cellars, Kite's Rest (Anderson Valley)

Breggo Cellars (Anderson Valley)

Copain Wines, Cerise Vineyard (Anderson Valley)

Greenwood Ridge Vineyards (Mendocino Ridge)

Handley Cellars (Anderson Valley)

Husch Vineyards (Anderson Valley)

La Crema (Anderson Valley)

Lazy Creek Vineyards (Anderson Valley)

Londer Vineyards (Anderson Valley)

MacPhail (Anderson Valley)

Phillips Hill Estates, Toulouse Vineyard (Anderson Valley)

Phillips Hill Estates, Oppenlander Vineyard (Mendocino)

Raye's Hill Winery, Cerise Vineyard (Anderson Valley)

Roessler Cellars, Savoy Vineyard (Anderson Valley)

Saintsbury, Cerise Vineyard (Anderson Valley)

High-End Anderson Valley Pinot Noirs, Mostly $50–$75

Adrian Fog Winery, Savoy Vineyard (Anderson Valley)

Breggo Cellars, Savoy and Donnelly Vineyards (Anderson Valley)

Copain Wines, Hacienda Secoya Vineyard (Anderson Valley)

Littorai, Savoy Vineyard and Cerise Vineyard (Anderson Valley)

Londer Vineyards, Paraboll Vineyard (Anderson Valley)

MacPhail, Toulouse Vineyard (Anderson Valley)

Williams Selyem, Ferrington Vineyard (Anderson Valley); *over $100*

Williams Selyem, Weir Vineyard (Yorkville Highlands, Mendocino County); *over $100*

Hot new Pinot Noir regions

Three regions in California have emerged in the last decade or so as excellent places to grow Pinot Noir:

- Sta. Rita Hills (Santa Barbara County)

- Santa Lucia Highlands (Monterey County)

- Sonoma Coast (Sonoma County)

Sta. Rita Hills (Santa Barbara County)

Until 2001, the area known as Sta. Rita Hills was part of the larger Santa Ynez Valley AVA (or about 99 percent of it was). But Sta. Rita Hills, on the western end of Santa Ynez Valley, is so different in climate — on average, 15 degrees cooler in the growing season than the eastern end of the Valley — that common sense dictated that it have its own AVA.

Few commercial wineries existed in the Sta. Rita Hills until the 1980s. Three early wineries — Clos Pepe, Sanford Winery, and Babcock Vineyards — led the movement to establish the Sta. Rita Hills AVA, which finally happened in 2001. Richard Sanford, who founded the region's first Pinot Noir vineyard (Sanford & Benedict Vineyard) in 1971 and Sanford Winery in 1981, is perhaps the name most associated with Sta. Rita Hills; Sanford's current affiliation is as the owner of Alma Rosa Winery and Vineyards.

Although the area is known as Santa Rita Hills, the official AVA name, which appears on wine labels, is Sta. Rita Hills, to protect the trademark of the Chilean winery Viña Santa Rita.

Sta. Rita Hills, one of California's smaller AVAs, now has over 1,700 acres planted, mainly with Pinot Noir and Chardonnay grapes, the classic cool-climate varieties. As with Santa Maria Valley (see "Santa Barbara County" earlier in this chapter), what makes the Sta. Rita Hills AVA unusual is its clear pathway of east-to-west rolling hills open to the Pacific Ocean, which provides morning fog, cool temperatures, and strong winds. These conditions lengthen the growing season, limit excessive crop levels, and contribute flavor concentration and acidity to the grapes.

Even though many of the Pinot Noirs from Sta. Rita Hills are being made in the opulent, powerful, modern style, a few winemakers, such as Ojai (pronounced *oh*-high) Vineyard's Adam Tolmach, continue to produce Pinots in the more traditional style. Tolmach's secret is that he picks his grapes early, before they become too ripe and sugar-laden. He believes that Pinot Noir's lovely perfumed aromas are lost when the grapes are picked late — as many winemakers are picking them today.

Currently, 23 wineries are located within the Sta. Rita Hills AVA, with another 48 wineries outside of the AVA sourcing grapes from this area — but both numbers are growing each year. Here, alphabetically within each price category, are our recommended Sta. Rita Hills Pinot Noirs.

Moderately Priced Sta. Rita Hills Pinot Noir, under $20

Babcock Vineyards, "Rita's Earth Cuvée (Sta. Rita Hills)

Moderate-Plus Sta. Rita Hills Pinot Noirs, $20–$50

Alma Rosa Winery (Sta. Rita Hills)

Babcock Vineyards, "Grand Cuvée (Santa Ynez Valley)

Badge Wines (Sta. Rita Hills)

Fiddlehead Cellars, Cuvée 728, Fiddlestix Vineyard (Sta. Rita Hills)

Flying Goat Cellars, Rio Vista Vineyard, Clone 2A (Sta. Rita Hills)

Ken Brown Wines, Clos Pepe, Cargasacchi, and Sanford & Benedict Vineyards (Sta. Rita Hills)

Kenneth-Crawford Wines, Clos Pepe Vineyard (Sta. Rita Hills)

Pali Wine Company, Turner Vineyard (Sta. Rita Hills)

Roessler Cellars, Peregrine Vineyard (Sta. Rita Hills)

Sanford Winery, Santa Rita Hills (Sta. Rita Hills)

High-End Sta. Rita Hills Pinot Noirs, Mostly $50–$75

Alma Rosa Winery, La Encantada Vineyard (Sta. Rita Hills)

Au Bon Climat, Sanford & Benedict Vineyard (Sta. Rita Hills)

Brewer-Clifton, Clos Pepe and Mount Carmel Vineyards (Sta. Rita Hills)

Clos Pepe Estate (Sta. Rita Hills)

Foxen Winery, Sea Smoke Vineyard (Sta. Rita Hills)

Gypsy Canyon Vineyards, Santa Rita Creek Vineyard (Sta. Rita Hills); *about $100*

Longoria Wines, Fe Ciega Vineyard (Sta. Rita Hills)

Loring Wine Company, Cargasacchi Vineyard (Sta. Rita Hills)

Ojai Vineyard, Clos Pepe and Fe Ciega Vineyards (Sta. Rita Hills)

Roessler Cellars, Clos Pepe Vineyard (Sta. Rita Hills)

Sea Smoke Cellars, Southing Vineyard (Sta. Rita Hills); *about $90*

Siduri, Clos Pepe and Cargasacchi Vineyards (Sta. Rita Hills)

Santa Lucia Highlands (Monterey County)

A decade ago, practically no one outside of Monterey County had ever heard of the Santa Lucia Highlands wine region. Now, thanks to recent acclaim for its Pinot Noirs, Santa Lucia Highlands is definitely a hot new region in California.

The Santa Lucia Highlands AVA, part of the larger Monterey County AVA, came into existence in 1991. The Highlands are on the eastern side of the Santa Lucia Mountain range, overlooking the Salinas River Valley, with vineyards at altitudes as high as 1,200 feet. The AVA is south of Monterey Bay, and it runs northwest to southeast for 18 miles, from the town of Gonzales in the north to the Arroyo Seco AVA to the south. It's only 1 mile wide.

Morning fog comes into this area from Monterey Bay, just 10 miles north. But especially in the higher vineyards, it burns off in time for plenty of early-day sunshine. Cooling ocean breezes come in like clockwork through Monterey Bay every afternoon. The ocean fog and breezes are responsible for Santa Lucia Highlands' having a Region I climate, the coolest climate zone. The average high temperature in August is only in the mid-70 degrees, and nights in the growing season can be up to 50 degrees cooler than days, locking in the necessary acidity in the grapes.

The cool climate, an extremely long growing season, and ancient glacial soil create ideal conditions for growing the two Burgundian varieties, Chardonnay and Pinot Noir. Chardonnay, the easier of the two grapes to cultivate, was the dominant variety in the Highlands at first, but as soon as growers discovered how and where to grow Pinot Noir effectively, Pinot became the darling: 2,500 acres of it now exist.

Although Spanish missionaries planted vineyards in Santa Lucia Highlands in the 1790s, the area really got started as a wine region in the early 1970s, with the establishment of Paraiso Vineyards, Sleepy Hollow Vineyards (now part of Robert Talbott Winery), La Estancia, and Smith & Hook (now Hahn Estates–Smith & Hook) — all of which started as vineyards and eventually added wineries.

Before the 1990s, larger wineries outside of Monterey County purchased most of the grapes grown in the Santa Lucia Highlands. In the 1990s, three vineyard owners, Gary Pisoni (Pisoni Vineyards), Gary Franscioni (Roar Wines), and Robert Talbott (Talbott Winery) began the single-vineyard movement in Santa Lucia Highlands, earning recognition and respect for the region.

Six top-value Pinot Noirs

These six Pinot Noirs, all $15 and under, are consistently reliable, and they're our picks as top values:

✔ Blackstone Winery (Sonoma Coast)

✔ De Loach Vineyards, "Cote De Loach" (California)

✔ Hangtime Cellars (Edna Valley, San Luis Obispo)

✔ Jekel Vineyards (Monterey County)

✔ Mark West (California)

✔ Red Truck, Cline Cellars (California)

Here are our recommended Santa Lucia Highlands Pinot Noirs, listed alphabetically in three price categories.

Moderately Priced Santa Lucia Highlands Pinot Noir, under $20
Hayman & Hill (Santa Lucia Highlands)

Moderate-Plus Santa Lucia Highlands Pinot Noirs, $20–$50
Campion Wines (Santa Lucia Highlands)

David Bruce Winery (Santa Lucia Highlands)

Estancia, Stonewall Vineyard (Santa Lucia Highlands)

Hope & Grace, Sleepy Hollow Vineyard (Santa Lucia Highlands)

Lucia Vineyards (Santa Lucia Highlands)

Lucienne Vineyards, Santa Lucia Highlands and Lone Oak Vineyard (Santa Lucia Highlands)

Morgan Winery, "Twelve Clones" and Rosella's Vineyard (Santa Lucia Highlands)

Paraiso Vineyards, Santa Lucia Highlands and "West Terrace" (Santa Lucia Highlands)

Roar Wines (Santa Lucia Highlands)

Siduri, Santa Lucia Highlands, Garys' and Rosella's Vineyards (Santa Lucia Highlands)

Tamayo Family Vineyards (Santa Lucia Highlands)

Tondre Wines, Tondre Grapefield (Santa Lucia Highlands)

Tudor Wines (Santa Lucia Highlands)

In our high-end list, you might notice some recurring vineyard names. The most renowned Pinot Noir vineyard in the AVA, from which many nonresident wineries purchase grapes, is Garys' Vineyard, which Gary Pisoni and Gary Franscioni founded in 1997. Two other top Santa Lucia Highlands Pinot Noir vineyards are (Franscioni's) Rosella's Vineyard and Pisoni Vineyards.

High-End Santa Lucia Highlands Pinot Noirs, Mostly $50–$75
A.P. Vin, Garys' Vineyard and Rosella's Vineyard (Santa Lucia Highlands)

August West, Rosella's Vineyard (Santa Lucia Highlands)

Bernardus, Rosella's Vineyard (Santa Lucia Highlands)

Belle Glos, Las Alturas Vineyard (Santa Lucia Highlands)

Loring Wine Company, Rosella's and Garys' Vineyards (Santa Lucia Highlands)

Miner Family Vineyards, Rosella's and Garys' Vineyards (Santa Lucia Highlands)

Miura Vineyards, Pisoni and Garys' Vineyards (Santa Lucia Highlands)

Pelerin, Rosella's Vineyard (Santa Lucia Highlands)

Pisoni Vineyard, Estate (Santa Lucia Highlands); *about $90*

Roar Wines, Garys' Vineyard (Santa Lucia Highlands)

Tamayo Family Vineyards, Sleepy Hollow Vineyard (Santa Lucia Highlands)

Testarossa Vineyards, Garys,' Pisoni, Sleepy Hollow, and Rosella's Vineyard (Santa Lucia Highlands)

Vision Cellars, Garys,' Rosella's, and Las Alturas Vineyards (Santa Lucia Highlands)

Sonoma Coast AVA

The Sonoma Coast is the largest AVA in Sonoma County. Its boundary runs along the Pacific Coast from the Mendocino County line in the north all the way down to San Pablo Bay and Marin County in the south — more than 500,000 acres, with about 7,000 acres under vine. It's an umbrella AVA in that it encompasses a number of other Sonoma AVAs.

Brice Jones, founder of the hugely successful Sonoma-Cutrer Vineyards, was the force behind the creation of the Sonoma Coast AVA. Jones saw the need for an AVA for "cold-climate" wine producers (like himself) who owned vineyards scattered throughout cool zones along the Sonoma Coast and who, until then, could not use the important *estate-bottled* term on their wines because their vineyards were in different AVAs than their wineries. (Chapter 3 explains the intricacies of using the term *estate-bottled.*)

Although the Sonoma Coast AVA began in 1987, in many ways, it's really the newest Pinot Noir region in California. Apart from the earliest vineyards such as Brice Jones's, vine plantings began in a serious way only in the early 1990s. Today, over 50 growers have vineyards in the AVA (most also have wineries), and another 60 or more wineries from elsewhere source grapes here. Almost all this growth has taken place within the last two decades. Pinot Noir and Chardonnay are the driving force behind this growth, with Syrah also expanding rapidly in plantings.

Big-name wineries producing Sonoma Coast Pinot Noir include Kistler, Marcassin, Peter Michael, Williams Selyem, Flowers, Littorai, and Martinelli. And large wineries such as Kendall-Jackson have bought land here.

The Sonoma Coast is California's most extreme wine region, climatewise. Growing season temperatures are almost as low as possible for grapes to ripen: Daytime highs are usually in the low 70s, and night temperatures are in the 40s. Cool Pacific fog and winds coming through the Petaluma Gap (an opening in the mountains at Bodega Bay) are responsible for the cool temperatures. The growing season is extremely long; most of the grapes are harvested from mid-October to November (quite a contrast to Napa Valley, where harvest typically begins in August). The vineyards — which are generally planted high in the Sonoma Mountains to catch the sun — have thin, shallow, very rocky soil. The thin soil plus the sunshine are key assets. But the Sonoma Coast is always a challenge to growers, with cold spring seasons (common), very small crops (also common), and fall rains (always likely).

We believe that the Sonoma Coast could eventually be regarded as the finest Pinot Noir region in the U.S. and perhaps the entire New World. The stressed vines produce meager crops of small, concentrated, ripe, flavorful grapes with low sugar levels. Pinot Noir wines made from these grapes tend to show greater complexity of aroma and flavor than most Pinots from other regions in the state. Sonoma Coast Pinot Noirs need two or three years' longer bottle aging than California's other Pinot Noirs, and our prediction is that they will age longer.

Because the Sonoma Coast AVA is so huge, it will probably divide into several smaller AVAs in the near future. The first will probably be Fort Ross-Seaview, in the southern coastal part of the larger area.

Here are our recommended Sonoma Coast Pinot Noirs in three price categories.

Moderately Priced Sonoma Coast Pinot Noirs, under $20
MacMurray Ranch (Sonoma Coast)
Schug Carneros Estate (Sonoma Coast)
Sebastiani Vineyards (Sonoma Coast)

Moderate-Plus Sonoma Coast Pinot Noirs, $20–$50
Alcina Cellars, Sonoma Coast; Sangiacomo and Ramondo Vineyards (Sonoma Coast)
Chasseur (Sonoma Coast)
David Bruce Winery (Sonoma Coast)
Dunah, Estate and Sangiacomo Vineyard (Sonoma Coast)
Dutch Bill Creek Winery (Sonoma Coast)
Failla (Sonoma Coast)
Flowers Vineyard (Sonoma Coast)
Fort Ross, Fort Ross Vineyard (Sonoma Coast)
Harrington Winery, Gap's Crown Vineyard (Sonoma Coast)
Hartford Court, Land's Edge Vineyard (Sonoma Coast)

Hirsch Winery, Estate, "The Bohan-Dillon" (Sonoma Coast)
Keller Estate, La Cruz Vineyard (Sonoma Coast)
La Crema (Sonoma Coast)
MacPhail Family Wines (Sonoma Coast)
MacRostie Winery, Wildcat Mountain Vineyard (Sonoma Coast)
Marimar Estate, Doña Margarita Vineyard (Sonoma Coast)
Patz & Hall (Sonoma Coast)
Roessler Cellars, "La Brisa" and "Griffin's Lair" (Sonoma Coast)
Siduri Wines, Sonoma Coast; Hirsch and Terra di Promissio Vineyards (Sonoma Coast)
Sonoma-Cutrer Vineyards (Sonoma Coast)
Stephen Vincent, Four Sisters Vineyard (Sonoma Coast)
W. H. Smith Wines, Sonoma Coast and Hellenthal Vineyard (Sonoma Coast)
Wild Hog Vineyard (Sonoma Coast)
Willowbrook Cellars, Kastania Vineyard (Sonoma Coast)

High-End Sonoma Coast Pinot Noirs, Mostly $50–$75

Aubert Wines, Reuling and UV Vineyards (Sonoma Coast); *both $200*

Benovia Winery (Sonoma Coast)

Bjornstad Cellars, Van Der Kamp and Hellenthal Vineyards (Sonoma Coast)

Drew Family, McDougall Vineyard (Sonoma Coast)

Dutton-Goldfield, McDougall Vineyard (Sonoma Coast)

Flowers Vineyard, Frances Thompson and Sea View Ridge Vineyards; also "Andreen-Gale Cuvée" (Sonoma Coast)

Freestone Vineyards (Sonoma Coast)

Halleck Vineyard, "Clone 828" and The Farm Vineyard (Sonoma Coast)

Hartford Court, Far Coast Vineyard (Sonoma Coast)

"J" Vineyards (Sonoma Coast)

Kistler Vineyards, Sonoma Coast and Hirsch Vineyard (Sonoma Coast); *each about $ 100*

Littorai Wines, Sonoma Coast and Hirsch Vineyard (Sonoma Coast); *mainly in restaurants*

Marcassin Vineyard, Marcassin Estate, Blue-Slide Ridge, and Three Sisters Vineyards (Sonoma Coast); *$200 to $500 for older vintages; recent vintages: mailing list only*

MacPhail Family Wines, Pratt and Goodin Vineyards (Sonoma Coast)

Merry Edwards Wines, Sonoma Coast and Meredith Estate (Sonoma Coast)

Pahlmeyer Winery (Sonoma Coast)

Peay Vineyards, "Pomarium" and "Scallop Shelf" (Sonoma Coast)

Radio-Coteau Wine Cellars, "La Neblina" and "Terra Neuma" (Sonoma Coast)

Sonoma Coast Vineyards (Sonoma Coast)

W. H. Smith Wines, Maritime Vineyard (Sonoma Coast)

Williams Selyem Winery, Sonoma Coast; Coastlands, Hirsch, Peay, and Precious Mountain Vineyards (Sonoma Coast); *single-vineyard wines over $75; available mainly through mailing list*

Pinot Noirs in other regions

Good Pinot Noirs exist in various regions of California other than the renowned Pinot Noir regions that we highlight earlier in this chapter. The least-known region is Marin County AVA, north of San Francisco's Golden Gate Bridge and south of the Sonoma Coast. Actually, Marin County's very cool climate is very much like that of Sonoma Coast.

We have violated our own guidelines and recommended a Pinot Noir that might be difficult to find — because it's so good: Willowbrook Cellars, Marin County. Its first vintage, 2006, is lean, pure, flavorful, and concentrated.

We've found one moderately priced Pinot Noir that, at $18, clearly qualifies as a best buy, and we name 11 of our other favorites in this disparate group.

Other Moderately Priced Pinot Noir, under $20

Pietra Santa Winery, Cienega Valley (San Benito County)

Other Moderate-Plus Pinot Noirs, $20–$50

Clos La Chance (Santa Cruz Mountains)

Domaine Alfred, Chamisal Vineyard (Edna Valley, San Luis Obispo)

Edna Valley Vineyard, Paragon Vineyard (Edna Valley, San Luis Obispo)

Laetitia Estate (Arroyo Grande Valley, San Luis Obispo)

Mount Eden Estate (Santa Cruz Mountains)

Talley Vineyards, Estate (Arroyo Grande Valley, San Luis Obispo)

Willowbrook Cellars (Marin County)

Other High-End Pinot Noirs, $50–$75

Dutton-Goldfield, Devil's Gulch Vineyard (Marin County)

Laetitia Estate, Les Galets and La Colline Vineyards (Arroyo Grande Valley, San Luis Obispo)

Talley Vineyards, Rosemary's and Rincon Vineyards (Arroyo Grande Valley, San Luis Obispo)

Thomas Fogarty Winery (Santa Cruz Mountains)

Chapter 8

Zinfandel

*W*hen we look back on all the Zinfandel wines that we've tasted, the two thoughts that come to mind — besides serious drinking satisfaction, of course — are fun and adventure: adventure, because the quest to discover the finest Zinfandel producers and their best vineyards has taken us to amazing patches of ancient gnarly vines all over the state; and fun because . . . well, fun just seems to be part of Zinfandel's nature. Something about this spicy, flavorful red wine brings a smile to wine drinkers' faces. We remember organizing a comprehensive wine-tasting of Zinfandels once and giving every taster a large, bright purple pin that read, "Commit Zinfandelity with someone you love!" We can't imagine ever being so playful over a bunch of Cabernet Sauvignons!

Zinfandel today has two faces: the dark, flavorful red wine that it's always been and the slightly sweet, flavorful pink wine that for over two decades was the second most popular varietal wine in the U.S. after Chardonnay. We cover the Zinfandel grape and red Zinfandel wines in this chapter, and we cover the pink White Zinfandel wines in Chapter 11.

Tracing California's (Almost) Native Grape

In the mid-1800s, Zinfandel vines came to California with Gold Rush emigrants from the East Coast, where a nurseryman named George Gibbs had imported that vine from Europe in approximately 1829.

Zinfandel adapted so well to California's terrain that it quickly became a favorite grape and occupied prime vineyards in the state. It also occupied less-favorable sites, where it produced grapes for inexpensive blended red wines. Grape growers prized the Zinfandel grape particularly for its ability to produce large crops, but the wines made from those grapes, presumably those from grapes in prime locations, were also prized. During Prohibition, Zinfandel grapes were a popular choice among home winemakers.

In the modern era of varietal wines, however, Zinfandel became a more marginalized grape as growers began cultivating Cabernet Sauvignon and other classic grapes of French origin. Some winemakers treasured the old Zinfandel vineyards that produced small crops of flavorful, concentrated grapes, but other Zinfandel vineyards fell out of favor. In the 1970s, Zinfandel production was in serious decline.

At this point, the storyline of Zinfandel forks off in two directions. One is the road of the original (red) Zinfandel wine, and the other is the road of White Zinfandel, the sweet pink wine. In 1975, Sutter Home Winery inadvertently made the first "White Zinfandel" when the fermentation of a dry pink Zinfandel wine stopped of its own accord, leaving residual sugar in the wine. That style went on to became hugely popular. In 2005, White Zin outsold red Zin 6.5 to 1.

The road less traveled is that of red Zinfandel. This wine had two things going in its favor: One was the quality of wines from grapes grown in good sites, and the other was the mystery that surrounded the grape's origins. Although wine experts knew Zinfandel wasn't a native American grape, they considered the wine uniquely American because the grape didn't seem to exist elsewhere in the world. The idea that the Zinfandel grape was an orphan that America could claim as her own gave the wines a special aura that enhanced their popularity. Even today, wine columnists recommend Zinfandel for Thanksgiving because the wine is so identified with America in spirit.

DNA testing solved the mystery of Zinfandel's heritage. In the early 1970s, scientists determined that Zinfandel is the same as Primitivo, a grape grown in the Apulia region of Southern Italy. In 1993, genetic testing showed that these two varieties are both clones of another variety, identity then unknown but related to a Croatian grape called Plavac Mali. In 2001, scientists determined that Zinfandel and Primitivo are both the same as Crljenak Kaštelanski (soorl-*yen*-ak kash-tel-*ahn*-ski), a red grape from coastal Croatia.

U.S. regulations recognize Primitivo as a synonym for Zinfandel, and some California wines are named Primitivo. Meanwhile, some producers of Primitivo in Italy have begun calling their wines Zinfandel. And would you believe it? No one at all seems to be calling the wine Crljenak Kaštelanski!

What's Special about Zinfandel

The Zinfandel vine is California's third most important, after Chardonnay and Cabernet Sauvignon, in terms of the quantity of grapes grown. Cabernet ranks higher than Zinfandel by only a fraction of a percentage point.

Red wines from the Zinfandel grape boast a unique combination of ripe berry flavors that give an impression of sweet fruitiness and a firm, dry texture that gives a spicy energy to play against that sweet fruitiness. The wines have plenty of flavor, but their appeal isn't just flavor: They balance that flavor with firm structure and a sturdy character that make the wines particularly satisfying.

Zinfandel wines are typically said to have flavors of *bramble berries* — berries from plants that contain thorns, such as blackberries and loganberries. They often have a distinctive spicy black-pepper note as well, which usually comes from blending in some Petite Sirah (read about Petite Sirah in Chapter 10). Some winemakers ascribe a chocolate note to Zinfandel's taste.

Compared to Cabernet Sauvignon or Merlot wines, Zinfandel wines are generally fruitier and more flavorful, and they have a personality that's slightly wild and untamed — the opposite of sedate and proper. Compared to Pinot Noir wines, Zins are less seductive in their fruity aromas and flavors, and they're leaner in structure, giving less of an impression of "roundness" in your mouth. If we had to pick a type of California wine that Zinfandel most resembles, we'd say Petite Sirah — although Zinfandel wines are far more available and more varied than Petite Sirah wines.

In describing what's special about Zinfandel, we have to mention the fun-loving attitude that the wine seems to invoke and the passion and commitment that many winemakers feel toward this grape and its wines.

Naturally, Zinfandel has an advocacy organization, because almost every unusual wine type in California seems to have one. Zinfandel's is called ZAP, which stands for Zinfandel Advocates and Producers (www.zinfandel.org). To its credit, ZAP, founded in 1991, was probably the original such group. Each January, ZAP organizes a huge Zinfandel wine-tasting event in San Francisco, drawing thousands of fans.

The Spectrum of Zin Styles

Although Zinfandel is truly delicious and compelling, its following isn't huge. Some winemakers theorize that what holds Zinfandel back from broader sales is that when you buy a bottle, you can't be sure which style you're going to get. That's because Zinfandel wines cover a range of styles, from lean and relatively restrained to rich and opulent and high in alcohol, resembling Portugal's Port wines. (*Port* is an alcohol-added dessert wine; we mention California's Port-style wines in Chapter 11.)

Many factors contribute to this diversity of style, including the usual suspects — winemaking techniques and climate differences in the vineyards — as well as Zinfandel's special issue of vine age. The old vineyards produce small crops of flavorful, concentrated grapes, so Zinfandels made from old vines taste more concentrated and less fruity than other Zins.

The Zinfandel grapevine has a few built-in issues that winemakers must deal with, each in his or her own way, and their methods can affect the style of the wine. These issues include the following:

- ✓ **Susceptibility to rot:** Zinfandel bunches are compact and the berries are thin-skinned, setting the stage for rot. Fortunately, that's not a serious issue in California except in rainy autumns.

- ✓ **Uneven ripening:** A more critical issue is that some berries on a bunch get nice and ripe while others remain unripe and some are overripe. Without careful vineyard management, the wine can have unripe flavors and overripe flavors at the same time.

- ✓ **Shrivelling:** After Zinfandel berries ripen, they quickly shrivel and lose their acidity, which results in huge, blousy (sloppy and unkempt) wines with overripe, jammy fruit flavors.

Wine lovers used to speak of *claret-style* Zins, which were leaner, trimmer, dry wines somewhat in the style of Cabernet Sauvignon. (*Claret* is the term that the British traditionally use for Cabernet-dominant wines from Bordeaux, France.) Today, the wave of super-ripeness that has swept through California's red-grape vineyards has brought Zinfandel wines that are richer and fuller than ever, and few truly claret-style Zins exist. Nevertheless, some Zinfandel wines today are dry and are relatively trim and lean in style. Examples include Green and Red Vineyard, A. Rafanelli, Nalle, Frog's Leap, and The Terraces.

Many Zinfandel wines today are made from extremely ripe grapes and are therefore very ripe, sweet, and high in alcohol, containing more than 16 percent alcohol in many cases. Often these wines have Port-like flavors of sun-baked fruit and raisins. Wine literature sometimes refers to the most extreme wines in this style as *late harvest* Zins.

And many Zins occupy the middle ground: They're medium- to full-bodied wines that have perceptible sweetness but technically qualify as dry, with firm tannin and exuberant but not excessive fruity flavor.

In choosing a Zinfandel, pay particular attention to the alcohol level that's listed on the label. The higher the alcohol, the higher the odds that the wine will be sweet, jammy, and powerfully rich. That's not our cup of tea, but it might be just what you're looking for — and many Zin fanatics will agree with you.

Zinfandel Country

Zinfandel grows all over California, and the style of the wine varies according to the wine region and the specific location of the vineyard, as well as the age of the vines for any particular wine. In general, the following holds true:

- ✔ The cooler areas, which include many of the coastal counties, tend to produce spicier, leaner, and more refined wines.
- ✔ The interior regions tend to make richer, lustier, more powerful Zinfandel wines.

The Central Valley is responsible for a big chunk of Zinfandel production, but most of those grapes make White Zinfandel or go into inexpensive blended red wines. Other areas — specific AVAs and certain counties of the state — specialize in growing the grapes for red Zinfandel wines, or they boast specific wineries that are renowned as Zinfandel specialists.

Specialist Zinfandel wineries often source grapes from vineyards in several different AVAs and make several vineyard-specific wines. One example is Ravenswood, which makes five Zins under single-county appellations (Sonoma, Napa, Lodi, Amador, and Mendocino) and eight single-vineyard Zinfandels in addition to producing a large quantity of "Vintners Blend" Zinfandel under the California state appellation. Another example is Rosenblum Cellars, which makes a California-appellation "Vintner's Cuvée" Zinfandel and 18 or more additional Zins under specific AVAs, reserve labels, or single-vineyard-designated labels.

Here are some specifics about Zinfandel acreage around the state:

- ✔ The counties that comprise the Central Valley region grow more than 60 percent of all the Zinfandel in California, much of it destined for White Zinfandel. San Joaquin County alone accounts for about 40 percent of all Zinfandel acreage, but included in that county is part of the Lodi AVA, which does produce a large amount of red varietal Zinfandel wine.

- ✔ Sonoma County (which includes the key Dry Creek Valley AVA), with about 10 percent of all Zinfandel acreage, is the leading coastal county for Zinfandel.

- ✔ San Luis Obispo County, which includes the Paso Robles AVA, accounts for about 4 percent of Zinfandel acreage.

- ✔ Napa, Mendocino, and Amador Counties, all known for their Zinfandels, each grow about 3.5 percent of the state's Zin crop. Amador is a warmer interior area.

Visiting Northern Sonoma

Northern Sonoma is downright vast, with more than one major hub and attractions branched off in virtually every direction. That said, each area does have its own distinct flavor and instant access to specific attractions, so read up and decide what works best for you.

The Russian River Valley wine region is home to the funky riverside town of Guerneville. Though it's a good 20 minutes west of the Highway 101 thoroughfare, it does offer relatively easy access to the region's wineries. However, this town of around 2,600 residents, which was explored by the Russians in the 1840s and became one of the busiest logging centers in the West in the 1880s, is now known for its casual cabin-like resort communities flanking the Russian River and its summertime popularity among the gay and lesbian community. Here, you can spend your days idling on inner tubes, canoeing, car camping, or hiking redwood trails. Accommodations tend to be old and funky, like the town and homes around it, but the relaxed summertime feel is pure old-fashioned fun. That said, if it's the ultimate wine country vibe you're after, you won't find it here, except for at the town's eastern entrance, which is home to Korbel Champagne Cellars.

North of the Russian River area is the greatly heralded wine region known as Dry Creek as well as the undisputed hub of Northern Sonoma wine country, the town of Healdsburg. A mere 30- to 45-minute drive from either Napa or Sonoma Valley (and 1½ hours from San Francisco) and just north of burgeoning suburban Santa Rosa, its centerpiece historic square, which has been the heart of the town since its inception in 1857, captures the quaint shopping and dining experiences of downtown Sonoma's plaza (only better in both areas). Its rural roads and country B&Bs have the same genuine backcountry appeal as its surrounding wineries, while the abundance of Victorian architecture gives it a bit of old-world charm. Adding to its intrinsic allure, Healdsburg is surrounded by all the premier viticultural areas, allowing easy access to Russian River, Dry Creek, Alexander Valley, and Chalk Hill.

Recently, Healdsburg has become a bona fide alternative to Napa Valley highlife due to the arrival of a few very sophisticated restaurants and hotels. (The wine scene here was already exceptional.) One hot culinary outpost is the Zinfandel-themed Zin Restaurant & Wine Bar (344 Center St., Healdsburg; phone 707-473-0946; Web site www.zinrestaurant.com). Locals and visitors flock to this downtown eatery, where talented, innovative young chefs fuse big-city ideas with country-comfort dishes. The seasonal menu does the wine country norm, pairing a top-notch wine list with local foods and produce. You'll have plenty of choices when you get to their exceptional Dry Creek, Russian River, and Alexander Valley focused wine list (15 to 17 picks by the glass, around 100 by the bottle).

Northern Sonoma doesn't have one major convention and visitors bureau representing the entire region. Fortunately, if you visit www.sonoma.com, it will direct you to the various visitors bureaus. Or if you roll into downtown Healdsburg off of Highway 101, you'll pass the Healdsburg Chamber of Commerce and Visitors Bureau (217 Healdsburg Ave., Healdsburg; phone 800-648-9922 or 707-433-6935; Web site www.healdsburg.com).

Frommer's Portable California Wine Country, 5th Edition, by Erika Lenkert; Copyright 2006 Wiley Publishing, Inc.; Reprinted with permission of John Wiley & Sons, Inc.

The Dry Creek Valley AVA in Northern Sonoma is a major region for Zinfandel, known for making fine Zins that are firm and structured. Other key Sonoma County AVAs for Zinfandel include Russian River Valley, Alexander Valley, and Sonoma Valley. Generally speaking, these areas make spicy Zinfandels with black pepper, blackberry, and black cherry aromas and flavors.

To find out about the characteristics of Zinfandels from various growing areas, consult the *Resource Guide to Zinfandel* available at www.zinfandel.org from ZAP. The descriptions tend to focus on the aromas and flavors of the wines from each area instead of describing the wines' weight, structure, alcohol levels, and so forth, but the array of descriptors will make your mouth water and perhaps inspire you to begin some firsthand research.

Recommended Zinfandel Wines

Our recommendations here are for red Zinfandels only (see Chapter 11 for White Zin). Most of the Zins fall into the two lower-priced categories: moderate (under $20 in wine shops) and moderate-plus ($20 to $50); just a couple of wines are high-end (over $50). We don't include wines that are available only in California, although some of our recommended wines do have limited availability nationally. We also recommend 20 top-value (under $15) red Zinfandels in a sidebar.

Moderately Priced Red Zinfandels, under $20

Alexander Valley Vineyards, "Sin Zin" (Alexander Valley)

Bonny Doon, "Cardinal Zin" (California)

Cline Cellars, "Ancient Vines" (Contra Costa County)

Dry Creek Vineyard, "Heritage Clone" (Dry Creek Valley)

Fife Vineyards, "Mendocino Uplands" (California)

Francis Coppola, "Diamond Series" (California) and "Director's Cut" (Dry Creek Valley)

Fritz Winery (Dry Creek Valley)

Gravity Hills, "Tumbling Tractor" (Paso Robles)

Kunin Wines, "Westside" (Paso Robles)

Lake Sonoma Winery (Dry Creek Valley)

Lolonis Winery (Redwood Valley, Mendocino)

Marietta Cellars (Sonoma County)

Mia's Playground, "Old Vines" (Dry Creek Valley)

Peachy Canyon Winery, "Westside" (Paso Robles)

Pezzi King Vineyards, "Old Vines" (Dry Creek Valley)

Quivira Vineyards (Dry Creek Valley)

Renwood Vineyards, "Old Vine" (Amador County)

Rodney Strong Vineyards, "Knotty Vines" (Sonoma County)

Sausal Winery, "Family Old Vines" (Alexander Valley)

Scott Harvey, "Mountain Selection"; "Old Vine" (Amador)

Sebastiani Vineyards (Dry Creek Valley)

Seghesio Family Estates (Sonoma County)

Starry Night (Lodi)

Trentadue Winery (Sonoma County)

Wente Vineyards, "Smith Bench Reserve" (Livermore Valley)

Moderate-Plus Red Zinfandels, $20–$50

Carol Shelton Wines, "Wild Thing" (Mendocino); "Monga," Lopez Vineyard (Cucamonga Valley); "Karma" (Russian River Valley); "Rocky Reserve," Rockpile Vineyard (Rockpile)

Chateau Montelena, Estate (Napa Valley)

Cline Cellars, Live Oak and Big Break Vineyards (Contra Costa County)

Dashe Cellars (Dry Creek Valley)

De Loach, "OFS" and "Forgotten Vines" (Russian River Valley)

Dry Creek Vineyard, "Old Vines" (Dry Creek Valley)

Eberle, Steinbeck/Wine Bush Vineyards (Paso Robles)

Edmeades, all single-vineyard Zins (Mendocino County)

Elyse Winery, Korte Ranch and Morisoli Vineyard (Napa Valley)

Frank Family Vineyards (Napa Valley)

Frog's Leap Winery (Napa Valley)

Gravity Hills, "The Sherpa" (Paso Robles)

Green & Red Vineyard, "Chiles Mill Estate" (Napa Valley)

Grgich Hills Cellar (Napa Valley)

Hartford Family Wines (Russian River Valley)

Hendry Winery, Hendry Vineyard, "Block 7" (Napa Valley)

Kenwood Vineyards, Jack London Vineyard and "Reserve" (Sonoma Valley)

Michael-David Winery, "Earthquake" (Lodi)

Mill Creek Vineyards (Dry Creek Valley)

Nalle Winery (Dry Creek Valley)

Neyers Vineyards, "High Valley" and Tofanelli Vineyard (Napa Valley); Pato Vineyard (Contra Costa County)

Papapietro Perry Winery (Russian River Valley)

Peter Franus Wines, Brandlin Ranch (Mt. Veeder) and "Napa Valley" (Napa Valley)

Peachy Canyon Winery, Snow Vineyard (Paso Robles)

Preston of Dry Creek, "Old Vines" (Dry Creek Valley)

Quivira Vineyards, Wine Creek Ranch and Anderson Ranch (Dry Creek Valley)

A. Rafanelli (Dry Creek Valley)

Ravenswood, Old Hill (Sonoma Valley) and all other single-vineyard Zinfandels

Renwood Vineyards, "Grandpère," "Grandmère," and "Fiddletown Vineyards" (Amador County)

Ridge Vineyards, Lytton Springs and East Bench (Dry Creek Valley); Ponzo Vineyard (Russian River Valley); Pagani Ranch (Sonoma Valley); York Creek (Napa Valley); Dusi Ranch (Paso Robles); "Three Valleys" (Sonoma County)

Robert Biale Vineyards, Aldo's Vineyard, "Napa Ranches," Old Cranes, Grande Vineyard, Black Chicken (Napa Valley); Monte Rosso Vineyard (Sonoma Valley)

Rosenblum Cellars, Monte Rosso Vineyard and "Maggie's Reserve" (Sonoma Valley) plus all other single-vineyard Zins

Rubicon Estate, "Edizione Pennino" (Napa Valley)

Saucelito Canyon (Arroyo Grande)

Sausal Winery, "Private Reserve" and "Century Vine" (Alexander Valley)

Seghesio Family Estates, Home Ranch and Lorenzo Vineyard (Alexander Valley); Cortina and Rockpile (Rockpile); "Old Vines" (Sonoma County)

St. Francis Winery, "Old Vines" (Sonoma County)

Storybook Mountain, "Mayacamas Range" (Napa Valley)

The Terraces Winery (Napa Valley)

Trentadue Winery, "La Storia" (Alexander Valley)

Turley Wine Cellars, Dusi Ranch, "Juvenile" and "Old Vines" (California); Duarte Vineyard (Contra Costa County)

High-End Red Zinfandels, over $50

Martinelli Winery, Giuseppe & Luisa and Jackass Vineyards (Russian River Valley)

Williams Selyem Winery, Baciagalupi, Feeney, and Forchini Vineyards (Russian River Valley)

Twenty top-value Zinfandels

These 20 red Zinfandels, all under $15, are our picks as top values:

✔ Alexander Valley Vineyards, "Temptation" (Alexander Valley)

✔ Bogle Vineyards, Old Vines (California)

✔ Cartlidge & Browne (California)

✔ Cline Cellars (Sonoma County)

✔ De Loach (Russian River Valley)

✔ Gnarly Head, Old Vine (Lodi)

✔ Jessie's Grove, "Earth, Zin & Fire" (Lodi)

✔ Kendall-Jackson, Vintner's Reserve (California)

✔ Kenwood Vineyards (Sonoma County)

✔ Peachy Canyon, "Incredible Red" (Paso Robles)

✔ Pedroncelli Winery, "Mother Clone" (Dry Creek Valley)

✔ Pepperwood Grove, Old Vine (California)

✔ Rabbit Ridge Vineyards (Paso Robles)

✔ Rancho Zabaco, "Dancing Bull" (California)

✔ Ravenswood "Vintners Blend" (California)

✔ Renwood Winery, "Sierra Series" (Sierra Foothills)

✔ Robert Mondavi "Private Selection" (Central Coast)

✔ Shenandoah Vineyards, "Special Reserve" (Amador County)

✔ Sobon Estate, "Rocky Top" and "Old Vine" (Amador County)

✔ Terra d'Oro (Amador County, Sierra Foothills); *formerly Monteviña*

The four Rs of Zinfandel

Four wineries are head of the class in red Zinfandel renown, and coincidentally, all their names begin with the letter *r*. Here's another thing all four have in common: Almost all their Zinfandels come from Sonoma County. Here are the wineries in alphabetical order:

✔ **A. Rafanelli:** Rafanelli's Winery is in Dry Creek Valley, and all David Rafanelli's Zinfandels — intensely flavored with great balance — are textbook examples of Dry Creek Zinfandel at its best.

✔ **Ravenswood:** Joel Peterson of Ravenswood, whose winery is in Sonoma Valley, makes about eight single-vineyard Zins, all but one from vineyards in Sonoma.

✔ **Ridge Vineyards:** Paul Draper of Ridge Vineyards makes one of the most famous Zinfandel-based wines of all, Geyserville. (Technically it can't be called Zinfandel because it's a blend of what grows in the Geyserville vineyard — about 70 percent Zinfandel along with Carignane, Petite Sirah, and Mataro/Mourvedre.) Apart from Geyserville, Ridge also makes about seven wines actually labeled as Zinfandel.

✔ **Rosenblum Cellars:** Kent Rosenblum, a former veterinarian, makes about 19 single-vineyard Zinfandels from all over California in any given vintage, but his best Zins come from Sonoma.

Part III
More Reds, Whites, Pinks, and Bubblies

"We're a boutique winery. We produce several single-vineyard Merlots and Cabs as well as a highly regarded glass cleaner."

In this part...

1 f you enjoy a change of pace now and then, or if you like to be the first in your crowd to taste what's new and different, the dozens of types of wines that we profile in this part are right up your alley. They include varietal white wines such as Pinot Grigio/Pinot Gris (which is unusual for California, at least), Viognier, Pinot Blanc, Chenin Blanc, Riesling, Gewurztraminer, and more, as well as blended California white wines from the likes of Marsanne, Roussanne, and other grapes. The red wines we cover include Syrah, Petite Sirah, Cabernet Franc, Tempranillo, all sorts of "Cal-Ital" wines from Italian grape varieties, and Rhône-style blends, among other wines. And that's just in the first two chapters!

Later in this part, you can read about California's world-class sparkling wines, its new dry rosé wines, its wildly popular sweet pink wines such as White Zinfandel, and its rich and exotic sweet dessert wines.

Chapter 9

Pinot Grigio, Rhône-Style Whites, and Other California Whites

● ●

In This Chapter

▶ Inspiration from Italy and France

▶ Viognier's stealth popularity

▶ Chenin Blanc, Pinot Blanc, Riesling, and Gewurztraminer

● ●

*F*or as long as we can remember, winemakers in California have talked about which white wine could have the potential to rival Chardonnay as a hugely popular choice, apart from Sauvignon Blanc. They're still speculating. But now a new prospect is on the horizon: the Pinot Gris grape, which makes varietal wines called Pinot Gris or, more frequently in California, Pinot Grigio. Of course, whether that wine will become a real star is up to wine drinkers. In this chapter, we tell you what to expect when you reach for a California Pinot Grigio/Gris.

Every other white grape in California is, frankly, an also-ran — but that doesn't mean that your choices of California white wines are nil. In most markets, you can find delicious Viognier wines, and with a bit of effort, you can try a Marsanne or Roussanne — all three being white varieties from France's Rhône Valley. And we have a few personal favorites among California's Chenin Blanc, Riesling, Pinot Blanc, and Gewurztraminer wines that we're eager to name. Join us as we explore the exotic side of California white wines.

Here a Grigio, There a Gris

The Pinot Gris grape came into existence as a mutation of the red Pinot Noir grape (Chapter 7 has details of California Pinot Noirs). It grows all over the world — in France, Italy, Germany, Austria, and several Eastern European countries, as well as many New World wine regions. Its white wines vary greatly in style, depending on the region of production and the style the winemaker is aiming for.

According to expert consensus, the Alsace region of France makes the world's best Pinot Gris wines; however, the northeastern regions of Italy make the world's most popular wines from this grape, and these are called Pinot Grigio (*grigio* means "gray" in Italian, and *gris* means the same in French). The grape has other names in Germany, Hungary, and other countries.

The grape's name is "gray Pinot" because the grape skins are closer in color to those of black (red) grapes than to the skins of most white grapes.

In America, both names — Pinot Gris and Pinot Grigio — are in use. In Oregon, where this grape is the state's leading white grape variety, Pinot Gris is invariably the name. In California, Pinot Grigio is more common. (We use either term for the wine, depending on the name the winery uses, but we use Pinot Gris as the grape name.)

The California face of Italy's leading white

Most wine drinkers in America have heard of Pinot Grigio because Pinot Grigio from Italy is the number one type of imported white wine in the U.S. Because of the popularity of the Italian version, Pinot Grigio in general — including both imported and domestic wines, but mainly imported — is the number two best-selling type of white wine in the U.S., after Chardonnay.

Given the name recognition of Pinot Grigio and the huge success of Italian Pinot Grigio wines, most California winemakers naturally choose that name for their wines made from the Pinot Gris grape. The success of Italy's Pinot Grigios, in fact, is probably the inspiration for the dramatic increase in Pinot Gris vineyards across California: Since 1999, the state's acreage of Pinot Gris vines has more than quadrupled.

What's dramatic about Pinot Gris in California today is not the quantity of vineyards or wine that exists but how fast that quantity is growing. Pinot Gris actually ranks only fifth among white wine grapes in California, after Chardonnay, French Colombard (used for inexpensive wines and for blending), Sauvignon Blanc, and Chenin Blanc (which we cover later in this chapter). Because the acreage of Chenin Blanc is static and that of Pinot Gris has grown at an average rate of 12 percent per year for the past five years, Pinot Gris is poised to overtake Chenin Blanc in the number four slot very soon. In comparison to Sauvignon Blanc, California's third most planted white variety (and second most important grape for varietal wine), only 60 percent as much Pinot Gris acreage exists — but Pinot Gris is increasing in acreage at a much faster pace than Sauvignon Blanc is. No wonder, then, that Pinot Gris is the rising star of California white wine.

Because California's commitment to growing Pinot Gris is so recent, a track record regarding which regions are most suited to this grape doesn't exist. Currently, Pinot Gris is growing mainly in the following areas:

- **The Central Valley:** Approximately half of all the state's acreage is in the warm, interior counties of Sacramento, San Joaquin, Stanislaus, Merced, Madera, Fresno, and Tulare. This is also where the largest increase in Pinot Gris plantings has occurred.

- **The Central Coast:** Approximately another quarter of the state's plantings are in the cool Central Coast area.

- **The North Coast:** This area has less than 10 percent of the state acreage, with more than half that amount in Sonoma County.

Warm climates aren't ideal for growing Pinot Gris because the grape's acidity can drop too far, resulting in heavy wines that aren't refreshing. However, the large-scale vineyards of the warm Central Valley can grow grapes more economically than other vineyard areas, and low price is key for wines that hope to compete with Italy's inexpensive Pinot Grigios. Most of the Pinot Grigio wines from these warm areas carry the simple California appellation. More distinctive Pinot Grigio/Gris wines carry appellations such as Napa Valley, Russian River Valley, or Sonoma County.

The taste of California Pinot Grigio/Gris

Theoretically, the name Pinot Gris suggests a wine made in the richer style of Alsace's Pinot Gris wines, and the name Pinot Grigio suggests a wine made in the lighter-bodied, less flavorful style of Italian Pinot Grigio wines. But in practice, this distinction doesn't always hold true. When you buy a bottle of California Pinot Gris or Pinot Grigio, you can't be sure from the name alone which style the wine will be.

Twelve top-value Pinot Grigio/Gris wines

These 12 Pinot Grigios/Gris, all under $12 and all with a California AVA, are consistently reliable, and they're our picks as top values for the money:

- ✔ Barefoot Cellars Pinot Grigio
- ✔ Estancia Pinot Grigio
- ✔ Fetzer Vineyards Pinot Grigio, "Valley Oaks"
- ✔ Francis Coppola "Bianco" Pinot Grigio
- ✔ McManis Family Vineyards Pinot Grigio
- ✔ Meridian Pinot Grigio
- ✔ Pepi Pinot Grigio
- ✔ Stone Cellars by Beringer Pinot Grigio
- ✔ Terra d'Oro (formerly Monteviña) Pinot Grigio
- ✔ Turning Leaf "Reserve" Pinot Grigio
- ✔ White Truck Pinot Grigio
- ✔ Woodbridge Pinot Grigio

Generally speaking, the lower the price of a California Pinot Grigio/Gris, the more likely it is to fall into the lighter style.

Lighter style

The lighter style — the Pinot Grigio style, whatever the wine's name — is the dominant style in California. Most of the Pinot Grigio/Gris wines that carry the statewide California appellation are in this style.

These wines are medium-bodied and fairly pale in color, and they have no smoky or toasty aromas and flavors because the winemakers use no oak in producing the wine. Although Italian Pinot Grigios are usually dry and very crisp, the California versions tend to be fairly soft with a slightly rich texture, and they generally aren't bone dry. The aromas and flavors of these wines are fruitier than you find in most Italian versions, but they usually don't suggest any particular fruit, except perhaps a very vague apple, pear, or lemon note. In some wines, the aromas are neutral — they smell mainly like wine.

Some winemakers use oak chips in their inexpensive Pinot Grigio wines to give a slight vanilla or confectionery note to the wine. And sometimes the wine feels a little prickly on your tongue because the winemakers trap a slight amount of carbon dioxide inside. But generally, the wines are fairly soft, ever-so-slightly sweet, easy-to-drink whites that go well with food because they don't have a lot of flavor that might compete with the food.

Richer style

The richer style of wine — the Pinot Gris style, whatever the wine is actually called — is fuller in body and richer in texture. It's more substantial and more flavorful than the lighter style. The wines' aromas and flavors can include apple, peach, orange, or pear, and the flavors and scents are easier to detect than in wines of the lighter style. The wines generally don't have any smoky, toasty, or spicy flavors from oak. In sweetness, these wines can be dry or slightly off-dry. Ferrari-Carano Pinot Grigio and J Wine Company Pinot Gris, both from Russian River Valley, are examples of this richer style.

Recommended California Pinot Grigio/Gris wines

We list our recommended California Pinot Grigio/Gris wines alphabetically in two price categories, moderately priced ($12 to $20) and moderate-plus ($20 to $30). After the name of each wine, we identify the American Viticultural Area (AVA) from which the grapes were sourced. We also have a sidebar titled "Twelve top-value Pinot Grigio/Gris wines" that names wines under $12, all of them very good buys.

Moderately Priced Pinot Grigio/ Gris, $12–$20

Balletto Pinot Gris (Sonoma Coast)

Cosentino Pinot Grigio, Stewart Vineyard (Solano County)

Gallo Family Vineyards Pinot Gris, "Sonoma Reserve" (Sonoma County)

Ferrari-Carano Pinot Grigio (Russian River Valley)

"J" Vineyards Pinot Gris (Russian River Valley)

Jacuzzi Family Vineyard Pinot Grigio (Sonoma Coast)

La Famiglia di Robert Mondavi Pinot Grigio (California)

Luna Vineyards Pinot Grigio (Napa Valley)

Martin & Weyrich Pinot Grigio (Central Coast)

Palmina Pinot Grigio, Alisos Vineyard (Santa Barbara County)

Taz Winery Pinot Gris (Santa Barbara County)

Moderate-Plus Pinot Grigio/Gris, $20–$30

Inman Family Pinot Gris, Olivet Grange Vineyard (Russian River Valley)

Long Vineyards Pinot Grigio, Laird Vineyard (Carneros)

Robert Sinskey Pinot Gris "Los Carneros" (Carneros)

Terlato Family Vineyards Pinot Grigio (Russian River Valley)

Viognier comes into its own

Viognier's production was once limited to a small area in the northern Rhône Valley of France, but in the past 20 years, it has increased significantly not only in France but also in California and elsewhere. Now Viognier wine is well enough known, and respected enough, that it commands its own category in many wine judgings instead of being grouped in the "other whites" category. Viognier's California acreage is small, however: less than one-third that of Pinot Gris and less than 3 percent that of Chardonnay. Because Viognier wine is so distinctive, you can often find Viognier wines on wine lists of top-quality restaurants.

As small as Viognier is in production (it grew on 2,773 acres statewide in 2007), it eclipses Roussanne, Grenache Blanc, and Marsanne, which claimed only 268, 111, and 84 acres respectively that year.

White Wines from Rhône Varieties

Just as some California winemakers are crazy about red wines made from grape varieties native to France's Rhône Valley (read about these reds in Chapter 10), white wines inspired by the same French region have a special following among winemakers and wine lovers. Sometimes these wines are varietal wines, made from a dominant Rhône Valley grape variety, and sometimes they're blends of several varieties.

The Rhone Rangers group, the promotional body for both white and red American wines made from Rhône Valley varieties, lists ten white grape varieties that grow in America, but six of them have fewer than 50 acres of vines in California and are definitely inconsequential at this point. (Just for the record, these varieties are Bourboulenc, Clairette Blanc, Picardin, Picpoul, Ugni Blanc, and the finest variety of Muscat, known as Muscat Blanc à Petits Grains, which makes sweet wines.) The four more important white Rhône Valley varieties are

- ✓ Viognier (pronounced vee-oh-nyay)
- ✓ Roussanne
- ✓ Marsanne
- ✓ Grenache Blanc

These grapes make delicious and unusual wines from California that are real changes of pace from Chardonnay, Sauvignon Blanc, and Pinot Grigio/Gris.

The four grape varieties differ somewhat in the regions in which they grow. More than half of California's Viognier vineyards are situated in warm interior areas; however, cool coastal areas such as Monterey, Santa Barbara, Sonoma, Mendocino, and Napa Counties are also key players, accounting for almost one-third of Viognier vineyards. Grenache Blanc grows mainly in warm interior counties. Both Roussanne and Marsanne grow mainly in coastal regions; Monterey alone claims more than 25 percent of the state's acreage of Roussanne.

The taste of white Rhône varietals and blends

Among the big four Rhône whites, the grape variety whose wine is the most different from the others in taste is Viognier. Writers frequently describe Viognier wines as "exotic." This white grape is rich in aroma and flavor, particularly floral notes and fruity notes such as apricot and peach, along with tropical fruit, apple, and (depending on where it grows) an earthy mineral note.

Viognier makes fairly full-bodied white wines that are soft in texture because their acidity is low, but they're high in alcohol. Generally, these wines are not oaky. Some producers do use oak in making the wine, but the oaked wines generally don't taste particularly smoky or toasty from the oak.

Here's how the other white Rhône varietal wines stack up:

- **Grenache Blanc:** Grenache Blanc is similar to Viognier in that it's a high-alcohol, full-bodied wine, but its aromas and flavors, generally described as green apple, are far less pronounced and exotic than Viognier's.

- **Marsanne:** This is a full-bodied wine that can have complex, delicate aromas and flavors of citrus fruits and flowers, but it's often simple instead.

- **Roussanne:** Roussanne wines have aromas and flavors that suggest lemon peel, ripe pear, or mineral notes. They're full-bodied and high in alcohol but also high in acidity. Some Roussanne wines are oaked, and some have noticeable sweetness.

Blends of Marsanne and Roussanne in nearly equal proportions are common in the Northern Rhône Valley, and such blends exist in California as well. In California, however, blends often combine Viognier with these two varieties, making a more flavorful wine. Grenache Blanc also figures in some white blended Rhône-style wines.

California white Rhône wines to try

More than half of all California white Rhône wines are Viogniers. We therefore give Viogniers their own listings, followed by lists of other recommended white Rhône wines in three price categories.

Moderately Priced Viogniers, $10–$20

Beringer Vineyards (Napa Valley)
Bonterra Vineyards (Mendocino County)
Bridlewood Winery "Reserve" (Central Coast)
Calera (Central Coast)
Clay Station (Lodi, Central Valley)
Cline Cellars (Sonoma County)
Clos LaChance (Central Coast)
Copain (Mendocino County)
Eberle Winery, Mill Road Vineyard (Paso Robles)
EXP "Toasted Head" (Dunnigan Hills, Yolo County)
Fess Parker (Santa Barbara County)
Holly's Hill Vineyards (El Dorado, Sierra Foothills)
McManis Family Vineyards (California)
Michael David Winery, "Incognito" (Lodi, Central Valley)
Pepperwood Grove (California)
Renwood, "Sierra Series" (Lodi)
Rosenblum Cellars, 'Kathy's Cuvée' (California)
Sobon Estate (Amador County)
Wild Horse Winery (Central Coast)
Zaca Mesa (Santa Ynez Valley)

Moderate-Plus Viogniers, $20–$30

Alban Vineyards (Central Coast)
Arrowood, Saralee Vineyard (Russian River Valley)
Calera, "Estate" (Mt. Harlan, San Benito County)
Cold Heaven, Sanford & Benedict Vineyard (Sta. Rita Hills)
Consilience (Santa Barbara County)
Domaine de La Terre Rouge (Shenandoah Valley, Sierra Foothills)
Graff Family Vineyards (Chalone, Monterey County)
Iron Horse Vineyard, "T-Bar-T Cuvée" (Alexander Valley)
Miner Family Vineyards, Simpson Vineyard (California)
Qupé, Ibarra-Young Vineyard (Central Coast)
Stags' Leap Winery (Napa Valley)
Turnbull Cellars (Oakville, Napa Valley)
Vinum Cellars, Vio Vista Vineyard (San Benito County)
Voss Vineyards (Carneros, Napa Valley)
Wattle Creek (Alexander Valley)
Westerly Vineyards (Santa Ynez Valley)

High-End Viogniers, $30–$50

Alban Vineyards, "Estate" (Edna Valley)
Bonaccorsi, Vogelzang Vineyard (Santa Ynez Valley)
Failla Wines, Alban Vineyard (Edna Valley)
Melville Winery, Verna's Vineyard (Santa Barbara County)
Paras Vineyard (Mount Veeder, Napa Valley)
Pride Mountain (Sonoma County)

The following lists indicate our recommended varietal Roussanne, Marsanne, and Grenache Blanc wines, as well as blended white Rhône-style wines.

Other Moderately Priced White Rhône Wines, $10–$20

Anglim Winery Roussanne, Fralich Vineyard (Paso Robles)

Beckmen Vineyards "Le Bec Blanc," Roussanne/Marsanne/Grenache Blanc, Purisma Mt. Vineyard (Santa Ynez Valley)

Bonterra Vineyards Roussanne (Mendocino County)

Cline Cellars Marsanne/Roussanne (Carneros)

Epiphany Cellars Grenache Blanc, Camp Four Vineyard (Santa Barbara County)

Truchard Vineyards Roussanne (Carneros, Napa Valley)

Other Moderate-Plus White Rhône Wines, $20–$30

Beckmen Vineyards Marsanne, Purisma Mountain Vineyard (Santa Ynez Valley)

Domaine de La Terre Rouge "Enigma," Marsanne/Viognier/ Roussanne (Sierra Foothills)

Edward Sellers "Blanc du Rhône," Marsanne/Viognier/Roussanne/ Grenache Blanc (Paso Robles)

Nadia "White," mainly Viognier/ Grenache Blanc, Santa Barbara Highlands Vineyard (Santa Barbara County)

Qupé Marsanne (Santa Ynez Valley)

Renard Roussanne (Santa Ynez Valley)

Robert Hall "Blanc de Robles," Roussanne/Grenache Blanc/Picpoul Blanc (Paso Robles)

Tablas Creek "Côte de Tablas Blanc," Viognier/Marsanne/Grenache Blanc/Roussanne (Paso Robles)

Zaca Mesa Roussanne (Santa Ynez Valley)

Other High-End White Rhône Wines, $30–$50

Elyse Winery "L'Ingenue" Naggiar Vineyard, mainly Roussanne/ Marsanne (Sierra Foothills)

Qupé Roussanne, Bien Nacido Vineyard (Santa Maria Valley)

Tablas Creek "Esprit de Beaucastel Blanc," Roussanne/Grenache Blanc/Picpoul Blanc (Paso Robles)

More California White Wines

The white wines that we group in this section — Riesling, Gewurztraminer, Chenin Blanc, and Pinot Blanc — are all made from world-famous grape varieties, but they're not among California's most important varietal wines. California does in fact make some excellent wines from these varieties, but these wines are specialties that some good producers focus on rather than wines to seek out from dozens of wineries.

Riesling, Gewurztraminer, Chenin Blanc, and Pinot Blanc not only vary a lot in style from one another but also vary within a variety from one producer to the next. Cookie-cutter they are not! To understand the style of a wine that you're considering buying, ask your wine merchant about the use of oak and the degree of sweetness in the wine. And have an adventuresome spirit — you could very well discover your new favorite wine.

Riesling

On the world stage, Riesling is much more renowned than Gewurztraminer, Chenin Blanc, or Pinot Blanc. It makes Germany's most prestigious wines and also excels in France's Alsace region, Austria, parts of Australia, parts of the U.S. (such as upstate New York), and elsewhere. It was once far more popular in California than it is now; its acreage slipped from 11,000 about 25 years ago to less than 2,900 today.

Riesling wines rely on the high acidity that cool climate regions endow to give them backbone and to balance any sweetness they might have. (Riesling can be completely dry but is often somewhat sweet.) Not many regions of California are naturally gifted in that regard. However, plantings of Riesling are increasing slowly but steadily again in California.

California's Riesling wines have fairly pronounced and complex aromas and flavors that can include fruity notes (citrus, peach, and apple) as well as floral and sometimes mineral accents. The wines are flavorful and usually not bone dry, even when they're labeled as *dry Riesling.* They're unoaked and go very well with food.

Our favorite producers, whose wines are on the dry side, include Smith Madrone, Trefethen, Stony Hill (Napa Valley); Greenwood Ridge (Mendocino Ridge); Handley (Mendocino County); Chateau St. Jean (Sonoma); Gainey (Santa Ynez Valley); and Claiborne & Churchill (Central Coast). Fetzer and Kendall-Jackson make best-selling Rieslings with more sweetness, and Ventana Vineyards produces an award-winning Riesling.

Gewurztraminer

Gewurztraminer is a niche grape. Its wines excel in the northern Italian province of Alto Adige, where it originated, and in the Alsace region of France. This grape makes exotic wines that will probably never be truly mainstream. Yet when they're good, they're very, very good — including a few California examples.

These wines are full-bodied and flavorful, with typical aromas and flavors of roses and lychee fruit; they're also fairly soft in texture and aren't oaky. Inexpensive versions are somewhat sweet, but the finest wines are dry. Look for Lazy Creek, Londer, Handley, Navarro (all from Anderson Valley); Gundlach Bundschu (Sonoma Valley); and Bargetto (Monterey).

Chenin Blanc

Chenin Blanc grows in France's Loire Valley, where it makes compelling dry and sweet wines under regional names, and it's also a staple in South Africa. In California, its acreage is substantial — similar to that of Pinot Gris and almost quadruple that of Riesling. But you don't see many varietal Chenin Blancs from the Golden State because the grape grows mainly in the warm interior at high crop levels (which strips the grapes of their character) to make inexpensive white wine blends. However, the Clarksburg AVA, in the northern part of the Central Valley, is emerging as a special area for varietal Chenin Blanc wines.

Good Chenin Blanc wines have an unusual combination of rich texture and high acidity, and they're not oaky. Their flavors are subtle, suggesting melon, grapefruit, or lanolin. Often the wines are slightly sweet, and they're usually medium-bodied. Recommended producers include Dry Creek Vineyards (Clarksburg); Chappellet (Napa Valley); and Husch (Mendocino).

Pinot Blanc

Pinot Blanc makes good varietal wines in Alsace and northern Italy, but it remains a fairly unsung variety. In California, most of the Pinot Blanc grapes go into sparkling wine (see Chapter 11), but a few wineries make varietal Pinot Blanc wines that we admire.

Neutral is a common aroma/flavor descriptor for Pinot Blanc wines, but that term doesn't do justice to the best wines, which have tart lemon or green apple notes and sometimes a mineral character. They can be fairly full-bodied and are sometimes slightly oaky. They're usually dry. Brands to look for include Laetitia (Arroyo Grande Valley); Robert Foley, Robert Sinskey (both from Napa); Chalone, Graff Family (both from Chalone AVA); and Alma Rosa (Sta. Rita Hills).

Chapter 10

Syrah, Petite Sirah, Other Varietal Reds, and Red Blends

In This Chapter

▶ The excitement surrounding Syrah today

▶ Petite Sirah's newfound legitimacy

▶ Blended wines inspired by France's Southern Rhône Valley

▶ Italian influences in California wine country

▶ Tempranillo, Cabernet Franc, Malbec, and other unusual treats

*W*hen we dine in a restaurant, our favorite section of the California wine list is *Other Reds*. Not that we have anything against Cabernet, Merlot, Pinot Noir, and Zinfandel. But the Other Reds arena is always full of discoveries and surprises, not to mention some welcome changes of pace from the standard red wines. This is the section where we find those Syrah-Grenache blends made in the style of France's Rhône Valley wines, those Cal-Ital wines from Italian grape varieties, and an occasional Tempranillo (Spain's number one red grape) or Cabernet Franc. And of course, this category also boasts Petite Sirah — a wine from a grape variety whose true identity for years was as mysterious as what happened to Tony Soprano when the television screen went black at the end of *The Sopranos'* six-season run.

This chapter is our Other Reds list. We hope that it brings you discoveries, surprises, and lots of great drinking!

California Syrah Comes of Age

If we could have plucked any one type of wine from the Other Reds category and given it a chapter of its own, it would be Syrah. Syrah is one of the world's most celebrated red grape varieties. It makes truly great wines in France's Rhône Valley (where the wines have place names such as Hermitage and Côte Rôtie), Australia (where it goes by the name of Shiraz), and elsewhere, as well as plenty of inexpensive wines for everyday drinking.

But in California wine circles, Syrah has been something of a fringe-dweller until fairly recently, and so we cover it here, with the Other Reds. Another reason for not giving Syrah its own spotlight is that the Syrah grape makes blended wines in California at least as much as it does varietal wines. We cover the blended wines in the section "California's Red Rhône-Style Blends," later in this chapter.

Number five in production but growing

In 2007, Syrah ranked fifth among red wine grapes in California in terms of the quantity harvested, trailing Cabernet Sauvignon, Zinfandel (much of which becomes pink wine, not red), Merlot, and Rubired (a grape variety that has dark juice, unlike most red grapes; winemakers use it to enhance the color of their red wines). About 40 percent more Syrah than Pinot Noir exists in California's vineyards, but Pinot Noir grapes, being in more demand, command more than triple the price per ton when wineries buy them from grape growers. Syrah production is growing, however. In 2007, California wineries crushed 25 percent more Syrah grapes than they did just five years earlier — and more than 200 times as much as they did in 1990!

One of the reasons interest in Syrah is growing, we believe, is the amazing success that Shiraz wines from Australia have had in the U.S. market. Back when the main role model for Syrah wines was the wines of the Northern Rhône Valley in France — which don't even carry the grape variety name — Syrah was a fairly unknown entity to wine drinkers in America. Australia's success changed all that. Even though most of the Australian versions are called Shiraz rather than Syrah, wine drinkers now have a reference point for Syrah.

It's impossible to know what portion of California's Syrah grape production ends up as varietal Syrah wine as opposed to becoming part of a blended wine with Grenache, Mourvedre, and other red grapes, as is the custom in the southern part of France's Rhône Valley. But we have to guess that varietal Syrah production is gaining because of the Aussie factor and the spinoff excitement surrounding Syrah wines from every imaginable wine-producing country, from Chile and Italy to New Zealand and Spain.

In California, likewise, Syrah is all over the place. The large Central Coast region was originally one of the key areas for Syrah production and today is still a hotbed for this variety. But many wineries in Napa Valley now make Syrah — as do even more wineries in Sonoma County. In fact, Joseph Phelps Vineyards in Napa Valley was a Syrah pioneer; it first made a varietal Syrah in the 1974 vintage.

Syrah versus Shiraz

The word *Shiraz* is simply a synonym for *Syrah*. In Australia, both the grape and the varietal wine made from it are known as Shiraz. The name is that of a city in Persia — today's Iran — where the grape was once thought to have originated; through genetic testing, experts now peg France as the origin of Syrah.

U.S. regulations recognize Shiraz as an alternate name for Syrah, and winemakers in this country are free to use either name. Because Australian Shiraz wines are extremely popular in America, many wineries choose that name for their wine, whereas other wineries use the more traditional name, Syrah. (We remember one winemaker from northern California telling us a few years ago that sales were sluggish for his Syrah, but when he changed the wine's name to Shiraz, sales suddenly took off.)

The name Shiraz on a California wine label often suggests a style of wine similar to that of the popular, inexpensive, mass-market Aussie Shirazes. These wines have a particular taste profile: They tend to be exuberantly fruity, suggesting berry fruit in particular, with soft texture and fairly little tannin. Although Australia's full-bodied, powerful Syrah wines are also called Shiraz, many wine drinkers associate the style of the less expensive wines with the name Shiraz.

We believe that the popularity of Australian Shiraz has created an opportunity for California Syrah, but some California winemakers see the situation differently. They believe the low prices of Aussie Shiraz — many selling for close to $10 a bottle — have undercut the market for inexpensive California Syrahs or Shirazes. California's varietal wines from the Syrah grape have tended to occupy the middle to upper price ranks.

The taste of California Syrah

The taste of Syrah and Shiraz wines from California varies perhaps more than that of any other red California wine. And no wonder, when you consider the following facts:

- ✔ **Dual role models:** Not one but two iconic models of great Syrah wine exist outside of California: the wines of France's Northern Rhône Valley (concentrated, firm wines that are built for aging, with complex aromas and flavors of dark fruits, black pepper, smoked meat, leather, and sometimes a vegetal note) and the elite Shiraz wines of Australia (powerful, densely textured, and opulent, with ripe dark-fruit flavors). Winemakers can model wines after either style.

- ✔ **Diversity of growing conditions:** Syrah grapevines are extremely adaptable to a range of climates and soil types; the grapes favor different styles of wine in different *terroirs*. (For info on the influence of growing conditions, see Chapter 3.)

- ✔ **Number of American Viticultural Areas (AVAs):** The Syrah grape grows in just about every region of California, from cool, coastal areas to warm, interior regions; different regions have potential for different styles of Syrah. (See the next section for some generalizations.)

- ✔ **Target markets:** The success of Australia's inexpensive Shirazes together with the renown of Australia's and France's high-end Syrah wines have established two separate price tiers for Syrah, each with a different taste profile in terms of readiness to drink and each with a different target customer.

But we can make certain generalizations about how Syrah wines from California taste. They're generally deep in color, dry to dryish, and fairly fruity, with what some winemakers describe as a "juicy" character to their fruitiness. (Exceptions are some wines from very warm parts of California that have a baked-fruit character rather than a juicy, fresh-fruit character.) Aromas and flavors generally include dark fruit, berries, and spice, and these flavors are rather pronounced: Syrah is a flavorful wine. Other aromas and flavors can include floral notes, coffee, chocolate, earthiness, and a smoky character.

California Syrahs tend to have fairly high acidity and yet can suggest roundness in your mouth compared to the leaner structure of Cabernet Sauvignon. Tannin is moderate to very high (in those wines that age in new oak barrels).

When California producers call their wine Shiraz, they're sometimes — but not always — communicating that the wine has a berry-fruity, flavorful, agreeable, low-tannin style similar to the inexpensive Australian wines that are so popular.

Compared to Merlot and Cabernet Sauvignon, California's Syrah wines are generally fruitier, spicier, and more succulent. Compared to Pinot Noirs, Syrahs are somewhat more tannic, are fleshier in texture, and perhaps have greater aging potential.

Today's hotbeds of Syrah and Shiraz

Is there a wine region in California that doesn't grow at least a little Syrah? Maybe not. The highly adaptable nature of the Syrah grape enables it to grow well in very cool climates (such as the Sonoma Coast and Anderson Valley), in moderately warm climates (such as Paso Robles), and also in very warm climates, such as the San Joaquin Valley.

In 2007, San Luis Obispo County, which includes the Paso Robles AVA, had the most acreage of Syrah vines in California, followed by San Joaquin County. Together, these two counties accounted for about 25 percent of California's Syrah acreage. Throw in the acreage in Madera, Sacramento, and Fresno counties (all warm, interior areas), and the tally totals more than half of the state's Syrah acreage. But the top-ten list also includes Sonoma, Monterey, Santa Barbara, Napa, and Mendocino counties, all of which are cool or include significant cool-climate portions. In fact, the excitement over Syrah is now so intense in several cool-climate AVAs that, were Pinot Noir not so hugely popular, growers might conceivably supplant their Pinot Noir vines with Syrah.

The concept of "cool-climate" Syrah already exists in Australia, where winemakers and marketing types use the phrase to differentiate the wines of certain growing regions from those of other regions. And many California winemakers have begun talking in these terms themselves (a few even name their wine "Cool Climate Syrah").

The precise definitions of "cool climate" and "warm climate" are debatable. In naming the regions that make Syrah in the cool-climate or warmer-climate style, we generalize, and exceptions do exist. Parts of Napa Valley, for example, are cool enough to make Syrah wines with flavor complexity and other cool-climate taste characteristics. Also, many Syrah wines are midway between the two styles.

Cool-climate California Syrah

We have often heard Syrah producers espouse the conviction that, contrary to much popular belief, the Syrah grape grows best in fairly cool climates. Today, some California winemakers are providing fodder for this argument by making fine Syrah wines from grapes that grow in western areas cooled by Pacific breezes and fog.

Twenty-two top-value Syrahs/Shirazes

These 22 Syrahs/Shirazes, all under $15, are consistently reliable, and they're our picks as top values for the money:

- Avila Vineyards Syrah (Santa Barbara)
- Beaulieu Vineyard Syrah and BV Coastal Estates Shiraz (California)
- Cline Cellars Syrah (California)
- Concannon Vineyard Syrah, Selected Vineyards and "Stampmaker's Red" (Central Coast)
- Cycles Gladiator Syrah (Central Coast)
- Domaine de la Terre Rouge Syrah, "Les Côtes de l'Ouest" (Sierra Foothills)
- Echelon Shiraz (Central Coast)
- Edna Valley Vineyard Syrah, Paragon Vineyard (Edna Valley)
- Estancia Shiraz, Lucia Range Ranches (Central Coast)
- Fetzer Vineyards Shiraz, Valley Oaks (California)
- Frey Vineyards Syrah, Organic (Mendocino)
- Hahn Estates Syrah (Monterey County)
- Hess Syrah (Mendocino/Monterey Counties)
- J. Lohr Estates Syrah, South Ridge (Paso Robles)
- Kendall-Jackson Syrah, Vintners Reserve (California)
- Lockwood Vineyards Syrah (Central Coast)
- Renwood Winery Syrah, Sierra Series (California)
- Robert Mondavi Syrah, Private Selection (Central Coast)
- Rosenblum Cellars Syrah, Vintners Cuvée (California)
- Sterling Vineyards Shiraz, Vintner's Collection (Monterey County)

Cool-climate Syrahs are higher in acid and firmer in tannin than Syrah wines from warmer climates and therefore tend to be tight in structure and ageworthy. They have complex aromas and flavors that run the gamut of the grape's repertoire, expressing bright, fresh notes of berry fruit, cracked black or white pepper, floral notes such as lilac or lavender, and gamey notes.

Regions of California that make cool-climate style Syrah wines include

- The Sta. Rita Hills and Santa Maria Valley in Santa Barbara County
- Northern Monterey County
- Sonoma Coast, Carneros, and Russian River Valley in Sonoma County
- Anderson Valley in Mendocino County

Producers committed to making this style of Syrah include Dehlinger, Failla, HdV, Jaffurs, JC Cellars, MacRostie, Melville, Novy Family Wines, The Ojai Vineyard, Peay, Qupé Wine Cellars, Radio-Coteau, and David Ramey.

Warmer-climate California Syrah

California Syrah has its origins in warmer climates, particularly the eastern part of Paso Robles. The rich, powerful style characteristic of warmer climates has been the state's most common style of Syrah, and this style has attracted many fans among both wine-makers and wine drinkers. Warmer-climate Syrahs are fuller-bodied than cool-climate Syrahs and slightly sweeter, with softer tannins and more velvety, fleshier texture; their aromas and flavors tend to express mainly very ripe, dark fruit and often toasty oak character, with only minor notes, if any, of spices or herbs.

Regions of California that produce Syrah in the warmer-climate style include

- Lodi
- Paso Robles
- Napa Valley (apart from Carneros)
- Alexander Valley
- Parts of Monterey

Those Syrah wines that carry only the state-designation, California, also usually hail from warmer, interior wine regions, but these wines are often less powerful and dense in texture than those of the regions we mention here.

Recommended Syrah wines

Although Paso Robles in San Luis Obispo might be considered the unofficial capital of Syrah country, we recommend excellent Syrah wines from every major region in the state — including Santa Barbara County, where Syrah has certainly been very successful, and the Sonoma Coast AVA, which is emerging as a key region for cool-climate Syrahs.

We list our recommended California Syrahs alphabetically in three price categories:

✔ **Moderately priced:** Under $20

✔ **Moderate-plus:** Between $20 and $50

✔ **High-end:** Mostly between $50 and $100 (three wines retail for over $100 in the high-end listing, and we give their approximate prices)

Don't miss our sidebar "Twenty-two top-value Syrahs/Shirazes" for a list of recommended California Syrahs that cost less than $15.

Moderately Priced Syrahs, under $20
Bishop's Peak, Talley (Edna Valley)
Bonterra Vineyards (Mendocino County)
Cline Cellars, "Los Carneros" (Carneros)
Jade Mountain (Lake County) and (Monterey County)
Melville Estate, "Verna's" (Sta. Rita Hills)
Michael and David Winery, "6th Sense" (Lodi)
Qupé (Central Coast)
Rabbit Ridge (Paso Robles)
Santa Barbara Winery (Santa Barbara County)
St. Francis Winery (Sonoma County)
Voss Vineyards (Napa Valley)
Westerly Vineyards (Santa Ynez Valley)

Moderate-Plus Syrahs, $20–$50
Alban Vineyards (Central Coast)
Ampelos Cellars, Gamma Ampelos Vineyard (Sta. Rita Hills)
Big Basin Vineyards, "Mandala" and "Rattlesnake Rock" (Santa Cruz Mountains)
Blue Rock Vineyards (Alexander Valley)
Brassfield Estate, Monte Sereno Vineyard (High Valley, North Coast)
Burgess Cellars (Napa Valley)

Copain Wines, Eaglepoint Ranch (Mendocino County)
Cuvaison (Carneros, Napa Valley)
Domaine Alfred, "Califa," Chamisal Vineyard (Edna Valley)
Domaine de la Terre Rouge, Sentinel Oak Vineyard (Shenandoah Valley, Sierra Foothills)
Edmunds St. John, Bassetti Vineyard (San Luis Obispo County) and Wylie-Fenaughty Vineyard (El Dorado County)
Failla, Phoenix Ranch (Napa Valley), Estate (Sonoma County), and Que Vineyard (Sonoma Coast)
Fess Parker, Rodney's Vineyard (Santa Barbara County)
Havens Wine Cellars (Napa Valley) and T block, Hudson Vineyard (Carneros)
Io, "Ryan Road" (Paso Robles) and "Upper Bench" (Santa Maria Valley)
Jade Mountain (Napa Valley)
Jaffurs Wine Cellars, Bien Nacido Vineyard (Santa Maria Valley) and Melville Vineyard (Sta. Rita Hills)
JC Cellars, Fess Parker Vineyard (Santa Barbara County)
Kendall-Jackson Highland Estates, Alisos Hills (Santa Barbara County)
Kenneth-Crawford, Lafond Vineyard (Sta. Rita Hills)
Kuleto Estate (Napa Valley)
Kunin Wines (Santa Barbara County)

Lafond Vineyard, SRH (Sta. Rita Hills) and Santa Ynez (Santa Ynez Valley)

Lagier Meredith (Mount Veeder, Napa Valley)

Longboard Vineyards, Russian River Valley and Dakine Vineyard (Russian River Valley)

MacRostie Winery, Wildcat Mountain Vineyard (Carneros, Sonoma)

Marimar Estate, Don Miguel Vineyard (Russian River Valley)

Miller Wine Works, Sage Canyon Vineyard (Napa Valley)

Neyers, Old Lakeville Road Vineyard (Sonoma Coast), Hudson Vineyard and "Cuvée d'Honneur" (Napa Valley)

Novy Family Wines (Napa Valley) and Christensen Family Vineyard (Russian River Valley)

Obsidian Ridge, Red Hills (Lake County)

The Ojai Vineyard, Melville Vineyard (Sta. Rita Hills) and Bien Nacido Vineyard (Santa Maria Valley)

Patianna Organic Vineyards, Fairbairn Ranch (Mendocino)

Qupé, Bien Nacido Vineyard and Bien Nacido "Hillside Select" (Santa Maria Valley)

Radio-Coteau, Las Colinas Vineyard (Sonoma Coast)

Renard, Peay Vineyard (Sonoma Coast)

Ridge Vineyards, "Lytton West" (Dry Creek Valley)

Rocca Family Vineyards (Yountville, Napa Valley)

Rosenblum Cellars, "Hillside" (Sonoma County)

Rusack Vineyards, Ballard Canyon Estate and Santa Barbara (Santa Barbara County)

Saracina Vineyards (Mendocino County)

Shadow Canyon Cellars (Santa Barbara County) and York Mountain (San Luis Obispo County)

Shannon Ridge (High Valley, Lake County)

Sonoma Coast Vineyards (Sonoma Coast)

Spencer-Roloson, La Herradura Vineyard (Napa Valley)

Stolpman Vineyards, Estate (Santa Ynez Valley)

Tallulah Wines, Bald Mountain Ranch (Mt. Veeder) and Sonoma Coast and Shake Ridge Ranch (Amador County)

Tablas Creek Vineyard (Paso Robles)

Truchard (Carneros, Napa Valley)

Turnbull Wine Cellars (Oakville, Napa Valley)

Viader Vineyards (Howell Mountain)

Vie Winery, Las Madres Vineyard (Carneros, Sonoma County)

High-End Syrahs, Mostly $50–$100

Araujo Estate, Eisele Vineyard (Napa Valley); *$135 and up*

Bonaccorsi, Bien Nacido Vineyard (Santa Maria Valley) and Larner Vineyard (Santa Ynez Valley) and Star Lane Vineyard (Santa Barbara County)

Dehlinger, Estate (Russian River Valley)

DuMol (Russian River Valley)

HdV (Carneros, Napa Valley)

Kongsgaard, Hudson Vineyard (Napa Valley); *$125 and up*

Pax Wine Cellars, Castelli-Knight Ranch and Walker Vine Hill Vineyard (Russian River Valley)

Peay Vineyards, La Bruma Estate (Sonoma Coast)

Ramey, Sonoma Coast and "Rodgers Creek" (Sonoma Coast)

Rubicon Estate, RC Reserve (Rutherford, Napa Valley)

Sean Thackery, "Orion Old Vines," Rossi Vineyard (St. Helena, Napa Valley); *over $100*

The Dark and Mysterious Petite Sirah

Everyone loves a good mystery — and over the past few decades, the Petite Sirah grape has provided just that for wine lovers, because speculation abounded over the precise origins of the grape. In this section, we cover Petite Sirah's history and popularity, and we discuss the flavor of the wine, key Petite Sirah regions, and our recommended wines.

The great identity search

Theories about Petite Sirah's identity were many. Was it actually a clone of Syrah, or was it related to Syrah, or was it something entirely different? Was it in fact one variety or a common name for three different varieties? Was it a California original?

The variety today known as Petite Sirah came to California from France in 1884. After the phylloxera louse decimated California's vineyards (the first time) in the 1890s, Petite Sirah became a popular variety to plant. During Prohibition (1920–1933), it was one of the grape varieties shipped from California's vineyards to home winemakers across the U.S. But historians believe that winemakers in those days used the name Petite Sirah for several different varieties.

In the 1970s, two renowned French ampelographers (grape researchers) identified Petite Sirah as the Durif grape; however, a highly respected professor from U.C. Davis, Harold Olmo, still believed that the name applied to three distinct varieties in California. In fact, some vineyards that at one time were said to contain Petite Sirah were later identified as Syrah vineyards.

Some of the confusion surrounding Petite Sirah's identity was due to the fact that many Petite Sirah vineyards in California are very old and, as was customary in the past, those vineyards contained other grape varieties in addition to Petite Sirah. Instead of blending *wines* from different varieties, winemakers used to plant their vineyards with various grapes and harvest them all together to make a wine that was actually a *field blend*.

Finally, in 1996, science solved the mystery. U.C. Davis professor Carole Meredith used DNA analysis to prove that Petite Sirah is Durif.

But what is *Durif?* Apart from its presence in California, the variety is an obscure one. It came into existence in France in 1880 through a cross pollination of two *Vitis vinifera* varieties, Peloursin (an old variety from the Rhône Valley) and Syrah. The fact that Syrah is a parent of Durif/Petite Sirah became known only in 1998, again through Dr. Meredith's genetic research.

When experts conclusively identified Petite Sirah as Durif and subsequently discovered Durif's genetic lineage, Petite Sirah could finally claim status as a "noble" variety, based on its parent Syrah (if not on the basis of Peloursin, a mediocre variety).

Petite Sirah's ups and downs

Through all the years of its confused identity, Petite Sirah rose and fell in vineyard acreage several times. From a high of about 14,000 acres in 1976 (when the grape was often used in blends such as California "Burgundy"), the grape fell to only about 1,400 acres in 1990. Now it's on the upswing again, with more than 6,000 acres in 2005.

Less than ten years ago, only 60 producers were making Petite Sirah wine in California. Today, over 370 producers make Petite Sirah, a 600-plus percent increase. What has given this wine such momentum? We can think of several reasons:

- ✔ Producers are making better Petite Sirahs, softening the wine's brutal tannin and making the wine attractive in its youth.

- ✔ The increased popularity of Syrah/Shiraz has made Petite Sirah more recognizable and acceptable.

- ✔ Wine drinkers in America are becoming more adventuresome.

- ✔ Petite Sirah remains reasonably priced.

- ✔ It tastes good!

The grape has its own advocacy group of 78 winery and trade members, which sponsors an informational Web site (www.psilove you.org) and conducts events and other marketing activities to promote Petite Sirah wines.

The taste of Petite Sirah

Petit Sirah wines are dark, gutsy, bold, and intense reds. Because of their decisive personality, these wines have always elicited a strong reaction from those who taste them. They're not the kind of wines that you feel neutral about. Those who love the wines tend to be passionate fans, and they constitute something of a cult following for the wines.

The aromas and flavors of Petite Sirah wines include fruits such as plum and blackberry as well as black pepper. In some wines, the aromas and flavors can be complex, verging into the red-fruit spectrum (cranberry, pomegranate) or having animal notes such as leather or refined notes from oak-aging, such as mocha or cinnamon. But in other wines, the aromas and flavors, although pleasant, are low key and not particularly distinctive.

More than aroma and flavor, the wine's structure — its tannin, high alcohol, robust body, and dense texture — and its gutsy, powerful, take-no-prisoners style are what particularly characterize Petite Sirah. (A common saying is that Petite Sirah is not Syrah, and it's definitely not petite!)

We remember the Petite Sirah wines from the 1970s that we drank together in the 1980s. They were somewhat rustic wines loaded with black pepper spiciness, and they were firm and austere due to their high tannin. No matter how long we let them lie in our cellar, they never seemed to be quite ready to drink. We definitely enjoyed them, but we always thought that they would have been even better with more age.

Although Petite Sirah is a high-tannin grape, its wines today require less aging than was the case 20 years ago. You can drink Petite Sirah wines that are two or three years old — their age when they're released from the winery — and find them very drinkable. They still can improve with some aging, but that aging isn't a requirement for enjoying them. Winemakers today are adept at limiting the amount of grape tannin that finds its way into the wine and at growing the grapes in such a way that the tannins are less aggressive.

Where Petite Sirah grows

We were amazed to read that, according to wine historian Charles Sullivan, Petite Sirah was the most planted grape in California's most prestigious wine region, Napa Valley, during the 1960s. In the 1970s, growers removed most of their Petite Sirah vines to plant Cabernet Sauvignon. Petite Sirah does grow in Napa Valley today, but it's a minor variety. Nevertheless, some Napa Valley winemakers are very dedicated to this variety — among them, Stags' Leap Winery, Quixote Winery, Markham Vineyards, and Girard Winery.

Mendocino County, north of Sonoma County (see Chapter 4), is a stronghold of Petite Sirah, particularly in the interior Redwood Valley AVA; Parducci Wine Estates has been a pioneer for this wine in Mendocino.

Sonoma County has Petite Sirah vineyards, particularly in Dry Creek Valley, where Pedroncelli grows this grape. Sonoma's Russian River Valley AVA to the south is the home of Foppiano Vineyards, where Louis Foppiano, one of Petite Sirah's strongest advocates, grows the variety and makes a fine Petite Sirah.

Other notable regions for Petite Sirah include the Central Coast AVAs of Paso Robles and San Luis Obispo; the Sierra Foothills AVA; Fair Play; Lodi; Lake County; and the San Joaquin Valley. Livermore Valley is of historical significance because Concannon Vineyard, an early advocate of Petite Sirah, is there.

Recommended Petite Sirah wines

Our recommended Petite Sirah wines fall into two price categories — moderate (under $20) and moderate-plus ($20 to $50). Many of our recommended wines cost less than $20, and a number of them are under $15! (At around $10, we consider Red Truck Petite Sirah a best buy.) And many wines in our higher tier cost less than $30 retail.

Some wineries label their Petite Sirah wines as Petite Syrah. Don't let that confuse you; it's just an alternate spelling that some wineries prefer.

Moderately Priced Petite Sirahs, under $20

Bogle Vineyards (California)

Concannon Vineyard, "Limited Release" (Central Coast)

David Bruce (Central Coast)

EOS Estate (Paso Robles)

Foppiano Vineyards (Russian River Valley)

Guenoc (Lake County)

Parducci Wine Estates (Mendocino County)

Pedroncelli (Dry Creek Valley)

Peirano Estate Vineyards (Lodi)

Red Truck (California)

Trentadue Winery (Alexander Valley)

Vinum Cellars, "Pets," Wilson Vineyards and Reserve (Clarksburg, Central Valley)

Moderate-Plus Petite Sirahs, $20–$50

Carver Sutro, Palisades Vineyard (Napa Valley)

Clayhouse Estate (Paso Robles)

Girard Winery (Napa Valley)

Lava Cap Winery, Granite Hill Vineyard (El Dorado County)

Markham Vineyards (Napa Valley)

Michael-David Vineyards, "Earthquake" (Lodi)

Quixote Winery, Stags Leap Ranch (Napa Valley)

Quivira Vineyards, Wine Creek Ranch (Dry Creek Valley)

Rosenblum Cellars, Pickett Road (Napa Valley) and Rockpile Road Vineyard, Reserve (Rockpile)

Shannon Ridge (High Valley, Lake County)

Stags' Leap Winery (Napa Valley)

Viña Robles, Jardine Vineyard (Paso Robles)

California's Red Rhône-style Blends

In the category of red *Rhône-style wines* — that is, wines made from grape varieties grown in France's Rhône Valley — California produces varietal wines from Syrah, Petite Sirah (technically not grown in the Rhône Valley but locally considered a Rhône grape because of its genetic link to Syrah), and to a minor extent, Grenache, Mourvedre, and Cinsault. But blends are actually the norm in the Rhône Valley, and California produces hundreds of red wines that are blends of various grapes native to or common in the Rhône Valley.

A range of styles

Rhône blends vary tremendously in style because they don't follow many rules: They can contain any number of grape varieties, from two to more than ten; any of the red Rhône varieties can be the dominant variety; and any of the approved varieties can be blended together, according to their availability and the winemaker's fancy.

The Rhone Rangers (www.rhonerangers.org), an association of producers of (mainly California) wines from Rhône varieties, categorizes the red blends with these words:

- ✔ **The Chateauneuf model (referring to a French wine, Châteauneuf-du-Pape):** Start with about half Grenache, add in a good proportion of Syrah and/or Mourvedre for oomph and aging, and round out the complexity with an amazing array of other red and even white grapes

- ✔ **The hot-weather model:** Various proportions of Grenache, Cinsault, and Carignan, designed to produce early-drinking wines

- ✔ **The Down Under model:** Shiraz and Cabernet Sauvignon, in various proportions

Note: Cabernet Sauvignon is not a Rhône Valley variety, but the organization includes it in one of the prototype blends. Cabernet-Shiraz blends are popular in Australia.

You can imagine — and we can confirm — that any one Rhône blend from California can vary considerably from the next. Some are soft, full-bodied, high-alcohol wines with baked-fruit and earthy aromas and flavors, whereas others are fairly vibrant reds with fresh-fruit flavors and a firm tannic structure, and still others are big, rich wines with spicy and very ripe fruit flavors and dense texture. Not even the dominant grape variety is a reliable predictor of the wine's style, because that variety can vary according to where it grows.

GSM, a classic grape trinity

If you begin exploring California's Rhône blends in your wine shop, in magazine articles, or on the Internet, you're sure to come across the term GSM. These initials stand for *Grenache, Syrah, and Mourvedre.*

These three grapes represent a classic blend in the Southern Rhône Valley, with Grenache generally the grape used in the highest proportion and Mourvedre used in the smallest. The French versions usually have place names, such as Côtes du Rhône; however, New World wines that blend these three varieties often carry the name of the grapes, which has led to the convenient abbreviation GSM. Sometimes GSM is actually the name of the wine, and sometimes it's just a term that people use to refer to that type of wine.

The bad news might be that you don't really know what you're getting when you buy a Rhône blend (unless you do your home-work in advance by reading reviews of the specific wine you intend to buy) — but the good news is that the category offers lots of opportunities for exploration and adventure.

When in Rhône: The grapes in Rhône blends

Although we can't describe the taste and style of every possible Rhône-style red blend, we can at least describe the grape varieties that are the building blocks of these blends. When you know how the component wines typically taste, you can extrapolate the likely style of a particular blended wine. In most cases, back-label information tells you which grape varieties are in the wine and sometimes gives you the relative percentages of each variety.

In the following list, we describe the main Rhône grapes and their wines in the order of their importance in Rhône blends:

✔ **Syrah:** Syrah is by far the most distinguished and highest quality grape used in Rhône-style blends, both in France and in California. In a nutshell, the grapes have deep color, thick skins, and a wide aromatic range. Wines are dark and are firm with tannin (unless produced by methods that limit their amount of tannin), and they express aromas and flavors that include black fruits as well as herbal, vegetal, spicy, earthy, and even floral notes. Generally, the wines are fresh and vibrant.

- ✔ **Grenache:** Almost the opposite of Syrah, this grape has thin skins, little color, and little tannin, and it ripens with high sugar levels to make full-bodied, high-alcohol, easy-drinking wines. Aromas and flavors can include raspberry, blueberry, raisins, spices such as pepper, and herbs such as rosemary — but frequently Grenache wines have far less flavor complexity than that. Only when the vines are old or when growers prune severely to achieve a low crop level are the wines fairly dark, rich, dense in texture, and flavorful.

- ✔ **Mourvedre:** Sometimes labeled as Mataro, this variety has small, dark, sweet berries and produces high-alcohol, tannic, sometimes rustic wines that can also be high in acid. A common descriptor for Mourvedre's aromas and flavors is "meaty"; the wines can also have blackberry flavors, and they tend to age well.

- ✔ **Carignan:** California has more than four times the acreage of Carignan than of Mourvedre, and most of the grapes end up in ordinary jug-wine blends. But some Rhone Rangers cultivate this grape for their wines. The grape is tannic and dark, with high acid and high tannin. It can contribute gutsy character to blended wines.

- ✔ **Petite Sirah:** This is a dark-skinned grape that makes tannic, robust wines with aromas and flavors of black pepper spiciness and dark fruits. (See the earlier section "The taste of Petite Sirah.")

- ✔ **Cinsault:** Cinsault makes wines that are fairly light in body and low in tannin, with fruity and spicy aromas and flavors.

- ✔ **Counoise:** A very minor variety in California, Counoise brings to a blend moderate alcohol, a medium amount of tannin, lively acidity, and flavors of berries and spice.

Another grape that winemakers sometimes use in Rhône style blends is Zinfandel, which is generally fruity and spicy, with ripe berry flavors. We devote all of Chapter 8 to this grape variety and its wines. Viognier, a very perfumed white grape, also makes occasional appearances in red Rhône-style blends; we discuss Viognier in Chapter 9.

Recommended California red Rhône blends

Just as almost every California wine producer who makes Cabernet Sauvignon also makes a Cabernet-based blended wine, most Syrah producers also make a blended red wine composed of Rhône varieties in various combinations. The Central Coast — primarily

Paso Robles and Edna Valley in San Luis Obispo County, plus Santa Barbara and Monterey Counties — is the main source for Rhône blends. Sonoma County also has some fine Rhône-style wines.

We list our recommended red Rhône-style blends alphabetically in two price categories, moderately priced (under $20) and moderate-plus ($20 to $50).

Moderately Priced Red Rhône Blends, under $20

Beckmen Vineyards, "Cuvée le Bec" (Santa Ynez Valley)

Cline Cellars, "Cashmere" G-S-M (California)

Edmunds St. John, "Rocks & Gravel" (California)

Fess Parker, "Frontier Red" (California)

Jade Mountain, "La Provençale" (California)

Rabbit Ridge, "Allure du Robles" (Paso Robles)

Red Truck, Red Wine (California)

Tablas Creek, "Côtes de Tablas" (Paso Robles)

Zaca Mesa, "Z Cuvée" (Santa Ynez Valley)

Moderate-Plus Red Rhône Blends, $20–$50

Bonny Doon Vineyard, "Le Cigare Volant" (California)

Copain Wine Cellars, "Les Copains," James Berry Vineyard (Paso Robles)

A Donkey and Goat Winery, "Three Thirteen" (California)

Epiphany Cellars, "Revelation" (Santa Barbara County)

Holly's Hill Vineyard, "Patriarche" (El Dorado, Sierra Foothills)

Io, Rhône blend (Santa Barbara County)

Joseph Phelps, "Le Mistral" (Monterey County)

Preston Vineyards, Sirah-Syrah and L. Preston (Dry Creek Valley, Sonoma)

Qupé Winery, "Los Olivos Cuvée" (Santa Ynez Valley)

Ravenswood, "Icon" (Sonoma County)

Sean Thackrey, "Pleiades XVI" Old Vines (California)

Tablas Creek, "Espirit de Beaucastel" Rouge (Paso Robles)

Terry Hoage Vineyards, "The 46" and "The Pick" (Paso Robles)

Vinum Cellars, "Red Dirt Red" (El Dorado, Sierra Foothills)

Zaca Mesa, "Z Three" (Santa Ynez Valley)

Cal-Ital: Italian Varieties in California

Considering how many Italian and Italian-American families settled in California since the 1800s, and considering what a crucial role wine plays in Italian culture, the Italian influence in California wine country has been considerable. Sometimes this influence plays out in the background, as part of a winery's culture; for example, Gina Gallo believes that food-friendliness, a prerequisite for Italian wines, is central to her winemaking at Gallo Family Vineyards. Sometimes the Italian influence dictates which grape varieties a winery plants — or which old vineyards it refuses to uproot; an example is the old plantings of Italy's Sangiovese grape that remain so cherished by the Seghesio family in Sonoma County.

Increasingly, some winemakers view their admiration for Italian grapes or Italian wines as something of a cause. The catchy name given to this movement of vino-loving winemakers and their Italianate wines is *Cal-Ital.*

The earliest plantings of Italian grape varieties in California date back to the 19th century, but the modern age began in the 1980s. Although nearly two dozen white and red varieties of Italian origin (or varieties that are mainly identified with Italy) now grow in California, the movement is a low-key one, because most of these varieties grow in small quantities.

Cal-Ital red grape varieties

The Cal-Ital red grape variety that dominates in terms of quantity produced is Barbera (bar-*bear*-ah), a grape from northern Italy's Piedmont region that was for many decades the most planted red grape variety in Italy. In California, Barbera quantitatively ranks seventh among all red varieties, behind Pinot Noir and just ahead of Ruby Cabernet (a California-bred crossing of Cabernet Sauvignon and Carignan).

But the red variety that dominates in terms of *image* is Sangiovese (san-joe-*vay*-say), a Tuscan variety (think *Chianti*) that in Italy overtook Barbera as the leading red grape. One of the reasons the Cal-Ital movement isn't bigger than it is, in fact, is that Sangiovese, the leader, is difficult to grow and to vinify. Winemakers in California have struggled to tame Sangiovese's firm tannins, for example, and to maintain deep color in the wine. Some once-committed wineries have now abandoned Sangiovese altogether — most notably Shafer Vineyards and Atlas Peak Winery, both in Napa Valley. Even when wineries produce decent Sangiovese wines, as many have learned to do, the wines are difficult to sell.

The 11 principal red grape varieties of Italian origin in California are the following, listed in terms of their tonnage, from most to least: Barbera, Sangiovese, Primitivo (recognized by U.S. authorities as a synonym for Zinfandel), Refosco, Dolcetto, Teroldego, Nebbiolo, Aglianico, Grignolino, Aleatico, and Freisa. Other Italian grape varieties that also grow in California include Lagrein, Montepulciano, Negroamaro, Nero d'Avola, and Sagrantino. However, apart from Barbera and Sangiovese, you aren't likely to encounter most of these wines in their California skin.

Some people include Charbono as a Cal-Ital variety, but California's Charbono is technically not an Italian variety. Although a grape called Charbono exists in Italy, the California grape of the same name is genetically unrelated.

Recommended Cal-Ital red wines

We believe that red Cal-Ital wines have a great future in California. The best is yet to come, as soon as winemakers figure out where to grow and how to handle Italy's great but extremely challenging red varieties, such as Nebbiolo, Sangiovese, and Aglianico. (It took Italian wine producers hundreds of years to decipher these varieties, and by their own admissions, they haven't mastered them yet.) Meanwhile, we'd like to see Californians concentrate on one red Italian variety that they have been able to grow successfully: Barbera.

We list our recommended red Cal-Ital wines alphabetically in two price categories: moderately priced (under $20) and moderate-plus ($20 to $50).

Moderately Priced Red Cal-Ital Wines, under $20

Boeger Winery Barbera (El Dorado, Sierra Foothills)

Bonny Doon Sangiovese, "Ca'del Solo" (Monterey County)

Brutocao Cellars Barbera, Feliz Vineyard, and Dolcetto, Feliz Vineyard (Mendocino)

Caparone Aglianico; Nebbiolo; and Sangiovese (Paso Robles)

Enotria Barbera; Dolcetto, Graziano Family (Mendocino)

Heitz Cellars Grignolino (Napa Valley)

Jacuzzi Family Vineyards Barbera (Carneros, North Coast), Primitivo (North Coast), and Sangiovese (Sonoma)

Martin & Weyrich Nebbiolo, "Il Vecchio" and Sangiovese "Il Palio" (Paso Robles)

Monte Volpe Sangiovese, Graziano Family (Mendocino)

Palmina Barbera (Santa Barbara County)

Pietra Santa Dolcetto; Sangiovese (Cienega Valley, San Benito County)

Renwood Barbera (Amador County, Sierra Foothills)

Shannon Ridge Barbera (Lake County)

Tamás Estates, Barbera; Sangiovese (Livermore Valley)

Terra d'Oro (formerly Monteviña) Barbera (Amador County)

Valley of the Moon Sangiovese (Sonoma County)

Moderate-Plus Red Cal-Ital Wines, $20–$50

Benessere Vineyards Sangiovese (Napa Valley)

Chiarito Vineyard, Nero d'Avola; Negroamaro (Mendocino)

Di Bruno Sangiovese, Stolpman Vineyard (Santa Ynez Valley)

Miner Family Vineyards Sangiovese, Gibson Ranch (Mendocino)

Palmina Nebbiolo, Stolpman Vineyard (Santa Ynez Valley)

Seghesio Family Vineyards Barbera; Sangiovese (Alexander Valley)

Stolpman Sangiovese, Estate (Santa Ynez Valley)

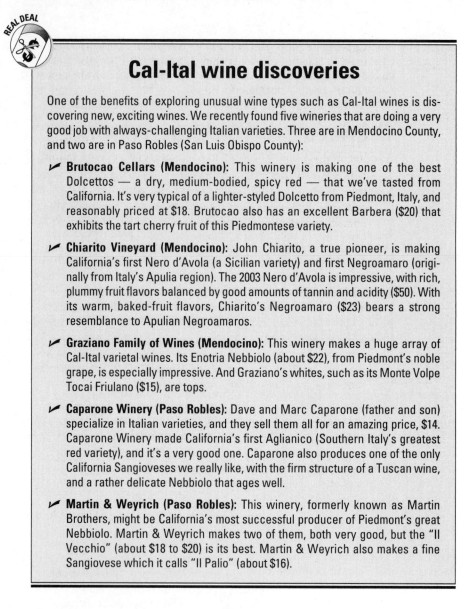

Cal-Ital wine discoveries

One of the benefits of exploring unusual wine types such as Cal-Ital wines is discovering new, exciting wines. We recently found five wineries that are doing a very good job with always-challenging Italian varieties. Three are in Mendocino County, and two are in Paso Robles (San Luis Obispo County):

✔ **Brutocao Cellars (Mendocino):** This winery is making one of the best Dolcettos — a dry, medium-bodied, spicy red — that we've tasted from California. It's very typical of a lighter-styled Dolcetto from Piedmont, Italy, and reasonably priced at $18. Brutocao also has an excellent Barbera ($20) that exhibits the tart cherry fruit of this Piedmontese variety.

✔ **Chiarito Vineyard (Mendocino):** John Chiarito, a true pioneer, is making California's first Nero d'Avola (a Sicilian variety) and first Negroamaro (originally from Italy's Apulia region). The 2003 Nero d'Avola is impressive, with rich, plummy fruit flavors balanced by good amounts of tannin and acidity ($50). With its warm, baked-fruit flavors, Chiarito's Negroamaro ($23) bears a strong resemblance to Apulian Negroamaros.

✔ **Graziano Family of Wines (Mendocino):** This winery makes a huge array of Cal-Ital varietal wines. Its Enotria Nebbiolo (about $22), from Piedmont's noble grape, is especially impressive. And Graziano's whites, such as its Monte Volpe Tocai Friulano ($15), are tops.

✔ **Caparone Winery (Paso Robles):** Dave and Marc Caparone (father and son) specialize in Italian varieties, and they sell them all for an amazing price, $14. Caparone Winery made California's first Aglianico (Southern Italy's greatest red variety), and it's a very good one. Caparone also produces one of the only California Sangioveses we really like, with the firm structure of a Tuscan wine, and a rather delicate Nebbiolo that ages well.

✔ **Martin & Weyrich (Paso Robles):** This winery, formerly known as Martin Brothers, might be California's most successful producer of Piedmont's great Nebbiolo. Martin & Weyrich makes two of them, both very good, but the "Il Vecchio" (about $18 to $20) is its best. Martin & Weyrich also makes a fine Sangiovese which it calls "Il Palio" (about $16).

Other Varietal Reds

If you live in California or you patronize wine shops and restaurants that specialize in California wines, you might come across other varietal wines beyond those that we discuss earlier in this chapter and in our previous red wine chapters. Here is a list of some of those unusual, exotic, or simply "other" red varietal wines. We describe the wines in what we consider their relative order of importance.

✓ **Cabernet Franc:** We mention Cab Franc as one of the grapes used in Bordeaux-style blends (Chapter 6). But Cabernet Franc also makes varietal wines in California, and those wines can be quite good. They tend to have fresh flavors of red fruits and are more flavorful than Cabernet Sauvignons.

✓ **Malbec:** Another grape that figures in Bordeaux-style blends, Malbec is far more popular in Argentina than in California. Varietal Malbecs are deep in color and can be quite tannic, with dark-berry and spicy flavors.

✓ **Petit Verdot:** Yet another Bordeaux blending grape, this one makes deep, dark wines with firm tannin and good fruit character concentration; the best wines have rich, fleshy texture.

✓ **Tempranillo:** Spain's flagship red grape variety is gaining a foothold in California. Tempranillo (tem-pra-*nee*-yo) wines are usually dark in color, low in acidity, and either soft-textured or very tannic, with rather low-key flavors of plum, blackberries, and coffee. They're considered inherently food-friendly.

✓ **Napa Gamay:** This is not the Gamay grape of Beaujolais fame but actually a southwestern France variety called Valdiguié (val-dee-gway) and increasingly labeled as such. It produces easy-drinking, low-tannin wines.

✓ **Alicante Bouschet:** This grape (pronounced al-eh-*cahn*-tay boo-*shay*) is used mainly to give color to other reds, but it has a following among fans of big, rustic, old-style California reds.

✓ **Tannat:** A variety from southwestern France and a signature varietal wine in Uruguay and Brazil, Tannat makes huge, gutsy, powerful reds.

Chapter 11

Bubbly, Rosé, and Dessert Wines

· ·

In This Chapter

▶ California's best bubbly *bruts*

▶ The return of rosé wines, this time dry

▶ Dessert wines for dessert

· ·

We love sparkling wines and drink them at every opportunity. California's top sparkling wines, often referred to as *sparkling bruts* because most are made in the *brut* (very dry) style, are generally excellent and deserve more attention than they receive. The best of them are among the best sparkling wines in the world; only some true Champagnes, from France, stand above them in quality — but of course you pay a hefty price for most Champagnes today!

In the world of table wines, we are very happy to see that dryer-style rosé (pink) wines are making a big comeback in the U.S. and throughout the world. Because of the popularity of White Zinfandel and other California *blush* (pink and sweet) wines, California's rosé wines have had a reputation — rightfully or wrongly — for being sweet and innocuous. That reputation is changing, as more and more California dry rosés become available. We name some of our favorite dry rosés in this chapter, and we also look at White Zinfandel and company. We conclude with a roundup of California dessert wines, in all colors and styles.

California's Sparkling Wines

California producers make sparkling wines in every major category: non-vintage bruts (bubblies blended from wines of several different years), rosé bubblies, *blanc de blancs* (from white grapes only), *blanc de noirs* (white or pink sparkling wines made entirely from red grapes), and vintage-dated bruts and rosés. You can even find California sparkling wines labeled *Spumante* that are sweet, flavorful wines in the style of Italy's famous sparkling wine, Asti. However, California's top sparkling wine producers use the varieties that are used in France's Champagne region as their main grape varieties: Pinot Noir and Chardonnay. (***Note:*** Pinot Blanc and Champagne's third important grape, Pinot Meunier, are minor components in a few California sparkling wines.)

All the better California sparkling bruts are made by the same method used in Champagne, called *méthode champenoise* or *classic method.* In this method, the wine's second fermentation, which gives the wine its bubbles, takes place in the bottle that you buy. However, some sparkling wines from larger wineries are the product of more economical methods, such as large-batch second fermentations in tanks or even the injection of gas directly into a wine. Labels of wines made using large-batch fermentation usually carry the term *charmat* method; wines made by the injection of carbon dioxide gas must be labeled as *carbonated* wines. Price can also be a guide: Wines costing under $8 are generally made using one of these two shortcut methods.

Considering the quality level of many California sparkling wines, we have always been mystified that they don't sell better than they do. Many top California sparkling wine producers have had to add table wines — Pinot Noir and Chardonnay — to their product line in order to stay in business, and quite a few just stopped making sparkling wine altogether. Of course, the sparkling wine business is highly competitive, with true Champagne from France wooing wine lovers on the luxury end and Spanish *cava* (the name used for most Spanish sparkling wines) and Italian Prosecco wines luring value-minded wine drinkers.

Characterizing California bubbly

California's different climates, soils, and other variables make California's sparkling wines different from France's Champagnes and all other sparkling wines in the world. Because California's bubblies tend to be made with riper grapes than those of Champagne and many other regions, they taste fruitier than these other wines. Also, California generally ages most of its sparkling wines a shorter time than the historic French region, Champagne, does; as a result, California bruts usually lack the toastiness or biscuity character that you can find in some aged Champagnes.

The fruitiness, exuberance of bubbles, and frothiness of California bubblies makes them perfect for less formal settings, such as parties, outdoor events, and casual eating. However, more and more serious, longer-aged, complex California sparkling wines are now available from such producers as Iron Horse and Schramsberg. (You can find many of these wines listed in our high-end recommendations in the following pages.)

Don't call it "Champagne"

California's top sparkling bruts are among the best in the world, and many are good values as well. But make sure you get the name straight! *Champagne* is the name of a region in northeastern France, from which the world's most famous sparkling wine, Champagne, originates. France and all other countries in the European Union recognize Champagne as a name that belongs only to the sparkling wines of the Champagne area.

Because U.S. labeling regulations consider *champagne* to be a semi-generic name (see Chapter 2), it's legal for California producers to use the term for their sparkling wines, provided that they modify it with the word *California* or a similar geographic indication. Quite a few producers do call their bubblies "champagne," including California's biggest producer of sparkling wines, Korbel. However, most top-quality producers don't use the term. Schramsberg dropped "champagne" from its sparkling brut labels a few years ago after having used the term for decades. Of course, half of the best California sparkling wine companies are owned by French Champagne houses, which doesn't hurt the cause!

French- and California-owned brands

Many of California's top sparkling wine companies are French-owned. Producers from the region of Champagne opened wineries in California for two reasons: They were running out of vineyard land in their home region, and they knew that Americans were very loyal to their own brands. (Even today, almost 70 percent of all wines sold in the U.S are domestic, and most of them are from California.)

Moët & Chandon, located in the town of Epernay in France, started the Champagne foray into California in 1973 when it opened Domaine Chandon — today the second-largest sparkling wine producer in California after Korbel. Other French producers from Champagne followed: G. H. Mumm (which founded Mumm Napa), Taittinger (which owns Domaine Carneros), and Louis Roederer (owner of Roederer Estate). Some came to California but have since left: Deutz (which had owned Maison Deutz), Veuve Clicquot (which had owned Scharffenberger, a brand now owned by Roederer Estate), and Piper-Heidsieck (former owner of Piper Sonoma, which is now owned by an importer, Remy Cointreau USA).

Other top California wineries producing sparkling wines are American-owned. These include Iron Horse, Schramsberg, J Wine Company, Laetitia Estate, and Korbel. The one exception to French or American ownership is Gloria Ferrer, owned by a huge Spanish producer, Freixenet.

REAL DEAL

Roederer Estate, the ultimate California bubbly

When French Champagne producers realized they were running out of vineyard land back home, many started buying vineyards in California and building wineries there. Most of these new operations were in Napa Valley or Sonoma. But Jean-Claude Rouzaud, the crafty boss of Champagne Louis Roederer (producers of the sublime *Cristal*) knew that top sparkling wine demanded a very cool climate, and in 1982 he found it 125 miles north of San Francisco, in Mendocino's Anderson Valley.

Roederer Estate debuted its first sparkling *brut* (a dry sparkling wine) in 1988, followed shortly by a delicately colored brut rosé. Both wines have been the critics' darlings since their introduction. In 1993, Roederer Estate introduced a premium vintage sparkling wine, L'Ermitage, which vintage after vintage vies for honors as the best sparkling wine in the world made outside of Champagne itself. Recently, a vintage L'Ermitage Rosé joined the line. If you shop around, you can find the non-vintage Roederer Estate sparkling brut for under $20, the brut rosé for about $25, the L'Ermitage for about $40, and the low-production, harder-to-find L'Ermitage Rosé for about $50.

Recommended sparkling wines

We list our recommended California sparkling wines — including rosés, blanc de blancs, and vintage bubblies — in three price categories, according to their typical prices in wine shops:

✔ **Moderately priced:** Under $30

✔ **Moderate-plus:** $30 to $50

✔ **High-end:** Over $50

Don't miss our sidebar titled "Top-value California sparkling wines," in which we name several California sparklers under $20 that we think are excellent buys.

Moderately Priced Sparkling Wines, under $30

Domaine Carneros Vintage Brut (Carneros)

Domaine Chandon Brut Classic and Blanc de Noirs (Napa Valley)

Gloria Ferrer Vintage Blanc de Blancs and Royal Cuvée (Carneros)

Handley Cellars Vintage Brut and Brut Rosé (Anderson Valley)

Iron Horse Vintage Brut and Blanc de Blancs (Green Valley, Sonoma)

"J" Vineyards Brut, "Cuvée 20" (Russian River Valley)

Korbel Vintage Brut "Natural" (Russian River Valley)

Laetitia Estate Brut (Central Coast)

Laetitia Estate Vintage Brut Rosé (Arroyo Grande Valley)

Mumm Napa Brut Prestige, Blanc de Noirs, "Cuvée M," and Vintage Blanc de Blancs (Napa Valley)

Piper Sonoma Brut Cuvée and Blanc de Blancs (Sonoma County)

Roederer Estate Brut and Brut Rosé (Anderson Valley)

Scharffenberger Brut (Anderson Valley)

Schramsberg Vintage Blanc de Blancs and Blanc de Noirs (North Coast)

Moderate-Plus Sparkling Wines, $30–$50

Domaine Carneros Vintage Rosé Brut (Carneros)

Étoile Brut and Étoile Brut Rosé, Domaine Chandon (Napa Valley)

J Vineyards Vintage Brut and Brut Rosé (Russian River Valley)

Mumm Napa, Vintage "DVX" (Napa Valley)

Roederer Estate Vintage Brut "L'Ermitage" (Anderson Valley)

High-End Sparkling Wines, over $50

Domaine Carneros, Le Rêve Vintage Blanc de Blancs (Carneros)

Gloria Ferrer, Carneros Cuvée (Carneros)

Iron Horse Vintage Blanc de Blancs "Late Disgorged" (Green Valley, Sonoma)

Iron Horse, Joy! magnum only (Green Valley, Sonoma); $147

J Vineyards, Vintage "Late Disgorged" Brut (Russian River Valley)

Roederer Estate Vintage Brut Rosé "L'Ermitage" (Anderson Valley)

Schramsberg Vintage Brut "Reserve"

J. Schram Vintage Brut (North Coast)

J. Schram Vintage Brut Rosé (North Coast); $125

Pretty in Pink: California Rosés, Dry and Sweet

Many wine drinkers dismiss the entire category of rosé wines because they consider the wines not serious, too sweet, or wimpy. But a revolution is underway: Many California rosé wines are now being made dry, and remarkably, they're in demand. Sales of rosé wines in the U.S. increased over 50 percent in 2007. Who would've thunk it?

Top-value California sparkling wines

These California sparkling wines, all under $20, are consistently reliable, and they're our picks as top values for the money:

✔ Ballatore Gran Spumante (California)

✔ Korbel Brut, Brut Rosé, and Blanc de Noirs (California)

✔ Mirabelle Brut and Brut Rosé, by Schramsberg (California)

✔ Sofia, by Francis Coppola, Blanc de Blancs (Monterey County), and Pinot Noir Rosé (Carneros)

Of course, California still makes plenty of White Zinfandel and other sweet rosés, often referred to as *blush* wines. These wines are inexpensive, easy-drinking, flavorful, and no, not serious. But there's definitely a time and a place to enjoy wines that don't take themselves too seriously — and there's certainly a place for any wine that has as many fans as White Zinfandel does.

Serious, dry rosés

Serious California rosés include all rosé wines made in a dryer style. They retail for over $10, generally in the $12 to $20 range — as opposed to sweeter rosés and blush wines, which are almost always under $10. They can come from any red grape variety, and they might or might not be labeled with the name of the grape. The varieties most frequently used for California rosés are Pinot Noir, Sangiovese, Grenache, and Syrah (the last two often blended together).

Two French terms you sometimes see on California rosé labels are *oeil de perdrix* (meaning "eye of the partridge") and *vin gris* ("gray wine"), both referring to color. These terms usually apply to very pale rosé wines that are often dryer than deeper-colored rosés.

Our recommendations of serious California rosé wines fall into two categories according to the wines' typical prices in wine shops: moderately priced ($12 to $20) and moderate-plus (over $20). And in the sidebar "Five top-value rosé wines," we identify five good California rosés for under $12 that we think are excellent buys.

Moderately Priced Serious Rosés, $12 to $20

A Donkey and Goat Winery, "Isabel's Cuvée," Grenache Rosé (McDowell Valley)

Alexander Valley Vineyards, dry Rosé of Sangiovese (Alexander Valley)

Ampelos Cellars, Rosé of Syrah (Sta. Rita Hills)

Bonny Doon, "Vin Gris de Cigare" Rosé (Santa Cruz Mountains)

Carol Shelton Wines, "Rendezvous Rosé," Carignane (Mendocino County)

Chateau Potelle, "Riviera Rosé" (Paso Robles)

Edmunds St. John, "Bone Jolly Rosé" Gamay Noir (El Dorado, Sierra Foothills)

Emmolo, Syrah Rosé (Napa Valley)

Etude, Rosé of Pinot Noir (Carneros)

Heitz Cellars Grignolino Rosé (Napa Valley)

Hitching Post, by Hartley & Ostini, Pinot Noir Rosé (Santa Barbara County)

I'M Wines (Isabel Mondavi) Rosé of Cabernet (Napa Valley)

Lucia Vineyards, "Lucy," Rosé of Pinot Noir (Central Coast)

Lynmar, Rosé of Pinot Noir (Russian River Valley)

Martin & Weyrich, "Matador Rosé" Tempranillo (Central Coast)

McDowell Valley Vineyards Grenache Rosé (McDowell Valley, Mendocino County)

Pietra Santa Rosato, Dolcetto (Cienega Valley, San Benito County)

Robert Hall Winery, "Rosé de Robles," Syrah/Grenache/Mourvèdre (Paso Robles)

St. Francis Winery Rosé, Merlot/Syrah (Sonoma County)

Saintsbury Pinot Noir Rosé (Carneros)

Scherrer Winery, Vin Gris Dry Rosé, Pinot Noir/Zinfandel (Sonoma County)

SoloRosa Rosé (Napa Valley)

Terra d'Oro (formerly Monteviña) Rosé, mainly Nebbiolo (Amador County, Sierra Foothills)

Valley of the Moon Rosato di Sangiovese (Sonoma County)

Ventana Vineyards, "Rosado" mainly Grenache (Arroyo Seco, Monterey County)

Vinum Cellars, Rosé of Cabernet Sauvignon (Napa Valley)

Moderate-Plus Serious Rosés, over $20

Lazy Creek, Rosé of Pinot Noir (Anderson Valley)

Tablas Creek Estate Rosé, Mourvedre/Grenache/Counoise (Paso Robles)

White Zinfandel and its blushing cousins

White Zinfandel isn't selling at the same frenzied pace that it did in the 1980s and 1990s, but it's still the third best-selling varietal wine in California, just slightly behind Cabernet Sauvignon and well behind Chardonnay. It outsells red Zinfandel by more than 6 to 1 (see Chapter 8 for info on red Zin).

Although wine connoisseurs scorn White Zinfandel as something more akin to a beverage than a real wine, it's certainly special to the many thousands who drink it. The wine offers sweetness, fruitiness, moderate alcohol levels, and no tannin, for a mild-tasting wine that doesn't bite. White Zinfandel is the perfect wine for you if you find most wines too dry or astringent.

Five top-value rosé wines

These five serious rosés, all under $12, are our picks as top values:

- Folie à Deux Winery, "Ménage à Trois" (California)

- Little Black Dress Syrah Rosé (California)

- Pedroncelli Zinfandel Rosé (Sonoma County)

- Pink Truck (Cline Cellars) Zinfandel/Grenache/Mourvedre (California)

- Toad Hollow Vineyards, "Eye of the Toad" Dry Rosé of Pinot Noir (Sonoma County)

White Zinfandel's color ranges from pale pink to a dark rose, and depending on the producer, the wine can vary in sweetness from off-dry to quite sweet. As a general rule, paler White Zins tend to be less sweet, and very pink ones tend to be sweeter. Regardless of hue, they're always soft in texture and low in alcohol. White Zin is a wine to drink cold, and it's a wine to drink while it's young and fresh; buy the most recent vintage you can find, and chill it.

The term *blush wine,* which came into vogue in the U.S. in the 1970s, is a general name for any sweet pink wine. White Zinfandel's success has given rise to many other blush wines in California, such as Cabernet Blush, or White Cabernet; White Merlot; and Grenache Rosé, or White Grenache. All blush wines are fairly similar in style.

Almost all blush wines, including White Zin, are inexpensive — in the $5 to $10 range, with most closer to $5. Most blush wines are produced from grapes grown in California's warm, inland San Joaquin Valley. California's leading White Zinfandels include the following:

- **Sutter Home:** The first commercial producer of White Zinfandel and still one of the most popular, selling more than 4 million cases a year

- **Beringer Vineyards:** The best-selling White Zinfandel of all; pale in color and dryer than most; Beringer also makes a white Merlot

- **De Loach Vineyards:** Definitely one of the driest, most complexly flavored White Zins; also one of the most expensive, at about $10

- **Woodbridge:** Another large producer and also one of the best

- **Terra d'Oro (formerly Monteviña):** A Zinfandel specialist; makes reliable White Zinfandels, not too sweet; owned by the Trinchero family, proprietors of Sutter Home

- **E & J Gallo Family Vineyard:** Very reasonably priced; lighter style; Gallo also produces Turning Leaf White Zinfandel

- **Fetzer, Valley Oaks:** Well-made, fruity, and not too sweet

- **Glen Ellen:** A well-priced White Zin in the sweeter style

- **Barefoot Cellars:** An affordable, non-vintage White Zin; also produces a sparkling White Zin

Sweet Dessert Wines

Sweet wines, also called *dessert wines,* date back to the earliest days of California wine production. Until the 1960s, they were more popular nationwide than dry table wines. Today, they represent just a small portion of California's wine production, but perhaps as a result, their quality is better than ever.

Dessert wines are a very varied group. Some of them have no more alcohol than table wines, for example, and others contain as much as 20 percent alcohol. Some of them are white, and some are red. They also come from many different grape varieties. But one characteristic that dessert wines all have in common is that they're highly flavorful and very rich. You can sip these wines with dessert or drink them after your dinner, as dessert itself.

California makes sweet wines in just about every style that exists, from a wide range of grape varieties. These styles include the following:

- **Late-harvest wines:** By the time the grapes for late-harvest wines are harvested, they've become so ripe on the vine that some of their sugar remains in the wine after fermentation. They're usually white wines from aromatic varieties such as Riesling, Gewurztraminer, and Sauvignon Blanc.

- **Botrytised wines:** *Botrytised wines* are late-harvest wines whose grapes were attacked by *botrytis,* a fungus that concentrates the grapes' sugar. In France's Sauternes region and in Germany's greatest Riesling vineyards, the botrytis attack occurs naturally when just the right combination of sunshine and humidity exists. In California, botrytis sometimes occurs naturally, and some wineries introduce botrytis to the grapes after harvest.

    The grape varieties for botrytised wines include Riesling, Sauvignon Blanc, and Semillon. Dolce by Far Niente and Robert Mondavi Sauvignon Blanc Botrytis are two of the state's most respected botrytised dessert wines.

- **Alcohol-added wines:** Alcohol-added (fortified) wines are sweet because the winemaker adds neutral alcohol to them during fermentation, killing the yeasts and therefore leaving sugar in the wines. They can be white or red. Quady's Essencia, from the Muscat grape, is an excellent wine in this category.

✔ **Port-style wines:** These are sweet alcohol-added wines made in the manner of Portugal's famous red Port wines: Alcohol is added to the wine during the early stages of fermentation to preserve natural grape sweetness, and the wine is subsequently aged in wood for varying periods, depending on the specific style of Port being made. Styles vary from young to aged and from simple to complex.

Port-style wines sometimes come from native Portuguese varieties grown in California, such as Touriga Nacional and Tinta Roriz, and in other cases come from Zinfandel, Charbono, Petite Sirah, or even Cabernet. Quady, Prager Port Works, Perry Creek, and Brutocao are top producers. Plenty of really inexpensive California "Ports" exist as well.

✔ **Sherry-type wines:** These are alcohol-added white wines that can be sweet or dry (when dry, they fall into the category of *aperitif* wines, for pre-dinner). Sweet Sherries actually ferment to dryness and are subsequently fortified with alcohol and sweetened.

Some styles have a yeasty character from a film of yeast that forms on the wine's surface as it ages in barrels. Other styles have a rich, nutty, and dried-fruit aroma and flavor that occurs when the wine is exposed to oxygen as it ferments and ages.

The best wines come from the Palomino grape that's used to make Sherry in its home region in Spain. Inexpensive versions come from more common grapes, such as Thompson Seedless. Sherry-type wines are usually not vintage-dated.

Dessert wines often come in half-bottles that contain 375 milliliters (compared to normal 750-ml wine bottles), and many of the best of them cost as much as you'd expect to pay for a full-size bottle of wine. But the extra cost is worth it. These wines go a long way: Generally, you have a smaller serving that you would of a table wine — about 2 or 3 ounces — because they're so very rich. Skimping on price will give you a wine that has sweetness and flavor but not the special quality that comes from using the best grapes and from the handcrafted winemaking processes that the top wineries employ.

Part IV
Enjoying California Wines

The 5th Wave
By Rich Tennant

"Oh, come on, you're just drinking it!
You're not even tasting it..."

In this part...

Yes, we know: There's only so much that you can discover from books. At some point, you have to get out there and start learning by doing. The first chapter in this part can guide you in matching California's wines to foods, in theory and in practice. You also find tips on glassware, serving temperatures, and wines to collect and wines to drink young, plus the ever-important issue of vintage. When the beauty and romance of California wine country calls you, our chapter on visiting wineries can come in handy and (we hope) make your visit all the more enjoyable.

Chapter 12

Pairing and Sharing California Wines

*I*f it hadn't been for sharing California wines, we might not be a couple today. True, we met at a dinner that featured Italian white wines, and our first date was a tasting of great Champagnes (French, of course). But in those early days, when we ate in, the wines were often special California Chardonnays, Cabernets, or Zinfandels from Ed's private stash. They captivated us, helped us delight in our meals together, and solidified new and old friendships with other wine lovers.

Great California wines also proved to us the wisdom of laying down special bottles to enjoy in the future — not only for the fond memories they bring but also for the fascinating discovery of how they age with time (or remain ageless, as is sometimes the case). To experience more great bottles in the future, we discovered which wines, in which vintages, were most reliable agers.

Enjoying California's wine bounty doesn't require older vintages or special, expensive wines or even, for that matter, particular types of food. But all those factors can be part of the fun. In this chapter, we offer suggestions for pairing California wines with food. We then delve into the topic of which California wines age best, followed by a discussion of the current state of recent California vintages.

Matching Wines to Foods

We spend plenty of time each month doing comparative wine-tastings, in which we sample similar wines side-by-side without food to experience the essential character of each wine. Such tastings serve a purpose for wine professionals. And they can be fun, because the clinical atmosphere brings out aspects of the wine that we might not notice otherwise. But that's no way to appreciate wine. Wine and food, on the table, together — now that's real fun, and you can do it on a daily basis! The nagging question, of course, is which type of wine to have with which type of food.

You could make an argument that a food-friendly wine is one that doesn't have much flavor to compete with the flavors in the food you plan to eat — a wine that just hangs in the background and offers refreshing acidity to cleanse your taste buds between bites of food. California doesn't make many wines like that (though some Pinot Grigios are an exception). The food-friendly currency that California wines trade in is flavor, lots of flavor, and a dynamic personality in the meal.

Dishes that are flavorful — the kind of foods that we Americans eat on a regular basis — require flavorful wines that don't wimp out next to the food's flavor. If that's the kind of food that you enjoy, you're ready to experiment with California wines on your table.

Elements of the match

The key to pairing wine and food, in our opinion, is not so much matching the specific flavors of the food and the wine — echoing the delicate fresh herbs and lemon on sautéed fish fillets with a herbal-tasting, citrusy Sauvignon Blanc, for example — as matching the food's flavor intensity with that of the wine. After all, many California Sauvignon Blancs are likely to be so intense in flavor that they overwhelm the flavor of the fish itself.

Although most California wines are flavorful, some are more so than others; here are some generalizations about the flavor intensity of specific types of California wine (refer to Chapters 5 to 10 for information on the various wines):

- ✔ **Very flavorful whites:** Richly oaky or richly fruity Chardonnays, most Sauvignon Blancs, Rieslings, Viogniers, and most Gewurztraminers

- ✔ **Less flavorful whites:** Most Pinot Grigio/Gris wines, most unoaked or subtly oaked Chardonnays, Rhône-style whites other than Viognier, and Pinot Blancs

- ✔ **Very flavorful reds:** Pinot Noirs, most Syrah/Shiraz wines, Zinfandels, and Petite Sirahs

- ✔ **Less flavorful reds:** Cal-Ital reds, many blended Rhône-style wines, Merlots, many Cabernets, and many Bordeaux-type blends

We also like to match the weight of the dish with the weight of the wine: The more substantial the food, the fuller-bodied and more substantial the wine should be. Using the weight of your dish as a guide, you can decide whether to serve a white, rosé, or red wine from California:

- ✔ **Substantial choices:** Red wines are generally more substantial than white wines, so they're the more logical choice with heavy meat and game dishes, meaty pasta entrees, and bean-based meals.

- ✔ **Lighter choices:** White wines generally complement lighter dishes, such as salads, fish, omelets, and light poultry dishes.

- ✔ **In-between options:** The heaviest white wines, the lightest red wines, and rosé wines straddle red-wine and white-wine territory and can go well with many dishes in both realms.

Two other factors that can affect your decision of what to drink with what food are sweetness in the wine and the tannin level of the wine. A wine with some sweetness can use a dish with fruity elements or elements of sweetness, such as balsamic vinegar. Very tannic red wines can match well with protein-rich foods such as rare beef or hard cheeses.

The serving-temperature factor

You might already know the usual advice: Serve red wines cool and white wines cooler but not very cold. A cool temperature is particularly important for California wines because the wines are often very high in alcohol, and the sensation of the high alcohol — which some people perceive as a burning sensation — diminishes when the wine is cool. Of course, cool temperatures can also reduce the intensity of flavor that you perceive, but given the high flavor quotient of most California wines, the wines still have plenty of flavor.

Bottles of red wine should be cool to the touch, and white wines, cold to the touch — but not so cold that moisture condenses on your wine glass when you pour the wine.

If you're thinking that this system of pairing California wine and food involves a bit of trial and error, you're right. Because every dish is different in its ingredients and preparation, and because every wine tastes at least slightly different from others of its type, no one can guarantee how well any one wine will go with any one dish. To us, that's part of the fun of sitting down to dinner with wine. It's a fresh adventure every evening.

Above all, your personal taste, not what other people tell you, must dictate your final choice of wine. We know people who always drink white wine, no matter what the food, because that's what they enjoy most. And although we would never pair White Zinfandel with pot roast, we believe that you should absolutely do that if you enjoy the combination.

Try this with that: Wine pairings for specific foods

Strict rules about wine and food pairings aren't valid, because everyone is ultimately guided by his or her own taste. But certain combinations of food and wine just seem to be naturals. Here are some of our favorite food pairings for California wines:

- ✔ **Egg and mushroom dishes:** Fine California sparkling wines

- ✔ **Cobb salad:** California Sauvignon Blanc

- ✔ **Brie cheese:** Viognier

- ✔ **Pan-fried fillet of flounder:** Pinot Blanc

- ✔ **Broiled lobster:** Oaky, flavorful California Chardonnay

- ✔ **Thanksgiving turkey:** California Pinot Noir (Choose a Pinot Noir that isn't very oaky or one that has lots of fresh fruitiness — as opposed to jammy fruitiness — to balance its oaky character); as an alternative, Barbera

- ✔ **Spicy chili or other fiery foods:** Syrah/Shiraz or Petite Sirah (The key in matching red wines with spicy dishes is a high degree of fruitiness in the wine and relatively low tannin levels; choose inexpensive Shirazes, and choose Petite Sirahs in the less powerful style.)

- ✔ **Grilled vegetables:** Red Zinfandel, Syrah, or a red Rhône-style blend

- ✔ **Barbecue ribs:** Red Zinfandel

- ✔ **Black-pepper steak (steak au poivre):** Cabernet Sauvignon

> ✔ **Turkey burgers:** A fruity Pinot Noir or a low-tannin red such as an inexpensive Shiraz
>
> ✔ **Pizza with red sauce:** A flavorful type of wine such as Syrah or Barbera (The cheesier the pizza, the more tannic the wine can be)

Aging and Collecting California Wines

You do not need to age your California wines to enjoy them! We'll say that again: It's perfectly okay to drink California wines without waiting for them to "come around." This is true for the vast majority of wines from the Golden State.

So why this section on aging and collecting California wines? Because some California wines do improve over time, and some people (we're two of them) enjoy laying wines down to enjoy in the future. If you have no interest in that activity, please fell free to skip ahead to our more general advice about recent vintages later in this chapter.

The right glass for the wine

We're firm believers in using good glassware for tasting and drinking wines. In fact, we admit to being a bit fanatical on this topic. Over dinner, it's not unusual for us to change the type of glass several times before we decide on the right glass for the wine we're drinking.

Over the years, we've come up with some general guidelines for choosing wine glasses. First, use high-quality glasses from a reputable producer who specializes in wine glasses. Also, note that large glasses invariably work better than small glasses. Here's how we match glass shape to various types of wines:

✔ For Cabernet Sauvignons, Merlots, Syrahs, Zinfandels, and Sauvignon Blancs, we generally prefer a glass with a large, fairly straight-sided bowl, commonly known as a *Bordeaux glass.*

✔ For Pinot Noirs and Chardonnays, we prefer a large, wider-bowled, apple-shaped glass, commonly known as a *Burgundy glass.*

✔ For sparkling wines, we use a large, elongated tulip-shaped glass rather than the narrow, flute-shaped glass that's fairly common for bubbly wines.

The more that you pay attention to the wine you taste, the more you notice the difference that the glassware makes. For more info on the right wine glass, refer to our book, *Wine For Dummies,* 4th Edition (Wiley).

When we first started collecting wines in the 1970s, we were a bit wary of collecting California wines because nobody knew how the wines would age. California wines didn't have the same kind of track record as wines from the world's classic regions, such as Bordeaux and Burgundy (France), Germany, Piedmont (Italy), or the Douro (home of Vintage Port, in Portugal). But our experiences over the years became that track record. We can now state with confidence that certain California wines age remarkably well. This is true especially in the "better" vintages — those years in which climatic conditions were superb. In this section, we name the California wines that age well — and in fact improve with aging — and the wines to drink soon rather than lay down for aging.

All our discussions about older wines and aging wines are based on the presumption that the wines have aged in proper conditions, such as a temperature-controlled cellar or a special wine-storage refrigeration unit. (For detailed information on how to keep wine under proper conditions, refer to *Wine For Dummies,* 4th edition.)

How different varietal wines age

Generally speaking, California red wines age much better than California whites. For practical reasons, we discuss only the six major California varietal wines here:

- ✔ **Cabernet Sauvignon:** Cabernet Sauvignon and Cabernet blends are definitely California's longest-lived wines, by a wide margin. We've recently tasted California Cabs from 1970 and 1974 that are perfect to drink now and still have some years left in them. Even those California Cabernets from the 1940s, 1950s, and 1960s that we've tasted were mostly still fine to drink. But of course, not every California Cabernet will age well; only certain wines from the better vintages can stand the test of time.

- ✔ **Zinfandel:** Red Zinfandels definitely age well; we've tasted 30-year-old Zinfandels that were delicious. But Zinfandel does lose its characteristic berry-like flavor with time and in fact comes to resemble Cabernet Sauvignon. If you like the taste of young Zinfandel, we recommend that you drink up your Zins within 15 years.

- ✔ **Merlot:** Not many California Merlots have been around long; before 1985, most winemakers used Merlot mainly as a blending wine. Generally, California Merlots are ready to drink sooner than California Cabernets; they're usually softer, fruitier, and less tannic than Cabernets. We believe that most Merlots will not age as long as Cabernets and are at their best within the first 12 to 15 years. Some Merlots that we've tried from the 1980s, however, have aged well.

✔ **Pinot Noir:** We've tasted wonderful 20-plus-year-old California Pinot Noirs. But generally speaking, Pinot Noir wines from a fairly low-tannin variety don't age as long as Cabernet Sauvignons. To be on the safe side, we generally prefer to drink California Pinots that are less than 10 years old so that all the wonderful, fresh aromas and flavors inherent in this variety are still at their peak.

✔ **Chardonnay:** A few of the very best California Chardonnays can age and even improve with up to 15 years of aging — the likes of Hanzell, Long Vineyards, Mount Eden, Matanzas Creek, and Stony Hill, for example. But generally speaking, California Chardonnays more than 10 years old disappoint us. We recommend that you drink Chardonnays within 10 years of the vintage — with the exception of those few Chardonnays that have a proven track record for aging.

✔ **Sauvignon Blanc:** California Sauvignon Blancs for the most part are best when they're young and fresh; most will not age well or improve after 5 or 6 years. Of course, there are exceptions: Robert Mondavi's very limited-production "I-Block" To Kalon Vineyard Fumé Blanc — from a vineyard planted in 1945, the oldest Sauvignon Blanc vineyard in the U.S. — can probably age for decades. Mayacamas Vineyards also makes a long-lived Sauvignon Blanc.

We've had limited experience with aged California sparkling wines because they haven't been around that long. Certainly, the better California bruts — such as Roederer Estate L'Ermitage and Iron Horse Late Disgorged Brut — can age well for 15 years or more.

California wines that have aged well

In California's fairly short wine history, only two varietal wines — Cabernet Sauvignon and Zinfandel — have established a clear record of aging well for 20 years or more. In this section, we name some specific wines that have stood the test of time.

Age-worthy Cabernet Sauvignons

Almost all California wines with a history of long aging are Cabernet Sauvignons from Napa Valley. We name here some Napa Valley Cabernet Sauvignons and Cabernet blends that have aged well in the past — and that, in current vintages, are still age-worthy wines:

✔ **Beaulieu Vineyards, Georges de Latour Private Reserve:** Since the first vintage in 1936, BV Private Reserve can boast a string of remarkable vintages. The 1951 and 1968 Private Reserves are among the greatest California wines ever produced. Also memorable are the 1970 and 1974.

- **Heitz Wine Cellars, Martha's Vineyard:** This is one of California's classic single-vineyard Cabernet Sauvignons, noted for its unique aroma of eucalyptus. Memorable vintages of Martha's Vineyard include the 1968, 1969, and 1974. Other age-worthy Heitz single-vineyard Cabernets are the Bella Oaks and Trailside Vineyard Cabs.

- **Robert Mondavi Reserve:** Robert Mondavi Reserve is produced from some of Napa Valley's finest vineyards. The 1968, 1969, and 1974 have been among California's best Cabernets, and the exemplary 2005 Mondavi Reserve Cab confirms the continuing excellence of this Cabernet Sauvignon.

- **Mayacamas Vineyards:** This mountain winery has always been renowned for its long-lasting Cabernet Sauvignons. Its 1970 and 1974 are still showing well.

Here are some other Napa Valley Cabernet Sauvignons/Cab blends that have aged well but hold slightly shorter track records:

- Anderson's Conn Valley
- Araujo Estate, Eisele Vineyard
- Beringer Private Reserve
- Cain Cellars "Cain Five"
- Cakebread Cellars
- Chappellet "Signature"
- Chateau Montelena
- Clos du Val
- Diamond Creek (all its Cabernets)
- Dominus Estate
- Dunn Vineyards, Howell Mountain
- Far Niente
- Forman Vineyard
- Freemark Abbey, Bosché and Sycamore Vineyards
- Frog's Leap
- Grgich Hills
- Hess Collection
- Joseph Phelps, "Insignia" and Backus Vineyard
- Opus One
- Rubicon Estate

> ✔ Shafer Vineyards
>
> ✔ Spottswoode
>
> ✔ Stag's Leap Wine Cellars "Cask 23"
>
> ✔ Trefethen

Outside of Napa Valley, two California Cabernet Sauvignons that have proven to age extremely well are the Laurel Glen "Estate" (Sonoma Mountain) and Ridge Vineyards "Monte Bello" (Santa Cruz Mountains). Ridge Vineyards has a track record of making fine Cabernet Sauvignons that dates back to the 1960s. Its 1970, 1971, and 1974 Monte Bello Cabernets are legendary.

Age-worthy Zinfandels

Besides Cabernet Sauvignon and Cab blends, the only other California wine with a significant track record for aging well is red Zinfandel. Most of the better red Zins are good agers. The two current Zinfandel producers with the finest and longest track records for aging are Ravenswood and Ridge Vineyards.

Joel Peterson, winemaker at Ravenswood, worked with iconic Zinfandel/Pinot Noir producer Joseph Swan in the 1970s. From Peterson's first Zinfandel in 1976, it was clear that he had the touch for making great red Zins. Ravenswood's finest single-vineyard Zin, in our opinion, is probably the Old Hill Vineyard, from Sonoma Valley.

Paul Draper, CEO and chief winemaker at Ridge Vineyards, is equally renowned for Cabernet and Zinfandel. Ridge's greatest Zinfandel — and the one with the longest track record — is Geyserville, a Zinfandel blend. Ridge produces about seven other fine Zinfandels, including the excellent "Lytton Springs."

A. Rafanelli and Rosenblum Cellars are two other Zinfandel producers making age-worthy red Zins.

Vintage Variations in California

The quality of the vintage year is not so vitally important in California as it is in European wine regions such as Bordeaux, Burgundy, Piedmont, and Tuscany, because those regions can have more dramatic swings in temperature and rainfall from year to year. Rain and hail, typical problems in Europe, seldom occur during California's growing season.

But it's *not* true that vintages don't matter in California. In some vintages, California's weather can be too hot, whereas in other years, it's quite cool. At times, spring frost can occur and impact the quality of the grapes.

Cool versus warm vintages

A year's relative warmth or coolness determines which varieties do well in that particular vintage. Here's how various grapes generally perform, depending on average temperatures during the growing season:

- ✔ Pinot Noir, Chardonnay, Syrah, and Merlot do better in cooler vintages.
- ✔ Zinfandel likes warmer years.
- ✔ Cabernet Sauvignon is like Goldilocks: It likes the temperature "just right" — not too hot but not too cool.

 We are firmly convinced that California's best vintages for its most important wines — with the exception of Zinfandel — are its cooler years, such as 2005. We have tasted some remarkably fine 2005 Cabernet Sauvignons, Pinot Noirs, and Chardonnays, for example, and we recommend buying the 2005 wines. (Coincidentally, it's also an excellent vintage in Bordeaux and Burgundy.) In the last 25 years, only 1991 and 1985, both cool vintages in California, are in the same league as 2005 for general excellence. But thanks to continual improvements in winemaking and viticulture, 2005 might prove to be even better than the earlier cool vintages. The 2006 vintage was fairly cool but warmer than 2005. We think that 2006 will generally prove to be a very good vintage as well.

In warm vintages, the wines often show well at first because they're rich and opulent, with higher than usual alcohol, but they age rapidly. The 1997 vintage is a classic example of the downside of warm-climate vintages: Most of the 1997 wines have faded. In our opinion, most of the wines produced in California from 2002 through 2004 also won't age well. For us, the 2005 vintage has been a refreshing change of pace for California wines.

Our California vintage ratings

In this section, we characterize California wine vintages back to 1990. We base our vintage preferences primarily on California's North Coast — Napa Valley, Sonoma, Mendocino, and Lake Counties — because there's generally more vintage variation in the North Coast than in the Central Coast.

Vintages from 2001 to 2007

Our remarks about vintages are generalizations, and they don't apply to every wine. We rate California's recent vintages with stars to indicate our appraisal of the quality of the wines in that year, up to four stars for the best vintages:

- ✔ **2007:** It's too early for a final judgment, but 2007 is shaping up as a good vintage, if not a great one. It was warmer than 2005 and 2006 but not overly warm. *Rating:* **No rating yet**

- ✔ **2006:** Generally a very good year, 2006 was not as cool as 2005 and therefore is better than 2005 for Zinfandel. Pinot Noir and Chardonnay are good but not quite as good as in 2005. For Cabernet Sauvignon, 2006 appears to be as good as 2005 and in some cases, better. But the 2006 wines seem to be precocious — they'll generally be ready sooner than the 2005s and might not have the great longevity of wines from 2005. *Rating:* ★★★

- ✔ **2005:** Our kind of vintage! The year 2005 was generally very cool for California, which resulted in a much longer growing season than usual. It was truly excellent for Pinot Noir, Chardonnay, and Syrah. And 2005 was also very good for Cabernet Sauvignon; the wines will be long-lasting. Only Zinfandel didn't do well in this super-cool (for California) vintage. We believe that 2005 could turn out to be California's best vintage of the past 30 years. *Rating:* ★★★★

- ✔ **2004:** This was a very warm year producing ripe, precocious wines generally high in alcohol. It was generally too hot for producing delicate, well-balanced Pinot Noirs and Chardonnays. Zinfandels fared better in 2004 than other varieties. If you enjoy big, fleshy, opulent Cabernet Sauvignons, this is the vintage for you. *Rating:* ★★

- ✔ **2003:** This year was generally even hotter than 2004, and wine quality is inconsistent. Only Cabernet Sauvignons from cooler areas will have any longevity. It wasn't a good year for most Pinot Noirs or Chardonnays, but 2003 was a fine year for Zinfandel. Not a favorite vintage for us. *Rating:* ★⁺

- ✔ **2002:** Another very warm vintage producing very ripe wines with limited aging potential. Only the very best Cabernet Sauvignons, Cabernet blends, and Merlots will age well. Generally, 2002 is a vintage to drink now. *Rating:* ★★

- ✔ **2001:** This was the first in a string of four warm vintages, but it's the best of the four. We've tasted several 2001 Cabernet Sauvignons and Cabernet blends that have been excellent for current drinking but will still age well for several more years. Wines from other varieties are ready now. *Rating:* **For Cabernet Sauvignons and Cabernet blends, ★★★ to ★★★★⁺; for all other wines, ★★⁺**

Vintages from 1990 to 2000

Going back in time to vintages before 2001 is an exercise that applies primarily to Cabernet Sauvignons and Cabernet blends, because these are the California wines that age the best and improve with aging. Only 1991 is a four-star vintage in this group:

- ✔ **2000:** Mediocre vintage; not for aging
- ✔ **1999:** The best vintage from 1997 through 2000; Cabernets are drinking well now but will keep for five years or more
- ✔ **1998:** Average year; drink now
- ✔ **1997:** Precocious, overhyped vintage; most '97s are showing their age
- ✔ **1996:** Good vintage; ready to drink
- ✔ **1995:** Very fine, underrated; many wines still need time
- ✔ **1994:** Good vintage, season a bit warm; drink now
- ✔ **1993:** Average vintage; drink now
- ✔ **1992:** Fairly good vintage; ready to drink
- ✔ **1991:** Cool vintage; the best wines are excellent; many still need time ★★★★
- ✔ **1990:** Opulent vintage; these wines were very good throughout the '90s but are now showing their age

Chapter 13

Making a Winery Pilgrimage

*E*ven though wine is our business and visiting wineries is technically work for us, we continue to tour wineries with excitement and enthusiasm. The reason is that trips to wine regions bring a special dimension to the understanding and appreciation of wine. Sampling a wine at a wine-tasting or drinking it with dinner is great, but seeing the wine region, walking into the winery, meeting the people who work at the winery — these are experiences that bring a wine alive forever after. Every time we visit wineries, we remember that wine is much more than just a beverage: It's a product of nature and of people who have real passion for what they do and where they do it.

Because wine is a technical subject and because wine contains alcohol, of course, visiting wineries and tasting the wines takes some advance planning. Should you hire a car and driver? How can you manage not to sound as inexperienced as you might think you are? In this chapter, we give you some tips about the ins and outs of the winery visit so your memories will be happy ones.

Knowing What to Expect on the Winery Visit

When you visit a winery in California, you can be sure of one thing, no matter which wine region you choose to visit: The scenery will be beautiful. Beyond that, the experience can differ quite a lot from one region to another and even from one winery to another within the same region. Some regions, such as Napa Valley, have wineries with very sophisticated facilities and programs for visitors. Other regions have wineries that for the most part greet visitors with a more down-home approach. Both experiences can be wonderful.

For some people, visiting a winery is all about tasting the wines, buying a few bottles to take home, and browsing the gift shop. For other people, a tour of the facilities is the key attraction. In this section, we discuss both aspects of the winery visit.

Hours and procedures vary from winery to winery, so check out the winery's visitor information before you go. Some wineries welcome visitors by appointment only. Other wineries have regularly scheduled tours that you can participate in, but it's a good idea to know when the tours start. Some wineries charge for tours, and others do not. Some wineries have shorter tasting room hours in the off-season. For some winery resources that can help you find the info you need, see the later section "Gather specific info on winery visits."

The winery tour

A winery tour is a behind-the-scenes look at the processes that turn the grapes into wine. Some wineries start their tours in the vineyards just outside the winery. If they do, you might also see the outdoor receiving area, where grape growers deposit the harvested grapes.

However, most tours focus on the internal part of the winery. You might see the *crushes* or *presses* (machines that convert the whole grapes into a semi-liquid or liquid form suitable for fermentation), and you get to see *fermentation vessels* (huge stainless steel tanks, generally) where the grape juice becomes wine. You follow the progress of a white wine and/or a red wine from the fermentation tanks to the *aging vessels,* which can be either tanks or oak barrels; some wineries have special rooms full of barrels for aging their red wines. And you might see the bottling room, where the wine enters the bottles and where the corks, labels, and other packaging are affixed to the bottle.

Someone from the winery guides you through this tour and explains what happens at every stage, giving you a history of the winery and its wines along the way. Often, you're part of a small group with other visitors. The tour guide welcomes your questions. Depending on the size of the winery and the number of questions that you or other people in your group ask, the tour can last about 20 minutes to more than half an hour.

To some extent, you see pretty much the same thing at every winery. But if you're the curious type and are eager to learn, you'll pick up new information at each winery and gain new insights into the winemaking process. In any case, winemaking is complex, and you most likely won't understand everything from just one winery tour.

The only part of winery tours that can tend to become repetitive is the bottling line. A common refrain among wine writers touring wineries as a group is "when you've seen one bottling line, you've seen them all!"

The tasting room and shop

Your tour of the winery usually ends at the winery tasting room. If you prefer not to tour the winery or if a tour isn't available, the tasting room is the place you spend all your time during your visit.

The tasting room, which can be very simple or very elaborate, is the winery's reception area for visitors. You'll see a bar where samples of the winery's wines are available for tasting. The people behind the bar who pour the samples are usually knowledgeable about their wines. These people might also be knowledgeable about wine in general, depending on the individual. Tastes of non-alcoholic beverages, such as grape juice, are usually also available for children or nondrinkers.

Art and wine in Napa Valley

Many beautiful wineries exist in Napa Valley — Opus One and Rubicon Estate come to mind — but two wineries have gone out of their way not only to create impressive wineries but also to fill those wineries with magnificent artwork. The two are The Hess Collection and Clos Pegase.

Donald Hess, a Swiss industrialist and art collector, opened his stunning winery, located in Mount Veeder, high up in the Mayacamas Mountains in 1986. The Hess Collection Winery (www.hesscollection.com) is best known for its exceptional Cabernet Sauvignons and Chardonnays, and that's a good enough reason to visit the winery. But the winery also displays about 20 percent of Donald Hess's modern art collection (the rest is in various museums around the world). For art lovers who are also wine lovers, or vice versa, The Hess Collection is a memorable place to visit.

Clos Pegase's founder, Jan Schrem, made his fortune in the publishing business in Japan. His wife had converted him into a wine lover, and Jan combined his love of art and wine to build a strikingly beautiful winery south of Calistoga, off Route 29, which was completed in 1987 (www.clospegase.com). All of Clos Pegase's wines are estate-bottled, and Chardonnay is its signature wine. The winery is filled with art treasures, with an emphasis on sculpture. Guided tours are available every day at 11:30 a.m. and 2 p.m., free of charge; reservations aren't necessary except for large groups. Along with The Hess Collection, it's a must-see wine destination in Napa Valley.

Tasting fees

Many years ago, you could taste wines in tasting rooms for no charge, but today the norm is to charge visitors a small fee for each taste, varying from a couple of dollars up to $10 for very special expensive wines. Sometimes wineries charge you for the glass that you taste in instead of charging for the wine, and you get to keep the glass. Sometimes you can apply the entire tasting fee toward the cost of a bottle that you purchase.

Choosing wines to taste

Depending on how many wines a winery has, certain wines might be available on certain days, or all the wines might be available for tasting all the time. Sometimes instead of tasting the wines one by one, you can taste a *flight* of wines, a group of several wines (generally three or four) that you sample side-by-side to understand the differences among them.

Usually, the tasting room personnel expect you to request a particular wine or type of wine to taste. Their goal is to serve you something that you'll like so you'll decide to purchase that wine. Be prepared to discuss your likes and dislikes in wine so they can help you find a wine that excites you.

Special offers

Many wineries have certain wines that they sell only in their tasting room, not in wine shops or restaurants. These wines are usually small-production items, such as wines from unusual grape varieties or experimental blends. It's a good idea to ask whether any such wines are available, because this is your only chance to taste them — and you sound like an insider for asking.

While you're at it, ask whether the winery has a *wine club*. Wine clubs are mailing lists of wine drinkers to whom the winery makes special offers from time to time (for instance, the winery might give them the opportunity to buy tasting-room-only wines or to attend special events). Usually membership is free, with no commitment on your part to buy wines. You wouldn't want to belong to the wine club of every winery that you visit, we imagine, but if you really take to a winery and its wines, joining its wine club can be a good way to stay connected to that winery.

The gift shop

In those parts of California where brisk winery tourism exists, the tasting room also houses a gift shop. The gift shops can be terrific. The first things we look for are our own wine books (just checking!), and then we browse all the wine gadgets (corkscrews, no-drip pouring aids, coasters, and the like), glassware, aprons, t-shirts and other clothing, and baseball caps. These items can be great mementos of your visit, not to mention thoughtful gifts for the person who is watching your kids at home.

Do's and Don'ts for Visitors

We've never worked at a winery or done stints pouring wine in tasting rooms, but we have visited enough wineries over the years that we have a good idea of which behaviors work and which ones don't work for visitors to wineries. Here we offer some suggestions to help you get the most out of your excursions in California wine country.

Discover something new

Everyone at every winery you visit wants you to have such a good time that you'll tell everyone back home about the experience and feel connected to that winery for years to come. But hospitality isn't the only service that wineries offer you: They also offer information and the opportunity to expand your knowledge of wine (specifically their own wines, of course).

The best visitor is a curious visitor. Your own knowledge of wine isn't important. What's important is your willingness to learn. Don't be afraid to ask questions for fear of sounding ignorant.

You're not the only one who benefits from conversation with the pourers. The tasting room staff is a source of valuable feedback for the management of the winery regarding how acceptable their wines are to the general public. They want to know your likes and dislikes about their wines and about wine in general.

Enter into a conversation with those who are serving wines in the tasting room, assuming they're not crazy busy. Tell them what you like in wine and what you don't. Give them your honest (and polite) reaction to the wines that you taste. If you really find a particular wine too dry or too tannic, tell them so, and they can then steer you to one of their wines that you'll like more. Ask what specifically makes one wine work for you and not the other; you could discover something about your own palate that will help you in all your future wine buying.

Here are some more questions that you can ask in a tasting room to help you gather information and understand wine better:

- 🖊 How do your wines differ from other wines of this area?

- 🖊 In what ways do your wines reflect the region(s) where the grapes grow?

- 🖊 Is your winery experimenting with any unusual grape varieties? Why that variety?

- 🖊 Which of your wines is the most versatile with food, and why do you think that is?

- 🖊 How would you rate the vintage of this wine?

You can also ask questions about the quantity of wine that the winery produces (the number of cases) and whether the winery has a distributor in your home state.

Don't trust your memory regarding your impressions of the wines you taste. Jot down your impressions as you taste the wines. Most tasting rooms provide you with a list of their wines that you can use for this purpose.

Embrace the etiquette of tasting and spitting

Part of wine tasting (at least if you're tasting to learn) is spitting the wine back out. You might find the idea of spitting out wine to be not only distasteful but also wasteful. We urge you to reconsider that position when you're planning your winery visits. After swallowing just four or five tastes of wine, most people begin to feel the alcohol. At first that's relaxing and pleasant, of course, but it quickly leads to a loss of focus on the business at hand and eventually an awkward situation for all involved.

Spitting wine samples in winery tasting rooms is absolutely acceptable — more than acceptable, in fact: You set yourself apart as someone experienced in tasting wines for learning purposes.

Ideally, you should spit all the wines you taste. Swallow only when a wine is so compelling that it's down the hatch before you even realize it! (And then buy that wine.)

A quick primer on how to taste wine

Tasting wine is a slower, more deliberate and more thoughtful process than simply drinking wine. Wine is a complex beverage, and when you simply drink it as you would any other beverage, you miss the wine's nuances. Here's a quick lesson on what to do to when you want to taste a wine the way the pros do. You don't have to use this procedure with every sip, all the time — just when you want to really examine the taste of a particular wine. With practice, describing what you smell and taste in a wine becomes easier — and it becomes a lot of fun, too!

1. **Smell the wine.**

   Rotate your (half-full) glass on the table so that the wine swishes around in the glass and mixes with air. As soon as you stop moving the glass, bring it to your nose (stick your nose into the air space above the wine) and inhale. Notice how strong or subtle the wine's aroma is; then try to describe in your mind what you smell. Common descriptors include all sorts of fruits, floral notes, spices, herbs, and so forth.

2. **Taste the wine.**

   Take a medium-sized sip of the wine. Move it around your mouth and notice its *texture* (whether it feels soft or firm or rough — thinking of how different fabrics feel can be helpful). Also note its weight, or *body* (how heavy or light it feels on your tongue). Open your lips slightly and draw some air in to release the wine's flavors; describe in your mind how flavorful the wine is (or isn't) and which specific flavors you notice. Often, the flavors are similar to the aromas you smelled.

3. **Swallow or spit.**

   If you're tasting several wines, we suggest you do what the pros do and spit the wine out to keep your head clear. But if you're tasting just a single wine, swallowing is fine. As the wine leaves your mouth, notice whether the wine's flavors persist across the whole length of your mouth or whether they stop short about halfway back. Stopping short is not considered a flaw in inexpensive wines, but fine wines should carry their flavor farther across your mouth.

If you don't see containers for spitting, ask for a cup or other container to use as a spittoon. We actually carry disposable 12-ounce plastic cups with us, because they make ideal individual spittoons. You can hold the cup right up to your mouth to spit discreetly and then empty the cup from time to time into a ceramic pitcher or other larger container where people are dumping their leftover wine. (If you feel insecure about spitting, practice spitting water at home in front of a mirror. And be assured that every respectable tasting room has napkins available for the errant dribble or spill.)

Drink water at the beginning and end of your tasting, if not even more frequently. Wine tasters know how important water is in helping to mitigate the effects of alcohol. Nibbling on crackers can also help you handle the alcohol better. Even when you spit the wine, you still absorb some alcohol into your system.

Beware the designated driver trap

No, we are not suggesting that having a designated driver is a bad idea. In fact, it's a great idea. But knowing that someone else is driving can have one downside: When you hire a car and driver (or a small bus) to take you and your friends around from winery to winery, or when you and your friends take turns being the designated driver over the course of several days, the risk is that you'll relax so much that the alcohol goes to your head even more easily than it would otherwise.

Staying sober and sensible when you're tasting wine requires constant vigilance. If you let your guard down because you know that you don't have to drive, you could dampen your whole experience and end up regretting your behavior. To stay vigilant, remind yourself that you're there to discover and learn, not solely to have fun. Don't worry; you'll still have plenty of fun in the process!

Preparing for Your Visit

We think that planning a vacation is almost the best part. That's when we get to fantasize about what we'd like to do when we get to our destination and figure out, in time to make a reservation, the very best restaurants for lunch and dinner. In these days of airline security restrictions, we also plan for what we'll do after we visit wineries — specifically, how we'll transport our bottles home.

This section provides hands-on info on planning your wine tour. See Chapter 4 for info on California wine regions and Chapter 15 for some of our favorite California wine destinations. And for the names of wineries that produce wines we recommend, check out Parts II and III of this book.

Gather specific info on winery visits

The more you know before you go, the more relaxed and efficient (and surprise-free) your winery visits will be. Make sure you gather visitor info, including addresses, hours, possible charges, and whether you need an appointment.

When we first wrote *Wine For Dummies* back in 1995, we advised readers who wanted to visit California wine country to get their hands on a magazine published by *Wine Spectator* that listed names, addresses, telephone numbers, and visiting hours of practically all the wineries in California. Since then, two things have changed: The number of wineries in California has continued to climb beyond a number that's feasible to include in one publication, and the Internet now exists.

Here are places where you might want to begin your search for specific info today:

- ✔ *Wine Spectator* (www.winespectator.com) is still a valuable source of information on California's wine regions, the wines they make, the top local restaurants, and so forth.

- ✔ *Wine Enthusiast* magazine (www.winemag.com) publishes regular wine travel features.

- ✔ The *Appellation America* site (www.appellationamerica.com) is an extremely valuable source of information on wine regions not only in California but also elsewhere in North America, including Canada. You find listings of wineries in specific regions, descriptions of the regions and the types of wines made there, and useful tourist information.

- ✔ Wine travel Web sites such as www.winecountry.com can not only spark your enthusiasm for your trip but also provide useful contact information for visits to specific wineries.

- ✔ A new Web site, www.landofwineandfood.com, has the specific purpose of aiding visitors in their travel to wine and culinary destinations in California. The site is sponsored jointly by the California Travel and Tourism Commission and Wine Institute, California's wine trade association.

- ✔ Wine or travel Web sites that have forums or message boards are also good places for your planning; for example, Frommer's (www.frommers.com) has viewer-initiated discussion threads about wineries in Santa Ynez Valley, Temecula, and other California wine regions.

- ✔ Your favorite wine blog could also be a good place to ask questions and get opinions from fellow wine lovers.

While you're researching which wineries to visit in a specific area, be sure to check out the Web site of the local winery association. All but the smallest wine regions have associations whose mandate is to promote the wines of their area. (You can find links to all these organizations on the Web site of Wine Institute, www.wineinstitute.org.) These promotional sites can give you useful information on the types of wines made in the area and on the wineries themselves. And sometimes you discover that the associations have tasting rooms where you can sample wines from multiple wineries. A key example of this is the Monterey County Vintners and Growers Association (www.montereywines.org), which operates two wine-tasting visitor centers, in Monterey and in Soledad.

Know the restrictions on transporting your purchases

You probably know that you can't carry bottles of wine with you onto an airplane. But the black-and-white of transporting wine home or having it shipped by the winery ends there. The regulations governing delivery of wine to consumers vary from state to state. And what's more, they're constantly changing.

A landmark case before the U.S. Supreme Court in 2005 at first seemed to simplify the whole picture of wine shipping: The Court ruled that no state can deny an out-of-state winery the right to ship to consumers in that state if it grants local wineries that right (which many states did and still do). Wine lovers envisioned a new land of free commerce in wine, but their (our!) hopes were naïve.

Although Internet commerce in wine seems easier than it once did, individual states are still refining their regulations, often with the apparent goal of restricting consumers from buying any wine that isn't already available locally through state-registered wine shops and distributors.

In some cases, wines that you purchase personally as a tourist enjoy a different status from wines that you order from a California winery over the telephone or Internet, and they can be shipped home.

If you're thinking of purchasing wine during your trip to California and asking the winery to ship it back home for you — or taking your purchases to a local UPS or FedEx store in California and sending it back to yourself — look into your state regulations first. Winery staff and shipping companies in California can tell you whether they'll ship wine to your state, but by the time you get to California and ask, you might not be able to come up with a Plan B.

If you discover that you can't ship your purchases, you might want to do what we do when we travel abroad: We take with us an empty cardboard wine shipping case with Styrofoam inserts (your local wine shop might be able to save one of these for you) and bring it back, filled with wine bottles, as checked luggage. We have never lost a bottle to breakage this way. But even if a bottle were to break, that would be a lot less distressing than if it had broken in our suitcase.

Part V
The Part of Tens

"This one's earthy but light, with undertones of blackberry, vanilla, and Scotchguard."

In this part...

*I*f you've got questions, we've got answers — at least if your question is an FAQ, such as whether those expensive, luxury California wines are worth the price or whether the critics' scores are worth following. We also have some California Dreamin' going on as we recommend ten wine country destinations where we really wish that we could be right now.

Chapter 14

Answers to Ten Common Questions about California Wine

*I*n our years of teaching about wine and helping customers in wine shops, we've noticed that the same questions about California wines arise frequently. Here are the questions and our answers.

What's the Best California Wine?

In our experience, this is undoubtedly the most common question about California wines. We usually respond with a few questions of our own before we answer, such as the following:

- ✔ Is price a consideration? In other words, do you want to know the "best wine under $50" or the best wine regardless of cost?

- ✔ The best red wine, white wine, or sparkling wine?

- ✔ If it's red wine, do you generally prefer Cabernet Sauvignon, Merlot, Pinot Noir, Syrah, Zinfandel, or something else?

As you can conclude, no one "best wine for everyone" exists. Your best wine depends on your own very personal taste, with the price of the wine often another important consideration. Any wines that we nominate as our favorite California wines might be wines that you don't like one bit!

The best direct answer that we can give to this question is that we believe California's best wines generally are Cabernet Sauvignons and Cabernet blends, with most of the best coming from Napa Valley, although a few great ones also come from Sonoma (such as Laurel Glen "Estate") and the Santa Cruz Mountains (such as Ridge "Monte Bello").

Do Vintages Matter for California Wine?

Yes, vintages do matter, although California generally doesn't experience the wide variability from year to year that you find in Europe. In plain English, California seldom has really poor vintages in which no decent wines are produced. The weather just doesn't get that bad during the growing season in California. The curve runs mainly from "average vintage" to "excellent vintage."

The cooler vintages seem to work best for almost all California wines (except Zinfandel, which does well in warm weather). The 2005 vintage, generally quite cool for California, seems to be a generally excellent vintage for most California wines. (See Chapter 12 for some of our other favorite vintages.)

Are Ratings Important in Buying California Wine?

Ratings — the scores that critics give to wines to indicate their assessment of the wines' quality — matter only if you know that your tastes in California wine are exactly the same as those of the critic who is doing the rating. Tasting and judging wine is such a subjective experience that it's quite a stretch to think that you'll like all the highly rated wines of all critics. For example, we often don't enjoy wines rated in the high-90s of some critics because our tastes are so different from theirs.

We strongly recommend that you buy just one bottle of a wine you haven't tasted, regardless of critics' ratings, and try it yourself before investing in multiple bottles. Otherwise, you might be stuck with wines that you don't enjoy!

How Long Should California Wines Age before I Drink Them?

Today, the goal of most winemakers in California and elsewhere is to produce wines that are enjoyable when you buy them. You don't find the harsh tannins that used to be present in many young red wines; tannins are softer and are well-balanced by ripe fruitiness. Therefore, most California wines are quite drinkable when young.

But the finer California red wines — especially Cabernet Sauvignons and Cabernet blends but even Pinot Noirs — often improve with a few years of aging. For example, most 2001 and 1999 California Cabernets are perfect for drinking right now. Chapter 12 can tell you more about how well wines age.

Are the $100+ California Wines Worth the Price?

We actually believe that many California wines, especially Cabernet Sauvignons and Cabernet blends, are overpriced. To be fair, expenses are extremely high in California: The cost of the vineyard and winery in prime regions, operating costs, labor, and so forth are among the highest in the world. But often, the high price of a wine is a question of status or peer pressure; some California producers have said to us, "If I don't charge this (high) price, consumers won't respect my wine" or "The quality of my wine is commensurate with wines in that (high) price tier."

Yes, we have tasted some wonderful California Cabernets priced over $100 that we believe warrant the price. You can find some of them in our wine recommendations in Chapter 6. But we've also tasted some excellent California wines in the $20 to $50 range. You don't have to pay over $100 to find top California wines.

Do California Wines Age Well?

Some California wines do age well; others don't. In general, California's dry red wines age much better than dry whites:

✔ **Cabernet Sauvignon:** These California wines have the best track record for aging. We don't know whether they'll age as long as red Bordeaux wines (whose record for longevity extends over 100 years for the best wines), but some California Cabs, among the few that were around in the first half of the last century, have aged well for 60 to 70 years.

✔ **Zinfandel:** Red Zinfandel has aged well, but old Zinfandels do lose their unique berry-like character that you find in young Zinfandels.

✔ **Chardonnay:** Most older California Chardonnays haven't aged well. However, now that California wine producers are planting Chardonnay in more suitable, cooler areas, we believe that current Chardonnays will be aging longer than earlier Chardonnays.

Other major California red wines — Syrah, Merlot, and Pinot Noir — haven't existed in quantity for more than 20 years, so it's impossible to say at this point how well they'll age.

Are California Pinot Noirs as Good as Red Burgundy?

Because of differences in *terroir* (primarily climate and soil), California Pinot Noirs are very different from red Burgundies, which are made entirely from the Pinot Noir grape. Generally, most California wine regions are somewhat warmer than Burgundy, which makes California Pinot Noirs taste more overtly fruity and feel more opulent on the palate. Burgundies tend to be leaner, dryer, and somewhat lighter-bodied, and they tend to taste earthier and more suggestive of the forest.

California Pinot Noirs vary widely, depending on the region; cooler regions such as the Sonoma Coast, the Carneros, parts of the Russian River Valley, Anderson Valley in Mendocino County, and Santa Maria Valley in Santa Barbara County tend to produce lighter-bodied, more delicately flavored wines than the heftier Pinot Noirs from the Santa Lucia Highlands in Monterey County.

The bottom line is that excellent Pinot Noirs are coming from California and from Burgundy; they're just different. (For more information on California Pinot Noirs, flip to Chapter 7.)

Are California Chardonnays Too Oaky?

Ten years ago, we would have answered that most California Chardonnays have too much of the smoky/toasty aroma and flavor of oak as well as too much oak tannin. But we're happy to say that California's winemakers seem to have listened to the complaints of consumers and wine writers and have gotten the message.

Today, there's a healthy trend away from the heavy-handed use of oak in Chardonnay. More and more California Chardonnays are being produced with a minimum of oak aging and less *new* oak (the oakiest oak) than before. And California Chardonnays are better than ever.

Of course, you'll still find some California Chardonnays made with lots of oaky flavor, and that's a good thing for those wine drinkers who favor that flavorful, powerful style of wine. But many of the better California Chardonnays, the ones we recommend in this book (see Chapter 5), now carry a much subtler stamp of oak in their taste.

Are California Rosés Sweet?

California has definitely made progress with its pink, or rosé, wines. At one time, just about every California rosé, whether it was White Zinfandel, another blush wine, or a plain old rosé, was overtly sweet — too sweet for many wine drinkers accustomed to the taste of dry European rosé wines. But we're now seeing a definite trend toward dryer California rosés, many of which we recommend in Chapter 11.

In truth, we'd like to see California producers make rosés as dry as most of the rosés from France, Italy, and Spain, and they're not there yet. But they are heading in the right direction. Certainly, almost all of California's rosé sparkling wines are dry enough for us.

What's the Story with California Merlots?

The implication behind this question is "Are Merlots as poor as their recent reputation suggests they are, and will I look foolish if I order a glass of Merlot?"

Merlot has had an interesting history in California. It went from a mere blending wine (strictly a supporting-cast player) to a varietal wine in its own right to *the* hot red wine in California. It seemed for a certain period of time that everyone was ordering either Chardonnay or Merlot, nothing else. Unfortunately, Merlot couldn't handle its sudden fame, and lots of inferior Merlot flooded the market, giving the once-hot variety a bad reputation. (Witness Miles, the main character in the film *Sideways*, spewing venom about Merlot.)

We are happy to report that Merlot is making a comeback. Producers who never lost faith in Merlot — such as Clos du Val, Duckhorn, Matanzas Creek, Newton Vineyards, Selene, Shafer Vineyards, Swanson Vineyards, and Trefethen — are making superb Merlots today. You can check out some of our picks for Merlots in Chapter 6.

Chapter 15

Ten Top Travel Destinations and Attractions

California is so rich in wine-related travel destinations that it's challenging to limit our list to just ten. Napa Valley alone provides dozens of wonderful opportunities to enhance your stay in this beautiful state. But California wine country is more than Napa Valley.

For a complete change of pace, we suggest that you visit the Sierra Foothills in Gold Rush Country. Or go off the beaten path, to San Luis Obispo and Paso Robles. We also recommend visiting beautiful Santa Barbara if you're heading south to the Central Coast wine regions. And no visit to Sonoma County would be complete without stopping in Healdsburg, located in the heart of one of Sonoma's best wine regions (Russian River Valley). We end our list of top ten destinations with a personal favorite: the quirky town of Mendocino and its offbeat wine region, Anderson Valley. Enjoy!

Yountville, Napa Valley

In addition to the city of Napa, Napa Valley has five main wine towns, all located off Route 29, which runs south to north through the heart of the Valley. Starting north of Napa, the towns are Yountville, Oakville, Rutherford, St. Helena, and the northernmost, Calistoga. Each town has its charms. St. Helena is the largest town, and it's the one that has the most real-life (as opposed to wine country idyllic) feel to it. But Yountville offers probably the widest range of places to stay and excellent restaurants, and it's close to many wineries.

One of the places we like to stay when we visit Napa Valley is the Villagio Inn & Spa (www.villagio.com), located on Washington Street, Yountville's main street. It's a sprawling country inn with cabins, gardens, a spa, and a swimming pool, plus an excellent breakfast. The nearby Vintage Inn (www.vintageinn.com), somewhat similar and affiliated, is also a wonderful place to stay. Yountville also has lots of smaller bed & breakfast places available.

Yountville is home to one of the finest restaurants in the U.S., The French Laundry (tables fill fast, so make reservations several months ahead). If you can't get into The French Laundry or prefer to dine a bit more simply, we suggest two wonderful French bistros — Bouchon and Bistro Jeanty — both on Washington Street. Other top Yountville restaurants include Mustards, Redd, Brix, and Bistro Don Giovanni.

One special winery to visit in Yountville is Domaine Chandon. You can arrange for a tour and tasting at what is the one of the oldest — and still one of the best — sparkling wine companies in California, plus enjoy an excellent lunch or dinner at *étoile,* the winery's renowned French restaurant.

In addition to great dining and lots of shopping, you can opt for a hot air balloon ride over Napa Valley in Yountville (www.nvaloft. com). Or to combine a round of golf with your winery visits, contact the Vintner's Golf Club (www.vintnersgolfclub.com).

The Ferry Building, San Francisco

San Francisco is one of the greatest cities in the U.S., and it's a must-stop for anyone heading to Napa Valley and/or Sonoma County. The Ferry Building Marketplace, located along the Embarcadero roadway on the San Francisco Bay, is one of the great culinary meccas in the country; you can buy wines, fruits, vegetables, meats, breads, cheeses, and other artisan foods and food-related merchandise. The marketplace also has several attractive cafés and bakeries.

The very best time to visit the Ferry Building is Saturday from 8 a.m. to 2 p.m. or Tuesday from 10 a.m. to 2 p.m., when the crowded Ferry Plaza Farmers Market is open.

The Ferry Building is also the place to catch inexpensive ferries to places such as Alcatraz, Angel Island, the beautiful AT&T Park (home of Major League Baseball's San Francisco Giants), the colorful town of Sausalito in Marin County, and Vallejo, the entry town to Napa Valley. You can catch a return ferry from Vallejo at sunset to view the glorious Golden Gate Bridge in San Francisco Bay.

Picnic Lunches in Wine Country

One of our personal treats in California wine country, especially in the summer, is to buy the makings of a picnic lunch and find a good location to relax and enjoy it. We often stop in the town of Sonoma and go to a good food shop, bakery, and cheese shop off the main square to load up on goodies.

For some fancier food and great wine, two fantastic food stores in Napa Valley, both on Route 29, are the renowned Oakville Grocery in Oakville (www.oakvillegrocery.com) and Dean & DeLuca in St. Helena (www.deandeluca.com).

Perhaps the most famous picnic stop in all of California is the V. Sattui Winery, a small, family-owned winery on Route 29, south of St. Helena. V. Sattui sells almost all its wine to the thousands of visitors who arrive there every year. When you visit, you can taste V. Sattui's award-winning wines and buy a bottle or two, along with deli fare — such as salami, cheese, olives, and salads — and then sit down at a picnic table on the grounds surrounding the winery.

The Napa Valley Wine Train

One of the best and most luxurious ways to see Napa Valley is to head to the city of Napa and take the unique Napa Valley Wine Train tour (www.winetrain.com). It's a leisurely three-hour journey through Napa Valley wine country in vintage railroad cars. This is a great way to see Napa Valley (if not actually visit wineries) without having to hassle with the traffic.

You can choose among several options on your tour, including a gourmet three- or four-course meal in a fine restaurant on the train, a wine tasting, and lunch with a local Napa vintner. You even have the option to tour several top Napa Valley wineries when your ride is over.

Calistoga's Hot Springs and Mud Baths

At the northern end of Napa Valley is the picturesque town of Calistoga, the least gentrified town in the Valley. This is the place where you can add a bit of personal pampering and perhaps recovery time to your extensive wine touring. Lots of spas featuring hot springs, mud baths, and massages are available here. One of the traditional places to stay is the Mt. View Hotel & Spa (www.mountviewhotel.com). Many bed and breakfast places, country inns, and good restaurants are located in Calistoga, and a dozen or so wineries are close by. The adventurous can schedule canoe and kayak trips during their stay.

The Sierra Foothills

Thinking of going to Yosemite National Park or Lake Tahoe? On the way, be sure to visit California's most unique wine region, the Sierra Foothills. Located in central California, directly east of San Francisco, the huge Sierra Foothills American Viticultural Area (AVA) spreads out over eight counties, with Amador and El Dorado Counties in the center. The main entry to the Sierra Foothills is the city of Sacramento, situated just west of the wine area.

Visiting the Sierra Foothills is like taking a trip into the past, to old California. The Gold Rush towns are still here (gold was discovered at Sutter Creek in 1849), some of them no more than ghost towns now. The majestic Sierra Nevada Mountains to the east provide lots of outdoor activities, such as hiking, whitewater rafting, and so forth. Small wineries, located in colorful areas such as Fiddletown, Placerville, Fair Play, and the Shenandoah Valley, sell most of their wines to visiting tourists.

The Sierra Foothills (along with a few vineyards in Sonoma) are the main location of the very old-vine Zinfandels; you can buy intensely flavorful red Zinfandels made from 100-year old vines in this region (see Chapter 8 for more on Zins and why vine age matters). Mainly a red wine region, the Sierra Foothills also feature Cabernet Sauvignons, Rhône-style reds, and Italian varieties. This is a laid back, rustic area, directly in contrast to the gentrification of Napa Valley.

San Luis Obispo and Paso Robles

In the most central part of California's Central Coast are the city of San Luis Obispo and the region's main wine town, Paso Robles, which is located exactly halfway between San Francisco and Los Angeles. Although Paso Robles is just 25 miles north of San Luis Obispo on Highway 101, the cities are actually the focus of two different wine regions. Both regions are wonderful to visit, because you don't have to compete with all the wine tourists that Napa Valley or Santa Barbara attracts.

San Luis Obispo, distinctly cooler, is close to the Arroyo Grande and Edna Valley AVA regions, which are important for Chardonnay and Pinot Noir production. Major nearby wineries include Edna Valley Vineyard, Alban Winery, Domaine Alfred, Talley Vineyards, and Laetitia Vineyard. The city is fairly small (population: 46,000), but it's a quite sophisticated college town (California Polytechnic State University is there) with lots of good restaurants, interesting shopping, hotels, and bed and breakfast places.

Nearby, on the coast, is beautiful Pismo Beach, with a good wine restaurant, Giuseppe's Cucina Italiana. A top hotel in Pismo Beach, The Cliffs Resort (www.cliffsresort.com), hosts a Pinot Noir Festival every March. To the north of Pismo Beach is the more tranquil Morro Bay, with its fine hotel, The Inn at Morro Bay (www.innatmorrobay.com), and an excellent wine restaurant with a breathtaking view, Windows on the Water.

The rapidly growing town of Paso Robles (population: 32,000) also offers excellent hospitality in terms of hotels — including the five-star inn Villa Toscana (www.myvillatoscana.com) — bed and breakfasts, and restaurants. The main difference from San Luis Obispo is that the Paso Robles region is a much larger AVA (over 170 wineries), and the emphasis is definitely on red wines: Rhône varieties, Zinfandel, Cabernet Sauvignon, and Italian varieties. The York Mountain AVA, a cooler area to the west of the city of Paso Robles, is also part of the Paso Robles AVA.

Near both Paso Robles and San Luis Obispo is one of California's top tourist attractions, the magnificent Hearst Castle. The castle is the historic house of William Randolph Hearst, the newspaper magnate who largely inspired the film *Citizen Kane* (www.hearst castle.org).

Santa Barbara

A visit to the Santa Barbara wine region should begin with a stop in the city of Santa Barbara, one of the most beautiful cities in the world. It offers its fortunate residents an outstanding lifestyle. The city has several colleges and universities, excellent restaurants, and stunning vistas at every turn.

If you want to be closer to Santa Barbara's wine regions, consider staying farther north, either in the city of Lompoc or in Santa Maria. Lompoc is at the western edge of the Sta. Rita Hills AVA, and to its east is Santa Ynez Valley AVA; both regions have lots of outstanding wineries. The city of Santa Maria, in the northwestern part of Santa Barbara County, faces Santa Maria Valley, which is home of some of the best Pinot Noir wineries in the state; it was featured in the film *Sideways*.

A must-stop while in Santa Barbara is a visit to one or both of the Hitching Post restaurants. The original Hitching Post Restaurant, famous for its barbecue as well as its wines, is in the village of Casmalia, south of Santa Maria. Hitching Post II, owned by the same (Ostini) family, is in Buellton, in the Santa Ynez Valley.

Healdsburg, Sonoma County

Sonoma County offers many attractions, and one key place to visit has to be the booming wine town of Healdsburg, in Northern Sonoma. Healdsburg, in the heart of the Russian River Valley and right next to Dry Creek Valley, is an ideal place to stay while touring some of the best wineries in the state, such as Jordan, J, Williams Selyem, Rochioli, Ferrari-Carano, Hartford Family, Simi, Gallo Family, Iron Horse, Ridge Lytton Springs, Seghesio, Martinelli, and A. Rafanelli.

Healdsburg is the home of some of California's best restaurants, including the top-rated Cyrus. It has lots of fine hotels and inns, great food shops, and some of the best shopping in wine country.

Mendocino, Anderson Valley

We love the town of Mendocino, on the North Coast, where all (well, many) of the old hippies of the late '60s settled, or so it seems. Mendocino is a quaint town whose Victorian houses give the feeling that you're in New England. We enjoyed staying in the MacCallum House Inn (www.maccallumhouse.com), which dates back to the 1880s and which also has an excellent restaurant. Another top place to dine in Mendocino is Café Beaujolais.

FROMMERS TRAVEL TIP

Healdsburg's best annual wine events

In March, right before heavy tourist season kicks off, Healdsburg tempts the wine-lover's taste buds with a barrel-tasting weekend at nearly 100 wineries along the Russian River Wine Road. And if you happen to fall in love with a wine you taste, you can secure your share of bottles — at discounted prices — long before they even exist, never mind sell out. (It's called buying *futures*.) Tickets are $20 online or $30 at the door. For information, visit www.wineroad.com or call 800-723-6336 or 707-433-4335.

A big June attraction is the ten-day Healdsburg Jazz Festival. Venues range from vineyards to restaurants to intimate theaters, and headliners sell out quickly. Admission prices vary. Tickets can be purchased via Web sites, mail, fax, or at the venue. For more information, please go to www.healdsburgjazzfestival.com or call 707-433-4644.

Frommer's Portable California Wine Country, 5th Edition, by Erika Lenkert; Copyright 2006 Wiley Publishing, Inc.; Reprinted with permission of John Wiley & Sons, Inc.

South of Mendocino, along the Pacific Coast and closer to the Anderson Valley wine country, is the Albion River Inn, in Albion (www.albionriverinn.com). It offers private cabins with decks overlooking the water and a dining room with a great view.

Just south of Albion is Route 128, which takes you through the magnificent California redwood trees into Anderson Valley. Among our favorite wineries to visit there are Roederer Estate (California bubbly at its best), Handley Cellars, Greenwood Ridge, Lazy Creek Vineyards, Navarro, and some promising newcomers that emphasize Pinot Noir, such as Londer Vineyards and Phillips Hill Estates. The place to stay and dine in the Anderson Valley is the Boonville Hotel (www.boonvillehotel.com) in the town of Boonville. It's another place that dates back to the 19th century, and it offers a lot of charm along with good food.

Index

Notes

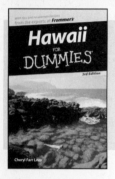
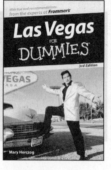